CONNECTIONS

A DEVOTIONAL COMPANION TO THE ONE YEAR CHRONOLOGICAL BIBLE NIV, 2011 EDITION

Daily Discover a Divine Connection
Between the Old and New Testament.

KAREN F. NORTON

WestBow Press books may be ordered through booksellers or by contacting:

WestBow Press
A Division of Thomas Nelson & Zondervan
1663 Liberty Drive
Bloomington, IN 47403
www.westbowpress.com
1 (866) 928-1240

ISBN: 978-1-4908-5339-0 (sc)
ISBN: 978-1-4908-5340-6 (hc)
ISBN: 978-1-4908-5341-3 (e)

Library of Congress Control Number: 2014917187

Printed in the United States of America.

WestBow Press rev. date:10/29/2014

I dedicate
"Connections"
to
Jesus Christ, my Wonderful Savior and Lord,
under whose wings I find shelter and refuge,
and to
Gene, my Loving Husband,
the wind beneath this sparrow's wings.

CONTENTS

PREFACE

I love God's Word, the Holy Bible. I love reading it, learning more about God and the love of Jesus Christ, and how it applies to my life. It is where I find daily encouragement and strength that can only come from Him.

God's truth spans all time and eternity. He never changes. I envision The Old Testament as the left hand and the New Testament as the right hand. The fingers neatly interlock like pieces of a puzzle. They are connected, interwoven, to produce a true picture of the heart of God. Each hand strengthens and reinforces the other. In each day's devotion, you will discover a connection with the opposite Testament. The Old Testament is just as important to our lives today as the New Testament. There is so much to learn from every page of the Bible!

Read the Bible completely through this year. If you've already done that, then do it again! "Connections" is meant to be used as a companion to The One Year Chronological Bible NIV, 2011 edition; consider it a side dish to your main course. Please read from this Bible first, and then read the day's devotion from "Connections" for additional insight or possible sermon seeds. May it expand and enlarge your thinking. One of the main purposes of "Connections" is to evoke thought, inspection and application. You'll find many questions to spur your serious consideration of the Scripture. That's the intention. Allow the Holy Spirit to fill in the blanks. Ask God to speak to you each day as you read His Word. He desires to communicate with you on a deeper level. Are you listening?

No devotional or any other Christian book should ever take the place of God's Word in your life. No other book is worthy of that honor; it doesn't matter what it is or who wrote it. The Bible is the only book on planet earth that is alive and that can impart life to you. Carve out and protect time each day to spend in His Word.

I will forever be a student of the Word. I am currently reading the Bible through for the 47th time. It is never boring to me, and I always learn something new and fresh from its pages, as the Holy Spirit illumines. It's one class from which I will never graduate! Time spent in God's Word and prayer is the most important part of my day. "Open my eyes that I may see wonderful things in your law." Psalm 119:18.

I submit "Connections" to God to use for His Glory. I pray He will use it in your life to cause you to fall more in love with Jesus Christ and His Word, and create an ever increasing hunger and thirst for Him. A daily intake of God's Word will change your life.

Karen F. Norton
August, 2014

JANUARY

January 1 – **It's God's Idea**

Marriage and family are important to God. That's an understatement! "That is why a man leaves his father and mother and is united to his wife, and they become one flesh." Genesis 2:24. Since the beginning of time, this truth has not changed. God has not changed His mind, and what's important to God should be important to us. "So they are no longer two, but one flesh. Therefore what God has joined together, let no one separate." Matthew 19:6. He's given us His handbook on marriage; it's called the Bible. I must read it to learn what He says about how to do life and marriage, believe that He is speaking to "me" personally, and then apply His truths to my life.

God knows what He is talking about! He invented marriage. He wrote the rules; and He has given us clear directions. Don't be one of those who thinks he can assemble a new toy without reading the directions first, or you'll get less than perfect results. Things won't fit together; pieces will be left over; it's not what the Manufacturer intends. You and I are not smarter than God! We must trust God and His directions. Read His Book this year; apply His truths to your life and your marriage. If you encounter a problem or make a mistake, there's still hope. Go back to the directions.

January 2 – **God's Favor**

"But Noah found favor in the eyes of the Lord." Genesis 6:8. He stands out; he does not follow the crowd. There is something different about Noah, and God notices. He refuses to allow the culture around him influence his walk with God. Perhaps as a child around the campfire, he listened intently to the stories about his great grandfather, Enoch, who walked with God right into glory (5:24), so Noah walks with God (6:9). Did his grandfather, Methuselah, share that story hundreds of times with his descendants? We know that Methuselah lived 969 years (the longest recorded life) and died the year of the flood; only God knows if that happened before or during. And look at verse 11; it could easily describe today's world: "Now the earth was corrupt in God's sight and was full of violence." However, "Noah did everything just as God commanded him." Genesis 6:22.

I believe humility and obedience characterize Noah and gain God's favor. Acts 7:46 reflects on David, "who enjoyed God's favor and asked that he might provide a dwelling place for the God of Jacob." A man after God's own heart, David humbly and obediently trusts in God's timing and promises concerning the kingship. A favor is a kind or helpful act and the state or condition of being approved. I want God's favor in my life. He wants to see a humble heart and obedience in me. So how are you doing in the arenas of humility and obedience?

January 3 – **He Remembers You**

God has an extremely good memory. He never forgets anything He says He will remember. I can't say that about my memory! How many times have I told someone I will pray for them only to forget I said that until the next time I see them? Perhaps Noah is sick and tired of so much water and wonders if

God has forgotten him. "But God remembered Noah..." "I will remember my covenant between me and you..." "...I will see it and remember the everlasting covenant..." Genesis 8:1, 9:15, 9:16.

Satan tries to convince us that God has forgotten us and moved on to more important people or projects. But there is no one more important to God than you. He has not forgotten you, your situation, your pain, or your prayers. Even during times when we forget God, He still remembers us. "He has helped his servant Israel, remembering to be merciful." Luke 1:54. "...God has heard your prayer and remembered your gifts to the poor." Acts 10:31. The only thing God does not remember is our confessed and forgiven sin, because He chooses to forget them. Aren't you glad! "For I will forgive their wickedness and will remember their sins no more." Hebrews 8:12.

January 4 – **Who's in Control?**

Genesis 11:4. Have you ever done something that was not God's plan for your life? Our ancestors at one time had a common language and a plan. They call a town meeting: "Come." The ringleaders reveal their plan: "Let us build ourselves a city." Sounds logical and innocent enough. This city will include a tower, and not just any tower, but "with a tower that reaches to the heavens." Why? "so that we may make a name for ourselves; otherwise we will be scattered over the face of the whole earth." This is obviously not God's plan, for He had already commanded Noah (9:1) "fill the earth," not just one city. God hears more than the words they speak. He hears their hearts saying, "We know what's best for us, and this is it. From now on, we'll call the shots."

God's Word tells us, "There is a way that appears to be right, but in the end it leads to death." Proverbs 14:12. "A person may think their own ways are right, but the Lord weighs the heart." Proverbs 21:2. "That is why I was angry with that generation;

I said, 'Their hearts are always going astray, and they have not known my ways.'" Hebrews 3:10. "...Great and marvelous are your deeds, Lord God Almighty. Just and true are your ways, King of the nations." Revelation 15:3. So today, are you uncertain about God's plan for your life? Read His Word; seek Him, and He will show you. Then walk in His ways.

January 5 – **Son of Promise**

"Then God said, 'Yes, but your wife Sarah will bear you a son, and you will call him Isaac. I will establish my covenant with him as an everlasting covenant for his descendants after him.'" Genesis 17:19. In his and Sarah's minds, this conception and birth would be a rare miracle in deed! Is Abraham truly able to comprehend the bigger picture here, the magnitude of God's covenant promise? Can I?

Some 1300 years later, Isaiah prophesies, "Therefore the Lord himself will give you a sign: The virgin will conceive and give birth to a son, and will call him Immanuel." Isaiah 7:14.

Another 700 years come and go. "But after he had considered this, an angel of the Lord appeared to him in a dream and said, 'Joseph son of David, do not be afraid to take Mary home as your wife, because what is conceived in her is from the Holy Spirit. She will give birth to a son, and you are to give him the name Jesus, because he will save his people from their sins.'" Matthew 1:20, 21. Jesus Christ is the Promised Son, the golden thread woven through Scripture from Genesis to Revelation.

January 6 – **There's No Question**

Since the time of Adam and Eve when God told Satan the woman's seed will ultimately crush his head (Genesis 3:15), Satan has attempted to thwart God's plan of redemption for mankind. We see it about the time Isaac is conceived. "Then God said to him in the dream, 'Yes, I know you did this with a clear conscience, and so I have kept you from sinning against me. That is why I did not let you touch her.'" Genesis 20:6. Satan has always attempted to destroy the promised Seed, even with a question mark: Is this *really* the promised one?

Satan knows Scripture; he knew Scripture declared the Messiah would be born of a virgin. He tries again to steal, kill, and destroy the divine plan – and fails – again. "But he did not consummate their marriage until she gave birth to a son. And he gave him the name Jesus." Matthew 1:25. God made sure these Scriptures were included in the Bible, so that all doubt is removed. The Holy Seed is forever pure and untainted.

Now in the twenty-first century, Satan continues his unrelenting attacks on the nation of Israel, the church (the bride of Christ), and anyone or anything resembling godliness. Why? It's the same reason: to stop God's plan of redemption for mankind. Satan will forever fail, and God's truth will forever prevail. "The Lord said to me, 'You have seen correctly, for I am watching to see that my word is fulfilled.'" Jeremiah 1:12.

January 7 – **God's Friend**

Unlike Jonah, Abraham does not run away; he obeys God. He probably doesn't sleep much that night, wondering if he had heard God correctly: "Sacrifice your son as a burnt offering." He concludes he did hear God clearly and so, early in the morning, begins the three day journey to Moriah. That must have been the longest three days of his life, with plenty of time to contemplate this latest conversation with God verses previous conversations: "It is through Isaac that your offspring will be reckoned." Abraham does the only thing he knows to do: trust and obey God. I wonder if Abraham is able to small talk with his son during the journey, or is he pre-occupied with his own thoughts. "God, it sure would be a good time to talk this over. Are you sure about this?" "Then he reached out his hand and took the knife to slay his son." Genesis 22:10.

Returning home, Abraham must have praised God for His faithfulness. Actually, they are faithful to each other. His relationship with God is more important than anything or anyone. He trusts God totally and proves it with his obedience. Is it any wonder God calls Abraham His friend? "But you, Israel, my servant, Jacob, whom I have chosen, you descendants of Abraham my friend." Isaiah 41:8.

It must have been very difficult for Abraham to just keep doing the next thing. Put yourself in his place. He passed the test of obedience. This test will come to all of us in some form during our lifetime. Jesus says to us today, "You are my friends if you do what I command." John 15:14.

January 8 – **Son of Promise**

God promises Abraham a son in his old age. "…and all peoples on earth will be blessed through you." Genesis 12:3. God always keeps His promises. "Abraham was the father of Isaac. The sons of Isaac: Esau and Israel." 1 Chronicles 1:34. Even though Abraham has a son, Ishmael, with Sarah's slave, Hagar, Isaac is the son of promise. After Sarah dies, Abraham marries Keturah and has six more sons, but Isaac is the son of promise. God repeats His promise many times to Abraham, Isaac, and Jacob (Israel). There is yet a Promised Son to be born.

Forty-two generations later, Jesus is born (Matthew 1:17). "The virgin will conceive and give birth to a son, and they will call him Immanuel (which means 'God with us')." Matthew 1:23. The birth of Jesus fulfills this prophecy given in Isaiah 7:14.

Jesus is the true Son of Promise, and through Him all peoples on earth are blessed because of the new life He gives. I'm thankful for God's Son of Promise. Because of Him my sins are forgiven; I've been born again, and I'm on my way to heaven. "His son by the slave woman was born according to the flesh, but his son by the free woman was born as the result of a divine promise." Galatians 4:23.

January 9 – **I Want It Now!**

Our 21st century generation is accused of being the microwave generation. We want what we want, and we want it now! No delayed gratification for us! Have you ever looked back to a time in your life when you regretted a hasty decision based solely on your desires in the moment? We often suffer the consequences of our stupid choices. If only…

Human nature hasn't changed much in 4,000 years. Esau, driven by an insatiable appetite for immediate satisfaction, exchanges his most precious possession, his birthright, for a measly bowl of soup. He listens to Satan's tempting lie: Doesn't that smell delicious? And it tastes so good! You will die if you don't eat some right now! "'Look, I am about to die,' Esau said. 'What good is the birthright to me?'" Genesis 25:32. No one forces Esau to do this. He just doesn't stop and think this through, but instead caves in to what feels good in the moment.

Don't rush into something; God may have a better plan. Learn to wait on the Lord, and teach your children and grandchildren this valuable truth. "Yet the Lord longs to be gracious to you; therefore he will rise up to show you compassion. For the Lord is a God of justice. Blessed are all who wait for him!" Isaiah 30:18. "But if we hope for what we do not yet have, we wait for it patiently." Romans 8:25.

January 10 – **Surprise!**

"When morning came, there was Leah! So Jacob said to Laban, 'What is this you have done to me? I served you for Rachel, didn't I? Why have you deceived me?'" Genesis 29:25. Jacob is not the innocent victim he so cunningly tries to make Laban believe. He has played the part of deceiver as did his grandfather and father before him. Deception sown; deception reaped.

I appreciate the fact that God includes the failures and sins of the superheroes of the Bible. We're in good company! We do reap what we sow, and there are consequences to our actions. However, God has the power to restore and make the good, bad, and ugly things in our lives work for His glory. He makes beauty from miserable ashes (Isaiah 61:3).

It's comforting to know that God loves me unconditionally. I refuse to believe Satan's lies: Just give up; you've messed up one too many times; just quit this God thing. It's not the end of the world! When the Holy Spirit convicts me of conniving, failures, mistakes and sin (yes, let's just call it what it is – sin), and I repent and receive God's love and forgiveness, give everything to Him, and continue walking with Him, He still creates blessing from cinders today.

The truth is we all need a Savior, and His name is Jesus. It doesn't matter where you are today or what you've done; believe in Jesus Christ. Give him your life, follow and obey Him. "And we know that in all things God works for the good of those who love him, who have been called according to his purpose." Romans 8:28.

January 11 – **Are You Comfortable?**

The mother eagle builds her nest high up and soft inside for her eaglets. As they hatch and grow, she meets their every need.

But there comes a time when she knows her babies are ready to soar. The eaglets, however, are comfortably content. Why should they leave the nest? They have it made! Besides, it's scary out there. They don't want to plummet into the deep unknown. Their mother knows they are created for more than this nest, so she gradually begins to remove some of the padding, and things get sticky. Their world is rocked! She wants them to fly and fulfill their purpose. She waits and remains close to catch them if they tumble.

Jacob recognizes that things are changing around him. The good life he has grown accustomed to for twenty years is shifting. "And Jacob noticed that Laban's attitude toward him was not what it had been." Genesis 31:2. It is as if God is whispering in his ear, "It's time. Move out and fulfill your destiny. Trust Me."

"Simon answered, 'Master, we've worked hard all night and haven't caught anything. But because you say so, I will let down the nets.'" Luke 5:5. Perhaps Simon Peter's fishing business has become unpredictable as of late, and he is beginning to question if there is more to life than fishing as he knows it. "…Then Jesus said to Simon, 'Don't be afraid; from now on you will fish for people.' So they pulled their boats up on shore, left everything and followed him." Luke 5:10, 11.

God doesn't create us to dwell in our private comfort zone all our lives and just watch the world go by. He wants us to take risks and trust Him. But sometimes we need a little incentive to take that first step of faith and follow Him, so He shakes things up. Our surroundings get uncomfortable in the workplace or in a relationship. Could it be that God is pulling away some of our security and insulation to get us to move? He is always nearby.

January 12 – **Adult Children**

"While Israel was living in that region, Reuben went in and slept with his father's concubine Bilhah, and Israel heard of it..."

Genesis 35:22. Yes, Reuben is an adult, but does Jacob confront his firstborn with this blatant sin against God, father, and son? Scripture doesn't tell us. The Word does tell us this sin cost Reuben the birthright and blessing of the firstborn (chapter 49). Jacob gives these to Joseph and Judah. A side note: We *never* get away with sin; it always costs more than we are willing to pay. Jacob is in good company with other Old Testament fathers such as David, Eli, and Samuel who fail to deal with the sins of their grown sons as well.

In Luke 15, Jesus tells the parable of the lost son. The father does not force his son to do the right thing, but he does continue to love his son and waits for him to return; he never disowns him. "So he got up and went to his father. But while he was still a long way off, his father saw him and was filled with compassion for him; he ran to his son, threw his arms around him and kissed him." Luke 15:20. This is a beautiful picture of our Heavenly Father's love for us. He always waits and watches for us to return when we drift away from Him.

There are no perfect parents or perfect children on this earth. There is and always will be only one perfect Father and one perfect Son. We are no longer responsible for our adult children. They are grown and responsible to God for their own relationship with Him. As parents, we continue to love, pray, watch, wait, and trust God. And then with open arms and kisses, we welcome them home.

January 13 – **Possessions vs. Promise**

I wonder if Jacob ever questions God when he looks at his brother Esau's descendants and wealth. "Hey, God, remember me? I'm the one you said you would bless and multiply. Why is Esau's family multiplying faster than mine, and he is growing richer more quickly than I am!" "Their possessions were too great for them to remain together; the land where they were staying could not support them both because of their livestock. So Esau (that is, Edom) settled in the hill country of Seir." Genesis 36:7, 8. Esau is already possessing his inheritance and making for himself a kingdom. Canaan is promised to Jacob and his descendants, but it will be a very long time before he takes possession. You will notice that only the names of Esau's sons and grandsons are recorded, not their history; and his genealogy goes no further than the third or fourth generation. It is from Jacob's seed that the promise will be fulfilled to the entire world. God's promise to Jacob begins to work late, but its effect remains forever and is completely fulfilled in the spiritual Israel, of which you and I are a part.

Psalm 73 discusses the prosperity of the wicked. "But as for me, my feet had almost slipped; I had nearly lost my foothold. For I envied the arrogant when I saw the prosperity of the wicked." Psalm 73:2, 3. There is no need to envy. What does it accomplish? The people of this world may have more in their hands, but they have nothing in hope. God's children have more in hope than they have in their hands. I'm reminded of Jesus' parable of the rich man and Lazarus. "But Abraham replied, 'Son, remember that in your lifetime you received your good things, while Lazarus received bad things, but now he is comforted here and you are in agony." Luke 16:25. I would rather have Jesus and hope that everything this world has to offer. Wait patiently for God's promise.

January 14 – **The Lord Was With Joseph**

Joseph is a braggadocios teenager who enjoys making his older brothers squirm – typical behavior for a little brother. But they don't appreciate it, and it lands Joseph in a pit, then in slave chains, then in a foreign country with the likelihood of never seeing his family again – better that than being murdered by his brothers.

It's safe to say that life is not good for Joseph at this point. But he starts to grow up quickly. Fast forward a couple of years, and we see a young man who works hard, serves God, and lives out his integrity – which lands him in prison. "…How then could I do such a wicked thing and sin against God?" Genesis 39:9.

Before and during Joseph's prison sentence, we read four times in one chapter, "The Lord was with Joseph." Genesis 39:2, 3, 21, 23. This tells me that even when God is with us, things can go very wrong for us if we look at our circumstances from the world's view. Lies can be told and believed about us, and the world finds us guilty as charged. We suffer unjustly; but it's really okay. We just can't see the whole picture yet; we don't understand God's eternal purpose and plan yet. Our part is to stay faithful to God, love Him, obey Him, and serve Him each day with what He's given us to do today. God will take care of the rest. We can trust Him completely. We decide to focus our energies (physical, mental, emotional, and spiritual) into what we know to do for Him and not allow worry, fear, and unforgiveness to deplete us. God is in control of all the things out of our control.

Please turn in your Bible and read Romans 12:17-21. Joseph lives this out, and we can too. "Do not take revenge, my dear friends, but leave room for God's wrath, for it is written: 'It is mine to avenge; I will repay,' says the Lord." Romans 12:19.

January 15 – **Reminders**

"But when all goes well with you, remember me and show me kindness; mention me to Pharaoh and get me out of this prison." Genesis 40:14. The memory is an interesting ability God has given us. When Joseph interprets the dreams of the pharaoh's cupbearer and baker, he probably remembers his own dream from years past and wonders if his dream will ever come true. But life gets busy for the cupbearer; he returns to his former job. He wants to do well; he puts the past behind him and sinks all his time and energy into pleasing Pharaoh. He thinks only about himself in this moment. After all, he never wants to go back to that dungeon.

Two full years pass when news of Pharaoh's dream reaches his ears. "Then the chief cupbearer said to Pharaoh, 'Today I am reminded of my shortcomings.'" Genesis 41:9. He suddenly remembers the promise he made and broke to Joseph. Now he has a decision to make: He can remain silent, or he can act on this memory. He does the right thing and sets the record straight.

"But the Advocate, the Holy Spirit, whom the Father will send in my name, will teach you all things and will remind you of everything I have said to you." John 14:26. God loves us. He reminds us of His Word and His promises to encourage us. He also reminds us of our shortcomings; He gives us another chance to do the right thing. Perhaps we need to repent or forgive someone. Perhaps we need to go to that person and reconcile. God reminds us for a reason. Then it's our choice to conveniently forget again or make it right before God and our brother or sister. "Though you already know all this, I want to remind you that the Lord at one time delivered his people out of Egypt, but later destroyed those who did not believe." Jude 1:5.

January 16 – **Hiding Sin**

Joseph's brothers must have talked with deep regret over the years about what they had done to their younger brother and for all the grief they caused their father. Hiding their sin takes its toll on the family. They never tell their father whom they love and respect the truth all those years. They really aren't evil men. They made a huge mistake but continue to cover up and feign innocence. Why cause their father more misery in admitting their guilt; his displeasure would be more than they can bear. So they live with the lie.

Now in Egypt, they try to convince themselves and the ruler of the land that they are honest men (Genesis 42:11, 31). Their guilt and shame surface; how many times have they had this conversation? "...Surely we are being punished because of our brother...Didn't I tell you not to sin against the boy? But you wouldn't listen! Now we must give an accounting for his blood." (Re-read Genesis 42:21, 22) "...God has uncovered your servants' guilt..." (44:16). "...and you may be sure that your sin will find you out." Numbers 32:23.

A lie will never morph into the truth; eventually the lie will be exposed and demand a response. God does this because He loves us; He gives us another chance to respond with repentance, so He can respond with forgiveness. "There is nothing concealed that will not be disclosed, or hidden that will not be made known." Luke 12:2. "The other guests began to say among themselves, "Who is this who even forgives sins?" Luke 7:49.

January 17 – **Distinctly Separate**

"God saw that the light was good, and he separated the light from the darkness." Genesis 1:4. God starts separating things at the beginning of creation. We need the distinctions, the clarity, the purity and no gray areas. God knows life works better with clear boundaries – a definitive yes and no with no maybe's. He separates the people at the Tower of Babel (Genesis 11:1-9). He commands Abram to leave his home so God can make him into a separate nation from which all the nations of the earth will be blessed.

When Jacob and all his descendants journey into Egypt to survive the famine, God arranges for Joseph's family to live in Goshen, situated in the delta of the Nile River far from the main centers of Egyptian life, where they will live in isolation and develop into a nation of people set apart for God's purpose. "Pharaoh said to Joseph, 'Your father and your brothers have come to you, and the land of Egypt is before you; settle your father and your brothers in the best part of the land. Let them live in Goshen..." Genesis 47:5, 6. "When Pharaoh calls you in and asks, 'What is your occupation?' you should answer, 'Your servants have tended livestock from our boyhood on, just as our fathers did.' Then you will be allowed to settle in the region of Goshen, for all shepherds are detestable to the Egyptians." Genesis 46:33, 34. The Egyptians' disdain for shepherds helps them to remain separate from the Egyptians and their ways.

God watches over His chosen people. Laws are established to protect them from the physically unclean and diseased. Even King Uzziah, who was a leper, lives separately from the people (2 Chronicles 26:21). The Israelites must separate themselves from the heathen around them in Ezra 10:11. God still admonishes His people today to live our lives apart from the world. Let there be a clear distinction between our lives and the world with no need for guesswork. "Do not be yoked together with unbelievers. For what do righteousness and wickedness have in common? Or what fellowship can light have with darkness?" 2 Corinthians 6:14.

January 18 – **Nonetheless a Promise**

"Jacob said to Joseph, "God Almighty appeared to me at Luz in the land of Canaan, and there he blessed me and said to me, 'I am going to make you fruitful and increase your numbers. I will make you a community of peoples, and I will give this land as an everlasting possession to your descendants after you.'" Genesis 48:3, 4. God gives Abraham, Isaac, and Jacob a promise. They rehearse it to themselves many times through the years. Nevertheless, none of them realize the fulfillment of that promise in their lifetime. They each receive the promise in faith. However, the promise is literally realized generations later – in God's perfect way and timing.

Parents pray fervently for wayward children, believing God's promise for their salvation, and the children come to Christ after their parents enter heaven. People pray and believe God for divine healing for loved ones, but God chooses to heal them in heaven. God's promises are God's promises; some are completed in this lifetime; some are achieved in heaven. God never says I will plainly see every promise He makes to me come to pass while I'm still walking this earth. "But do not forget this one thing, dear friends: With the Lord a day is like a thousand years, and a thousand years are like a day." 2 Peter 3:8.

Abraham, Isaac, and Jacob – and untold others – receive God's promises fulfilled in eternity. His promises are true, whenever He chooses to fulfill them. "And so after waiting patiently, Abraham received what was promised." Hebrews 6:15.

January 19 – **The Right Thing**

Just when Job thinks nothing else could possibly go wrong, it does. Have you ever felt like that? Most of us will never experience the tragedy, pain, and grief that Job endured. But look at Job 1:22. "In all this, Job did not sin by charging God with wrongdoing." I find this very impressive about Job's character. Most of us look for someone to blame when things go south.

It is traditionally believed among Bible scholars that Job and Abraham could have possibly been contemporaries – Abraham from Ur; Job from Uz, east of Ur by several hundred miles. Each never knew the other existed; however, I find that Abraham and Job view the One True God in much the same way. Abraham says in Genesis 18:25, "...Will not the Judge of all the earth do right?"

When I find myself walking through heartache, storms, and situations I don't understand, it is comforting to know that God always does the right thing. He never makes a mistake; He does understand; He is in control, and I can trust Him. "All this is evidence that God's judgment is right..." 2 Thessalonians 1:5.

January 20 – **Friends?**

As if things are not bad enough for Job, Satan makes sure that extreme mental anguish and continual emotional pain are inflicted on him by his so called friends. It is included in Satan's package deal. He excels at kicking a man when he is down. Satan has not changed his tactics. Emotional pain is the icing on Satan's cake. "Consider now: Who, being innocent, has ever perished? Where were the upright ever destroyed?" Job 4:7. What we have here is flawed thinking from Eliphaz. There's still a lot of that circulating today. Error mixed with truth equals error. These friends are relentless in their verbal pummeling of Job in his "unrelenting pain." (6:10). With friends like these, who needs enemies?

We know that Jesus' closest friends desert Him in His greatest hour of need on the earth. The Apostle Paul shares with Timothy his similar dilemma. "You know that everyone in the province of Asia has deserted me..." 2 Timothy 1:15. "for Demas, because he loved this world, has deserted me..." 2 Timothy 4:10. "At my first defense, no one came to my support, but everyone deserted me. May it not be held against them. But the Lord stood at my side and gave me strength..." 2 Timothy 4:16, 17. "...but there is a friend who sticks closer than a brother." Proverbs 18:24. This look at friendship begs me to ask myself this question, "What sort of friend am I?"

January 21 – **The Bridge**

Job wrestles with God, trying to make sense of catastrophe; and he is getting nowhere fast. He realizes his need for a mediator.

"If only there were someone to mediate between us, someone to bring us together." Job 9:33.

Today we know that "Someone" is Jesus Christ. Because of Who He is, the One and only Son of God, and what He did by taking our sin upon Himself, dying on the cross in our place, and resurrecting from the grave, we can now have relationship with Almighty God. Jesus Christ, 100% man and 100% God, bridged that vast expanse separating us from God with His own blood. And He was the only One in heaven and earth Who could.

"For there is one God and one mediator between God and mankind, the man Christ Jesus, who gave himself as a ransom for all people. This has now been witnessed to at the proper time." 1 Timothy 2:5, 6. I'm thankful that Jesus is my Lord, my Defender, my Redeemer; the One Who puts His nail-scarred hand on me and leads me to the Father.

January 22 – **Breath and Life**

"In his hand is the life of every creature and the breath of all mankind." Job 12:10. God is there when we take our first breath, and He knows exactly the day and moment of our final breath.

He's there when every creature – great or small, on the highest mountain top or in the depths of the ocean – is born into the world and when it dies. He creates each snowflake distinct from every other snowflake since the beginning of time. He watches as it falls to earth and knows exactly where it falls and where it melts. He watches the tiniest of flowers bloom lodged between two boulders. He observes each leaf fall to the forest floor. He creates millions of stars that human eyes will never see. Why? Because He can. He's God, and He takes great delight in His creation, which includes you. Absolutely nothing misses His attention. What a mighty God we serve!

May we not resemble the foolish rich man in Luke chapter 12 who lives only for himself. "But God said to him, 'You fool! This very night your life will be demanded from you. Then who will get what you have prepared for yourself?'" Luke 12:20. We only have this one life in which to get it right. He knows our beginning and end, because He is the Beginning and the End. "I am the Alpha and the Omega, the First and the Last, the Beginning and the End." Revelation 22:13.

January 23 – **Don't Be a Know-It-All**

"Listen to me and I will explain to you; let me tell you what I have seen." Job 15:17. This sounds like the words of a know-it-all! Eliphaz continues to exude his wisdom, and Job is tired of hearing it. "I also could speak like you, if you were in my place; I could make fine speeches against you and shake my head at you." (16:4). The diatribes continue until God decides it's time to intervene and set the record straight. And He *always* sets the record straight; His truth and justice *always* prevail, if not in this life, in the next.

"So, if you think you are standing firm, be careful that you don't fall!" 1 Corinthians 10:12. God admonishes us to remain humble and teachable at all times. The opposite of being teachable is arrogance. Does Job do life perfectly? No, and neither will you or I. There is always room for improvement in our lives and in our walk with the Lord. There is always more to learn about God. Will you keep a teachable and humble spirit even after many years of being a Christian, even with all your popularity, success, education, wealth, and position?

"This is what the Lord says: 'Let not the wise boast of their wisdom or the strong boast of their strength or the rich boast of their riches, but let the one who boasts boast about this: that they have the understanding to know me, that I am the Lord, who exercises kindness, justice and righteousness on earth, for in these I delight,' declares the Lord." Jeremiah 9:23, 24.

"For the foolishness of God is wiser than human wisdom, and the weakness of God is stronger than human strength." 1 Corinthians 1:25.

January 24 – **I Will See God**

Night and day, death's unflinching stare grips Job. Yet throughout this excruciating ordeal, Job maintains his deep faith and hope in God. "I know that my redeemer lives, and that in the end he will stand on the earth. And after my skin has been destroyed, yet in my flesh I will see God; I myself will see him with my own eyes – I, and not another. How my heart yearns within me!" Job 19:25-27. Job emphasizes three times in this brief passage, "I will see God; I myself will see him with my own eyes – I, and not another." He was sure of it, and oh, how he longed for that day!

Unbelievers do not have this assurance; they do not possess this peace and hope that comes from knowing the One True God and His Son Jesus Christ. Everyone will experience suffering and heartache in this life. The difference is this: Do we hold a faith, hope and trust in the One Who can navigate us safely to the other side? Everyone will experience physical death; but for the believer, it's not the end of life but a new and glorious beginning.

Put your faith in Jesus Christ today. Believe. Confess your sin and your need for a Savior. Receive His forgiveness and new life which He purchased for you on Calvary's cross. "For he says, 'In the time of my favor I heard you, and in the day of salvation I helped you.' I tell you, now is the time of God's favor, now is the day of salvation." 2 Corinthians 6:2. "They will see his face, and his name will be on their foreheads." Revelation 22:4.

January 25 – **God is Sovereign**

Throughout God's Word, God speaks of Himself as sovereign; the Old Testament prophets refer to Him as sovereign. The Webster Illustrated Contemporary Dictionary defines sovereign as "exercising or possessing supreme jurisdiction or power." However, in God's case, it's not "or" and "or" but "and" and "and."

"But he stands alone, and who can oppose him? He does whatever he pleases." Job 23:13. God is in a class by Himself; no one or no thing can ever be compared to Him. "Remember the former things, those of long ago; I am God, and there is no other; I am God, and there is none like me." Isaiah 46:9. To oppose God is to fail. Even Gamaliel, a Pharisee and teacher of the law, recognizes this. "But if it is from God, you will not be able to stop these men; you will only find yourselves fighting against God." Acts 5:39. We know that in the last days the antichrist will set himself up as God and will ultimately fail and be thrown into the lake of fire. God wins! Just read the end of His book. God is sovereign; He does whatever He pleases; His ways are always just and righteous.

"Each of the four living creatures had six wings and was covered with eyes all around, even under its wings. Day and night they never stop saying: 'Holy, holy, holy is the Lord God Almighty, who was, and is, and is to come.'" Revelation 4:8.

January 26 – **Is It Really Hidden?**

Job is a very learned man and knowledgeable of ancient mining techniques. In chapter 28:1-10, he shares his insight of the tunneling technology of his day. His description is easily verified by modern day archaeological discoveries, one of which is an eighth-century B.C. inscription at Jerusalem's Pool of Siloam authenticating the underground tunnel, the brain-child of King Hezekiah, which redirected water into Jerusalem from the Gihon spring, cut through solid rock with picks for 1,750 feet. Impressive.

Job then reverts back to his discourse about God. Does verse eleven belong more to the first ten verses of the chapter or to the verses following? "They search the sources of the rivers and bring hidden things to light." Job 28:11. The "they" in this verse can also be God.

There is absolutely nothing in this world hidden from God's eyes. He sees all and knows all, even those things we think we've buried deep in our hearts, away from God, others, and ourselves. However, the pain and sin are still there, covered by layers of time and lies. "For there is nothing hidden that will not be disclosed, and nothing concealed that will not be known or brought out into the open." Luke 8:17. "...He will bring to light what is hidden in darkness and will expose the motives of the heart..." 1 Corinthians 4:5. "Nothing in all creation is hidden from God's sight. Everything is uncovered and laid bare before the eyes of him to whom we must give account." Hebrews 4:13.

January 27 – **The Unstrung Bow**

"Now that God has unstrung my bow and afflicted me, they throw off restraint in my presence." Job 30:11. Job compares his present circumstances to his bow being unstrung. Let's take a closer look at his analogy. In the ancient world, a man's bow and arrows are vital to his livelihood. They are used in hunting food (Genesis 27:3), defending in battle (1 Chronicles 5:18), protecting homes and families (Nehemiah 4:13), and even for recreational purposes (1 Samuel 20:35, 36). Warriors spend many hours training for accuracy and become proficient shooting arrows with both hands (1 Chronicles 12:2). God unstrings Job's bow. In other words, Job loses everything important to him, everything he has worked so hard to acquire, in a moment of time. He feels helpless.

On any given day, we could experience God unstringing our bow; none of us are immune from this possibility. However, God can also restore everything we lose – and more – just like He does for Job. Rest assured; God restores and gives back to His children so much more, if not in this life, in heaven and for all eternity. Like Job, we must maintain a strong faith in God always, through blessed and difficult days alike.

Here's something else to consider. Zechariah foresees the Messiah as the battle bow. "From Judah will come the cornerstone, from him the tent peg, from him the battle bow, from him every ruler." Zechariah 10:4. "I saw heaven standing open and there before me was a white horse, whose rider is called Faithful and True. With justice he judges and wages war." Revelation 19:11. Jesus Christ is the victorious King, the Warrior-Messiah.

January 28 – **I Am the Ransomed One**

"...Spare them from going down to the pit; I have found a ransom for them." Job 33:24. I doubt Elihu understands the truth of these words he speaks so neatly lodged in the middle of his tirade against Job. Satan holds us captive because of our unrepented sin, which separates us from God. I cannot escape; I cannot free myself from Satan's grip. But God "finds a ransom" for me in His one and only Son. He exchanges the life of Jesus for me. He buys my freedom and your freedom with the holy blood of Jesus Christ. How He must love us to pay such a high price!

"For God so loved the world that he gave his one and only Son, that whoever believes in him shall not perish but have eternal life." John 3:16. The kidnapper/destroyer of our souls looks at Jesus and screams, "Not again!" Our Savior proclaims, "He's My child now. Set him free. I take his place." Satan shutters and lets the ransomed one go. He is reminded once again of his final doom before God's Holy and all powerful Son.

"For even the Son of Man did not come to be served, but to serve, and to give his life as a ransom for many." Mark 10:45.

January 29 – **Whose Spotlight Is It?**

"Bear with me a little longer and I will show you that there is more to be said in God's behalf." Job 36:2. Really? Is Elihu's pride talking here? The Apostle Paul's words in 1 Corinthians 2:1-5 offer a striking contrast to the words of Elihu. "...When I came to you, I did not come with eloquence or human wisdom as I proclaimed to you the testimony about God. For I resolved to know nothing while I was with you except Jesus Christ and him crucified. I came to you in weakness with great fear and trembling. My message and my preaching were not with wise and persuasive words, but with a demonstration of the Spirit's power, so that your faith might not rest on human wisdom, but on God's power."

Elihu disappears from the story after his discourse. Does he walk away at that point thinking, "I guess I dazzled them with my wisdom"? Does he leave the premises stuck on self and miss God altogether?

As the proclaimer of Good News, let's approach the pulpit or the friend with a humble heart, so that others see and hear Jesus Christ. So often, our deepest thought is, "I'm so glad you're here today, so I can astound you with my wit and wisdom." God won't bless that. Whose praises are the people singing as they leave the building? "Didn't he do a great job today? He's so articulate!" Or... "Praise the Lord! God spoke to me today! I felt His presence! He touched my life!"

Let's get out of God's spotlight long enough for Him to do what only He can do. Remember, God shares His glory with no one (Isaiah 42:8 and 48:11).

January 30 – **God's Pop Quiz**

I never did like a pop quiz in school. I was usually caught off guard, and my brain immediately started scrambling for lessons learned. God confronts Job with His own pop quiz. Seriously? Right in the middle of the greatest storm of his life – a test in the middle of his test?

"Then the Lord spoke to Job out of the storm. He said:" Job 38:1. What follows is a series of 52 questions which God asks Job (chapters 38 and 39). The answers are not up for debate and clearly not multiple choice. Most answers are either "No" or "God." Why not take the test and see how you do? Compare your answers with mine at the bottom of this page.

Jesus gives His own pop quiz in the middle of a storm (Luke 8:22-25). It was one question worth 100 points! "Where is your faith?" verse 25.

Here are a few lessons we can learn from today's reading: 1) God wants to teach us some things when we're in a storm. 2) The Lord is always with us in a storm. 3) He is the Master Teacher; He's all-wise and all-knowing. 4) He knows all the answers, and He is the Answer.

Am I a teachable student, and am I ready for His next pop quiz?

Answers: No – 32 times; God – 14 times; God knows – 3 times; Yes – 1 time; Job – 1 time; Nowhere – 1 time

January 31 – **Restoration**

"Then I myself will admit to you that your own right hand can save you." Job 40:14. "After Job had prayed for his friends, the Lord restored his fortunes and gave him twice as much as he had before." 42:10. "The Lord blessed the latter part of Job's life more than the former part..." 42:12. What correlation is there between these verses, if any? Only God can save a soul, so what can our own right hand do when we are walking through a deep and extended trial?

As Job obeys God and intercedes for his three pseudo-comforters, God honors those prayers, and blessings begin to flow in Job's direction. This is not to say that I will experience financial and material prosperity every time I pray for others, be it friends, enemies, those in authority, the lost, or the suffering. God's touch in my life may look differently. But if my heart is in the right place as I pray for others, God will definitely touch my spirit. Notice that up to this point in Job's trial, his attention was turned inward on himself and his problems. However, when his focus shifts to others, God begins to pour His blessings out on Job.

Whenever difficult days wrap around my life, it is very easy to become self-absorbed: "Oh, woe, is me!" As Jesus walked the earth, He was not self-centered; He was and is all about others. I want to be more like Jesus.

"The Lord blessed the latter part of Job's life more than the former part." That's a good report for all of us, because the best is yet to come! "And the God of all grace, who called you to his eternal glory in Christ, after you have suffered a little while, will himself restore you and make you strong, firm and steadfast. To him be the power for ever and ever. Amen." 1 Peter 5:10, 11.

FEBRUARY

February 1 – **God is Concerned**

"So God looked on the Israelites and was concerned about them." Exodus 2:25. "...and I am concerned about their suffering. So I have come down to rescue them..." Exodus 3:7, 8. God has not forgotten His children. He loves His people; He sees their suffering and declares that He will rescue them. But circumstances get much worse for the Israelites before they get better. God is working; He is bringing about deliverance, but the people find it difficult not to question, fear, and doubt in the middle of their suffering. However, God is faithful to His Word, and in His perfect time and will, He delivers the people He loves.

God still orders events in the lives of His children in ways that will give Him the most glory. Our questions, fear, and doubt, can get in the way of our trusting Him. "Grace and peace to you from God our Father and the Lord Jesus Christ, who gave himself for our sins to rescue us from the present evil age, according to the will of our God and Father, to whom be glory for ever and ever, Amen." Galatians 1:3-5. And that's all we need to know.

February 2 – **Worship Before**

The children of Israel are enslaved and living in cruel bondage. Moses and Aaron talk with the elders of the Israelites and explain to them God's plan to deliver them. "and they believed. And when they heard that the Lord was concerned about them and had seen their misery, they bowed down and worshiped." Exodus 4:31. The people have not yet experienced the answer to their suffering; nevertheless they worship God.

Don't wait for God to answer your prayers and perform His Word to you before you worship Him. He is worthy of our worship at all times, even in the waiting and living by faith moments of our lives. Will you worship Him today for Who He is, or will you withhold your worship, praise and devotion until circumstances turn around and start going your way? Wherever we are in our journey, He is worthy of our worship, always, and at all times. Let's practice today and every day what we will do in heaven for all eternity: worship the Lord. "the twenty-four elders fall down before him who sits on the throne and worship him who lives for ever and ever. They lay their crowns before the throne and say: 'You are worthy, our Lord and God, to receive glory and honor and power, for you created all things, and by your will they were created and have their being.'" Revelation 4:10, 11.

February 3 – **God's Finger**

"the magicians said to Pharaoh, 'This is the finger of God.' But Pharaoh's heart was hard and he would not listen, just as the Lord had said." Exodus 8:19. Pharaoh's magicians can see what Pharaoh cannot. They recognize the power in this finger and know there is more where that comes from! What about the power in God's hand – arm – both arms – voice – His entire being! If this is just His finger, we better watch out! Pharaoh doesn't listen.

God's finger inscribes the Ten Commandments on tablets of stone and gives them to Moses (Exodus 31:18). He crashes King Belshazzar's party by writing the King's doom on the wall (Daniel 5:5). There is more power in God's fingertip than we can possibly imagine.

Jesus says in Luke 11:20, "But if I drive out demons by the finger of God, then the kingdom of God has come upon you." God's finger still has more power today than all the demons in hell.

February 4 – **I Am the Lord**

"that you may tell your children and grandchildren how I dealt harshly with the Egyptians and how I performed my signs among them, and that you may know that I am the Lord." Exodus 10:2. With everything that happens in our lives – the good and the bad – the overarching truth God wants us to learn and understand and remember is that "I am the Lord." (Exodus 12:12). He wants us to know Him and know Him better today than we did yesterday.

"And when your children ask you, 'What does this ceremony mean to you?'" Exodus 12:26. The exodus and Passover are not just great Old Testament stories we tell our children; they contain much significance and implication for our lives today – "that you may know that I am the Lord." God still delivers His people from bondage. You become His when you believe in Him and give Him your life. The Passover points to the supreme sacrifice of the ages, Jesus Christ, who shed His blood for us on the cross so that we can truly live. When His pure and holy blood is applied to the doorposts of our hearts, the enemy must pass over us; he can't touch us, because the blood of Jesus covers us. Oh, the life-giving power of His blood!

"But these are written that you may believe that Jesus is the Messiah, the Son of God, and that by believing you may have life in his name." John 20:31.

Lord Jesus, I believe in You and Your sacrifice on the cross for my sin. Forgive me. Wash me. I give You my life. Cover my heart and life with Your precious blood. I want to know You as Savior, Lord, Deliverer, Mighty God. Thank You for saving me.

February 5 – **His Way**

"Moses answered the people, 'Do not be afraid. Stand firm and you will see the deliverance the Lord will bring you today. The Egyptians you see today you will never see again. The Lord will fight for you; you need only to be still.'" Exodus 14:13, 14. There are times in our lives when we feel just like the Israelites: surrounded and hemmed in on every side by the enemy, and we don't see a way out. God says the same thing to us today: "Do not be afraid; stand firm (in your faith); I will fight for you; you need only to be still."

"All that night" (v 21) God works, and the Israelites can't believe their eyes! God makes a way (a highway through the Red Sea) where there was no way the day before! What God uses to deliver His people, He uses to destroy the enemy. God does a complete work; every one of His children is safe, and every single enemy is destroyed.

God still makes a way today for His children. We don't see it; He sees it. Our view of our situation is so limited, much like tunnel-vision. He sees our situation from every possible angle; He sees people and circumstances we can't possibly see. He knows how to intervene and meet our needs in ways that will bring Him the greatest glory (vs. 17, 18).

The God we serve today is the God of the Exodus. His love, provision, and power have not diminished. He still does miracles today when we trust and obey Him. With the Israelites, we can sing, "The Lord is my strength and my defense; he has become my salvation. He is my God, and I will praise him, my father's God, and I will exalt him. The Lord is a warrior; the Lord is his name." Exodus 15:2, 3.

"Then Jesus came to them and said, 'All authority (power) in heaven and on earth has been given to me.'" Matthew 28:18.

February 6 – **Heaven's Bread**

I love the smell of homemade bread fresh out of the oven. There's nothing better than to cut off a piece of hot bread, smear it with butter and honey, and then just sit back and enjoy. Mmmmm good!

"Then the Lord said to Moses, 'I will rain down bread from heaven for you. The people are to go out each day and gather enough for that day. In this way I will test them and see whether they will follow my instructions.'" Exodus 16:4. God provides daily bread for the Israelites; it's healthy, delicious (tastes like honey), and even gluten-free! They must gather the manna each morning, double the amount on the sixth day. When they disobey God and attempt to survive on left-overs, there's a stench; "…but it was full of maggots and began to smell…" (v 20).

"Jesus said to them, 'Very truly I tell you, it is not Moses who has given you the bread from heaven, but it is my Father who gives you the true bread from heaven.'" John 6:32. Jesus Christ is the Living Bread/Word; the Holy Bible is His Written Bread/Word. We must have fresh Bread every day in order to maintain that sweet aroma. Time spent with Jesus and His Word on a daily basis keeps us well fed and smelling good. Those who teach or preach God's Word should always offer mouth-watering, tantalizing, fragrant, fresh from heaven's kitchen – bread; nothing stale, moldy, or wormy will satisfy. What do people smell in your presence? Heaven's perfume or a pungent odor. Jesus says, "I am the bread of life." John 6:48.

February 7 – **Healthy Fear**

"Moses said to the people, 'Do not be afraid. God has come to test you, so that the fear of God will be with you to keep you from sinning.'" Exodus 20:20. This is what I call a healthy fear of God. If I have this in sufficient quantity in my heart, I will think twice about the temptation to sin, and walk away. "The fear of the Lord is the beginning of wisdom, and knowledge of the Holy One is understanding." Proverbs 9:10.

There is very good reason to fear God and Him only. Jesus says to us in Luke 12:4, 5, "I tell you, my friends, do not be afraid of those who kill the body and after that can do no more. But I will show you whom you should fear: Fear him who, after your body has been killed, has authority to throw you into hell. Yes, I tell you, fear him." We are nowhere told to fear the devil, but to steadfastly resist him (James 4:7). May we stand in awe of God's majesty and holiness and his wrath against sin.

February 8 – **Superstition**

"Do not cook a young goat in its mother's milk." Exodus 23:19, 34:26, and Deuteronomy 14:21. I've often wondered what in the world this means. Why is this command written three times in the Pentateuch? We must be careful not to attach a disconnected connotation to something we don't understand, or in other words, don't make God's Word say something He never intends to say. Following a little research, I discover the Israelites know exactly what God is saying to them. They are accustomed to seeing this superstitious ceremony among the Egyptians who seethe a kid in its mother's milk, and sprinkle the broth as a magical charm upon their gardens and fields, to make them more fruitful next year. Israel must abhor such foolish customs and depend upon the Lord God for their next harvest. This unnatural custom is also practiced by the Canaanites, in whose land they will soon invade, as a magic potion to promote fertility. God warns His people not to be like other nations who do not know and serve the One True God. God goes on to say in Deuteronomy 14:21, "But you are a people holy to the Lord your God."

As Christians today, we have a responsibility to reflect the holiness of the God we know and serve by walking in His ways. "Therefore come out from them and be separate, says the Lord. Touch no unclean thing, and I will receive you. And, I will be a Father to you, and you will be my sons and daughters, says the Lord Almighty." 2 Corinthians 6:17, 18.

February 9 – **The Precious Cornerstone**

Everywhere one looks in God's Word, one sees reflections of Jesus Christ. Even the priestly garments mirror the beauty and value of our Lord and future home in heaven; but they still don't scratch the surface of the true description of our Savior's worth. "the second row shall be turquoise, a lapis lazuli and emerald;" Exodus 28:18. It is in some cases uncertain what kind of stones the Hebrew words for these twelve jewels signify.

The word diamond does not appear in the NIV; however, it appears four times in the KJV. In Exodus 28:18, 39:11, and Ezekiel 28:13, turquoise is substituted for the word diamond. In Jeremiah 17:1, the point of a diamond is referred to as a flint point in the NIV. The history of diamonds reveals they were first discovered in Southern India in the 9th century BC, some 500 years after the exodus. Once believed to be the tears of God or splinters of stars, diamonds are rare and precious.

"So this is what the Sovereign Lord says: 'See, I lay a stone in Zion, a tested stone, a precious cornerstone for a sure foundation; the one who relies on it will never be stricken with panic.'" Isaiah 28:16. "For in Scripture it says: 'See, I lay a stone in Zion, a chosen and precious cornerstone, and the one who trusts in him will never be put to shame.'" 1 Peter 2:6. Jesus Christ is that chosen and precious cornerstone. "The foundations of the city walls were decorated with every kind of precious stone..." Revelation 21:19.

February 10 – **Consecration**

I want to speak to the preachers and teachers of God's Word for a few moments. We can learn much from the dedication of Aaron and his sons to the priesthood. God's format may have changed from the old covenant to the new covenant, from the Old Testament to the New Testament, but His truth and principles remain the same. He hasn't changed His requirements to accommodate you or me!

"Whenever they enter the tent of meeting, they shall wash with water so that they will not die…" Exodus 30:20. Whenever you meet with God, do you first examine your heart and life and ask God to wash away anything unclean? "he saved us, not because of righteous things we had done, but because of his mercy. He saved us through the washing of rebirth and renewal by the Holy Spirit." Titus 3:5. Ask God to wash you and renew His Holy Spirit within you daily.

"Aaron must burn fragrant incense on the altar every morning when he tends the lamps." Exodus 30:7. God's Word is a lamp to our feet. Every morning certainly means every day. "For we are to God the pleasing aroma of Christ among those who are being saved and those who are perishing." 2 Corinthians 2:15. (Read 2

Corinthians 2:14-16.) Don't lose the aroma of Christ. God may want to use you today to lead someone to know Him as their personal Savior and Lord!

"Take the anointing oil and anoint him by pouring it on his head." Exodus 29:7. "So Samuel took the horn of oil and anointed him in the presence of his brothers, and from that day on the Spirit of the Lord came powerfully upon David. Samuel then went to Ramah." 1 Samuel 16:13. God wants to pour His Holy Spirit on you and use you powerfully to do His work. Submit to Him daily and ask Him to anoint you.

Consecration literally means association with the sacred. It is dedicating one's life, time, etc. to the specific purpose of serving and worshiping God. Now that I think about it, today's thought pertains to every Christian who loves and serves the Lord.

February 11 – **God's Anger**

"And he passed in front of Moses, proclaiming, 'The Lord, the Lord, the compassionate and gracious God, slow to anger, abounding in love and faithfulness.'" Exodus 34:6. Moses is, at this moment, in an up-close and personal encounter with the Holy God. God is revealing Who He is to Moses. He is compassionate, gracious, loving and faithful to the greatest degree. He is also slow to anger. Scripture bears this truth out in multiple passages: Number 14:18; Nehemiah 9:17; Psalm 86:15, 103:8, 145:8; Joel 2:13; Jonah 4:2; and Nahum 1:3 which states, "The Lord is slow to anger and great in power; the Lord will not leave the guilty unpunished. His way is in the whirlwind and the storm, and clouds are the dust of his feet."

The Scripture teaches us that God is slow to anger; it doesn't say that God never gets angry. Jesus experiences anger. "He looked around at them in anger and, deeply distressed at their stubborn hearts, said to the man, 'Stretch out your hand.' He stretched it out, and his hand was completely restored." Mark 3:5. What makes Jesus angry? Counterfeit holiness. Hypocrisy. Religious leaders playing games. People may not be able to perceive the difference, but the Lord is never fooled. He sees and knows the heart of man. The question we must ask ourselves: Does God see genuine devotion and love for Him when He looks at my heart?

February 12 – **The Fourth Commandment**

I have to be honest with you; I have always struggled with the fourth commandment (Exodus 20:8-11). Can I blame it on my personality? I enjoy working; I can always find something to do with my time; it's difficult for me to do "nothing." However, as I've grown older, I am listening to my body more when it tells me, "If you don't stop right now, I am going to crash and burn on you, and you'll be sorry!"

"For six days, work is to be done, but the seventh day shall be your holy day, a day of sabbath rest to the Lord. Whoever does any work on it is to be put to death." Exodus 35:2. You read right: put to death. Aren't you glad we're no longer under the law? In this fast paced world in which we live, how many of us would still be alive today?

"It will be a sign between me and the Israelites forever, for in six days the Lord made the heavens and the earth, and on the seventh day he rested and was refreshed." Exodus 31:17. If God needed a little R & R after He created the world, it's important that we rest and refresh as well. He fashioned our bodies, and He knows what we should do in order to obtain optimum performance. If we neglect proper rest and relaxation, it will catch up with us. Not only will we suffer physically, but mentally, emotionally, spiritually, and relationally. There are times when the most holy thing we can do is go take a nap! None of us are supermen or superwomen. A husband and wife need that down time together.

Parents and children need to have fun without distractions from work or technology. Turn it off! Go fishing! Take that week of vacation – or two weeks – or a month sabbatical. Rest, refresh, relax, reflect, revive, renew, restore, and regroup – so you can be the best at what God has called you to do. We eventually burn out when we burn the candle at both ends. Our bodies and brains just work better when they're rested. All work and no play make Jack a dull boy! The point is this: Take one day off each week to rest and refresh.

"Then, because so many people were coming and going that they did not even have a chance to eat, he said to them, 'Come with me by yourselves to a quiet place and get some rest.'" Mark 6:31.

February 13 – **The Mirror of God's Word**

"They made the bronze basin and its bronze stand from the mirrors of the women who served at the entrance to the tent of meeting." Exodus 38:8. I find this Scripture interesting for two reasons. One is the fact that women are serving God in a visible way at the place of worship, even in the early days of Moses' leadership. It may be for purposes of devotion or that they keep watch there during the night – possibly both. It reminds me of Anna in the temple the day Mary and Joseph bring baby Jesus in for dedication. Women of God always find ways to love and serve God by serving others inside and outside the church walls.

These women freely give their mirrors, which are of fine burnished brass, for the use of the tabernacle, particularly for the laver where the priests wash and then check their reflections for cleanliness before entering for service. Many of these women have already parted with their ornaments, now their mirrors. Need I say how important a mirror is to a woman? However, these women nobly sacrifice their incentives to pride to the service of their God.

This bronze basin signifies the provision made by Jesus Christ for the cleansing of our souls from sin, that we may serve our Holy God. As such, we then need the mirror of God's Word for self-examination. "Anyone who listens to the word but does not do what it says is like someone who looks at his face in a mirror and, after looking at himself, goes away and immediately forgets what he looks like. But whoever looks intently into the perfect law that gives freedom, and continues in it – not forgetting what they have heard, but doing it – they will be blessed in what they do." James 1:23-25.

February 14 – **The Temple**

"So all the work on the tabernacle, the tent of meeting, was completed. The Israelites did everything just as the Lord commanded Moses." Exodus 39:32. There is a progression in Scripture of God's presence filling the temple. First there is the tabernacle in the wilderness. "Then the cloud covered the tent of meeting, and the glory of the Lord filled the tabernacle. Moses could not enter the tent of meeting because the cloud had settled on it, and the glory of the Lord filled the tabernacle. Exodus 40:34, 35. Next, there is Solomon's temple. "And the priests could not perform their service because of the cloud, for the glory of the Lord filled his temple." 1 Kings 8:11.

In today's world, Christians are the temple. "Do you not know that your bodies are temples of the Holy Spirit, who is in you, whom you have received from God? You are not your own; you were bought at a price. Therefore honor God with your bodies." 1 Corinthians 6:19, 20. As Moses, Solomon, and the Israelites obey God and construct His dwelling place according to His specifications, God is faithful to bless His people with His

Holy Presence. Obedience is just as important today if we desire our churches and our lives to be filled with God's Holy Spirit. We must honor God with our bodies, for His glory abides where His word is living and obeyed.

February 15 – **God Speaks**

Moses completes the dedication of the altar. He then enters the tent of meeting to speak with the Lord – and the Lord speaks to Moses. "When Moses entered the tent of meeting to speak with the Lord, he heard the voice speaking to him from between the two cherubim above the atonement cover on the ark of the covenant law. In this way the Lord spoke to him." Numbers 7:89.

Our Creator God always enjoys communion with His creation. From the Garden of Eden to the present day, God desires to speak to man. We will hear His voice when we seek Him and spend time in His Word. "Come near to God and he will come near to you..." James 4:8. As with any relationship, listening plays a very important part. So the next time you pray, don't do all the talking; turn on your spiritual ears and hear what He wants to say to you. As you read the Bible, slow down and take time to listen to His Spirit speak to your spirit. "Here I am! I stand at the door and knock. If anyone hears my voice and opens the door, I will come in and eat with that person, and they with me." Revelation 3:20.

February 16 – **A Pleasing Aroma**

"...It is a burnt offering, a food offering, an aroma pleasing to the Lord." Leviticus 1:9. What pleases God? Sacrifice given in obedient faith. Jesus Christ pleased His Father. "Follow God's example, therefore, as dearly loved children and walk in the way of love, just as Christ loved us and gave himself up for us as a fragrant offering and sacrifice to God." Ephesians 5:1, 2.

What does sacrifice given in obedient faith look like for us today? How do we please God? Paul says this in Philippians 4:18: "I have received full payment and have more than enough. I am amply supplied, now that I have received from Epaphroditus the gifts you sent. They are a fragrant offering, an acceptable sacrifice, pleasing to God." We please God with sacrificial financial giving to support missionaries and the work of the Lord. "And do not forget to do good and to share with others, for with such sacrifices God is pleased." Hebrews 13:16. How will you please God today?

February 17 – **Confession: Good for the Soul**

"when anyone becomes aware that they are guilty in any of these matters, they must confess in what way they have sinned." Leviticus 5:5. Before the birth, death, and resurrection of Christ, God institutes the law and sacrifices so that man can know forgiveness and reconciliation with God. Today, we must believe in the supreme sacrifice Jesus Christ made for us and place our faith in Him.

Man is born with a sin nature, and God has always required confession of sin before He forgives. We must take full responsibility of our sin, confess it to God, repent (turn away from) and ask God to forgive us. "If we confess our sins, he is faithful and just and will forgive us our sins and purify us from all unrighteousness." 1 John 1:9. We must first confess, and then the Lord will do what He says He will do. He is true to His Word. What sweet relief it is – forgiveness!

February 18 – **Urim and Thummim**

Have you ever questioned what the Urim and Thummim actually were? People are still wondering. "He placed the breastpiece on him and put the Urim and Thummim in the breastpiece." Leviticus 8:8. "Also put the Urim and Thummim in the breastpiece, so they may be over Aaron's heart whenever he enters the presence of the Lord." Exodus 28:30. The English equivalent for these two words is light and perfection. They can also be defined as illumination and truth. The Urim and Thummim are already familiar to Moses and the people and connected naturally with the functions of the high priest. Scripture does not reveal their exact description.

The Urim and Thummim are used to ascertain the will of God regarding any important matter. One theory is that they are three stones, on one of which is written Yes, on another No, while the third was left neutral or blank. These are used as lots, and the high priest decides according as to which stone is drawn out. Casting lots is widely used in the Bible. Reliance on this unique means of revelation seems to have ceased after David's reign. An attempt to revive the practice occurs during the fifth century B.C. (Ezra 2:63 and Nehemiah 7:65).

Jesus Christ is now our High Priest and the perfect embodiment of light, perfection, illumination, and truth. There is no need for casting lots today, because Jesus knows the truth in every situation, and His decisions and judgments are always righteous and final. The Book of Hebrews has much to say about our High Priest. "For this reason he had to be made like them, fully human in every way, in order that he might become a merciful and faithful high priest in service to God, and that he might make atonement for the sins of the people." Hebrews 2:17.

February 19 – **Be Holy**

God teaches His children important lessons about health, infection, disease, and treatment. There are no medical doctors in this congregation, only priests who oversee the spiritual and physical health of the people. God's laws are for the wellbeing of His people; also, to distinguish them from the immoral and sinful lifestyles of the nations surrounding them. He loves His children and always has their best interest at heart. "I am the Lord, who brought you up out of Egypt to be your God; therefore be holy, because I am holy." Leviticus 11:45.

Jesus Christ fulfilled the law; however, God still expects Christians today to be separate and holy, rejecting ungodliness in the culture around us. Do we reflect the God we serve in our appearance, words, and actions? Can others clearly see Jesus Christ living in us?

God is holy; therefore, His people must be holy. "But just as he who called you is holy, so be holy in all you do; for it is written: 'Be holy, because I am holy.'" 1 Peter 1:15, 16. "Make every effort to live in peace with everyone and to be holy; without holiness no one will see the Lord." Hebrews 12:14.

February 20 – **Hear, Do, Walk**

"The priest is to take some of the blood of the guilt offering and put it on the lobe of the right ear of the one to be cleansed, on the thumb of their right hand and on the big toe of their right foot." Leviticus 14:14. This is a very interesting passage of Scripture that details the cleansing and restoration of the leper. We notice in Leviticus 8:23, 24 that this ceremony resembles the consecration of the priests. Both the priest and the common man are to be cleansed and set apart to the service of their covenant God. Another point worthy of consideration is found in 14:17 in which the priest is directed to apply the oil "...on top of the blood of the guilt offering."

Is there any significance here for us today? The particularly horrible disease of leprosy can only be cured by a divine miracle of God. Leprosy can also be regarded as a type for indwelling sin curable only through the blood of Jesus Christ. When we believe in Him and His atoning work on the cross, when we receive Him as our Savior and Lord, He washes and cleanses us from all sin. Our God is the only One Who has the power to do this. Next, the oil is placed on top of the blood. Wow! The oil, a symbol of the Holy Spirit in the New Testament – the baptism of the Holy Spirit – can only happen after we are saved by the blood of Jesus. "and asked them, 'Did you receive the Holy Spirit when (after) you believed?...'" Acts 19:2.

As Christians, we are set apart unto Christ, to serve and represent Him in the earth. As such, we must guard our lives from sin that would contaminate and bring reproach upon Him. Let us be careful what and who we listen to; may our hands (actions) further His Kingdom; may we follow in His footsteps and not walk in the ways of the world. His blood and Holy Spirit have been applied not only to our hearts, but to our ears, hands, and feet. Christ lives in us; may we be good stewards of His dwelling place. "reject every kind of evil." 1 Thessalonians 5:22.

February 21 – **Our Sin Offering**

"This is how Aaron is to enter the Most Holy Place: He must first bring a young bull for a sin offering and a ram for a burnt offering...having made atonement for himself, his household and the whole community of Israel." Leviticus 16:3, 17. Confession and repentance are always important to God. God requires His priests to offer a sacrifice for their own sin first before they intercede for their families or community.

By confessing and repenting (turning away from) my sin, I submit my life to God and acknowledge that He is in control; I'm not. This life is not about me; it's about Him, His ways, and His agenda. If I'm not careful, I can become preoccupied with confessing others' sins to God to the neglect of my own. God did not set it up that way! Each one is responsible for their sin before God. No one else can confess and repent of my sin; I must take ownership.

Sin separates us from God. "But your iniquities have separated you from your God; your sins have hidden his face from you, so that he will not hear." Isaiah 59:2. Jesus experiences that separation from God on the cross when He carries the sins of the world. God the Father cannot look upon His Son in that moment because of my sin and your sin. "About three in the afternoon Jesus cried out in a loud voice, 'Eli, Eli, lema sabachthani?' (which means 'My God, my God, why have you forsaken me?'") Matthew 27:46.

Sin separates. Before we enter His Presence, we must get rid of our sin through confession and repentance. How can we realistically hope to effectively intercede for others or minister to others in our households and communities until we follow God's protocol first?

February 22 – **Sexual Sins**

I had a brief conversation several years ago with a very intelligent gentleman who was railing against God for being so cruel. He had been reading the Old Testament and simply could not understand how God could destroy entire nations of people – men, women and children. Reading portions of God's Word may create more questions than it answers. That's why it is imperative that we prayerfully read His Word in its entirety and ask Him to give us His Biblical worldview.

"Do not defile yourselves in any of these ways, because this is how the nations that I am going to drive out before you became defiled. Even the land was defiled; so I punished it for its sin, and the land vomited out its inhabitants." Leviticus 18:24. God has just given us a list of sexual sins (vs. 6-23) that defile a person as well as their land. Sexual sin works the same way today. God is very clear about this. "You must not do as they do in Egypt, where you used to live, and you must not do as they do in the land of Canaan, where I am bringing you. Do not follow their practices." Leviticus 18:3.

"Speak to the entire assembly of Israel and say to them: 'Be holy because I, the Lord your God, am holy.'" Leviticus 19:2. As ministers of the Gospel, we need to kick it up a notch and speak boldly to our congregations about sin. Our nation is in danger of vomiting out its inhabitants! Do our people understand the requirements of a Holy God? Are we giving our congregations opportunities to meet God in the altars? God help us! "It is God's will that you should be sanctified: that you should avoid sexual immorality...The Lord will punish all those who commit such sins, as we told you and warned you before. For God did not call us to be impure, but to live a holy life." 1 Thessalonians 4:3, 6, 7.

February 23 – **God's Face**

"I myself will set my face against him and his family...I will set my face against anyone..." Leviticus 20:5, 6. Here God denounces Molek worship and human sacrifice in which many historians believe babies were placed into the metal arms of idols and burned alive. God condemns the practice of turning to mediums and spiritists to predict the future. Sin in any form causes God to turn His face away from people, and worse yet, set His face against them. "Then they will cry out to the Lord, but he will not answer them. At that time he will hide his face from them because of the evil they have done." Micah 3:4.

"Restore us, O God; make your face shine on us, that we may be saved." Psalm 80: 3. "The Lord bless you and keep you; the Lord make his face shine on you and be gracious to you; the Lord turn his face toward you and give you peace." Numbers 6:24-26.

Today we see the face of God when we peer into the eyes of Jesus Christ. "For God, who said, 'Let light shine out of darkness,' made his light shine in our hearts to give us the light of the knowledge of God's glory displayed in the face of Christ." 2 Corinthians 4:6.

"For the eyes of the Lord are on the righteous and his ears are attentive to their prayer, but the face of the Lord is against those who do evil." 1 Peter 3:12. Oh, for the day when we will always behold the face of God! "They will see his face, and his name will be on their foreheads." Revelation 22:4.

God forgive me of any and all sin in my life. I want Your face turned to me; I want Your eyes on me.

February 24 – **Compassion**

"When you reap the harvest of your land, do not reap to the very edges of your field or gather the gleanings of your harvest. Leave them for the poor and for the foreigner residing among you. I am the Lord your God." Leviticus 23:22. This is a picture of God's compassionate heart in action, and He expects no less from His people. The Israelites experienced poverty, enslavement, and displacement in Egypt. God wants them to remember where they came from and treat others with kindness and respect.

The world says, "Get all you can; can all you get; and sit on the can." It is very easy for us to forget what God has done for us and become self-centered, never noticing the plight of others. He wants us to open our eyes and hearts to those less fortunate, and share what He has given to us with others, because everything comes from Him anyway. "The poor you will always have with you..." Matthew 26:11.

God instructs us not only to share with others our material blessings but spiritual blessings as well. His grace is a free gift to us. Can we not freely share grace with others? "Heal the sick, raise the dead, cleanse those who have leprosy, drive out demons. Freely you have received, freely give." Matthew 10:8.

February 25 – **A Choice**

God loves the children of Israel so much that He gives them the freedom of choice. God does not make robots. He wants His creation to love, serve, and obey Him because they choose to do so. God never forces anyone to love Him. Man has been given the option by God to obey Him and be blessed or to disobey His laws and incur punishment. It's up to us. "If you follow my decrees and are careful to obey my commands," Leviticus 26:3. Then God outlines His blessings which include, "I will put my dwelling place among you, and I will not abhor you. I will walk among you and be your God, and you will be my people." (vs. 11, 12).

"But if you will not listen to me and carry out all these commands," Leviticus 26:14. God then describes the evils more fully than the blessings previously promised. God will deal with Israel exactly as she deserves. However, God is a God of mercy. "But if they will confess their sins...I will remember my covenant..." (vs. 40, 42). The implication is that He will restore them to the land promised to their fathers.

"It is for freedom that Christ has set us free. Stand firm, then, and do not let yourselves be burdened again by a yoke of slavery." Galatians 5:1. As long as there is breath and life in the body, God will give each one the freedom to choose Him and His ways or reject Him. As one Bible commentator so precisely states: The price of rejecting God and His righteous standards is enormous. To be in His will, in His presence and in His care are the greatest blessings of life.

February 26 – **The Yoyo Effect**

As a child, I enjoyed the yoyo. I was never very good with it but loved trying. Some of my friends excelled in the pastime and impressed me with their tricks. I, on the other hand, spent most of my time untangling and rewinding. The Old Testament children of Israel remind me of the yoyo. So many times, they escape the Master's hand, descend, get tangled up, repent, and the Lord takes them back – when all the while, the Master desires to amaze the world with His grace, mercy, beauty, and plan for mankind. I love reading when Israel actually gets it right! "The Israelites did all this just as the Lord commanded Moses." Numbers 1:54. "So the Israelites did everything the Lord commanded Moses…" Numbers 2:34.

What are a few lessons we can garner from these first two chapters? 1) Numbers are important to God – so important that He calls this book Numbers. Each number represents a person. 2) Leadership. God handpicks the leaders for each tribe and calls them by name. Jesus handpicked His 12 disciples. 3) Organization. God organizes the tribes in specific areas around the Tent of Meeting. 4) Order. God knows how to accomplish the task at hand, and there is no confusion when His children comply. "For God is not a God of disorder but of peace…" 1 Corinthians 14:33. 5) His plan is the best plan. When we follow God's will and plan for our lives, we will accomplish all that He created us to do. "and teaching them to obey everything I have commanded you. And surely I am with you always, to the very end of the age." Matthew 28:20. May it be said of us, "They did everything the Lord commanded."

February 27 – **Why?**

When our children are small, we hear "Why?" fall from their tiny lips often. We tell them to do something. Why? We tell them not to do something. Why? Sometimes we explain the reason behind the instruction; sometimes we don't. We want them to learn to trust us and know we love them, so we protect and care for them. These are small lessons in obedience to prepare them for the greater challenges in life.

"Count the Levites by their families and clans. Count every male a month old or more." Numbers 3:15. The Levites aren't counted in the first census of all the males 20 years and older. Doesn't God already know this number anyway? Of course, He does. Why doesn't He just tell Moses the number? Think about it; this is a big job. Moses doesn't have computers or an easy way to accomplish this task. "So Moses counted them, as he was commanded by the word of the Lord." (v. 16). Moses has learned he can trust God to know what He's doing. He obeys the Lord without asking God to explain Himself.

In all reality, God is not obligated to explain anything to us. He is God, and we're not! He's already given us everything we need to know contained in His Word. Our job is to obey Him in all things. "Simon answered, 'Master, we've worked hard all night and haven't caught anything. But because you say so, I will let down the nets.'" Luke 5:5. It doesn't make sense to Simon Peter, but because Jesus says it, he does it. As we obey the Lord in small and big ways, our faith and trust in Him grows, so that we are better prepared to face the bigger challenges in life.

February 28 – **Our Sin Offering**

The Bible is full of interesting stories and information that at first glance seem totally unrelated to our present day lives and may leave us with a puzzled look and a healthy "Huh?" So it is with the account in Number 5:11-31, a provision probably intended only for the wilderness journey, because there is no reference to such a practice in later parts of the Bible.

If a man becomes jealous and suspects his wife of adultery without her having been caught in the act or without his having witnesses to prove her supposed guilt, then he is required to bring her to the priest, along with an offering. "…He must also take an offering…because it is a grain offering for jealousy, a reminder-offering to draw attention to wrongdoing." Numbers 5:15. Dust is taken from the tabernacle floor and mixed with holy water, which the woman drinks. If she is guilty, the curse pronounced against her comes true causing bitter suffering and the inability to have children. If she is innocent, the water does not harm her; she is cleared of guilt and is able to have children. God is protecting innocent women from false accusations in a male-dominated legal system. In clear cases of adultery, the penalty for the man and woman is death (Leviticus 20:10).

Jesus Christ is our offering for sin. "For what the law was powerless to do because it was weakened by the flesh, God did by sending his own Son in the likeness of sinful flesh to be a sin offering. And so he condemned sin in the flesh," Romans 8:3. Jesus paid the price for my sin with His own blood on the cross. "Therefore, there is now no condemnation for those who are in Christ Jesus." Romans 8:1.

MARCH

March 1 – **I Wear His Name**

"So they will put my name on the Israelites, and I will bless them." Numbers 6:27. God instructs Moses to tell the priests to bless the Israelites and put His name on them. What does it mean to have God's name on me? Yes, God says He will bless me. Praise God!

"...The disciples were called Christians first at Antioch." Acts 11:26. I am a Christian for I wear the name of Christ. Blessing is not the only thing I can expect for having His name on me. "However, if you suffer as a Christian, do not be ashamed, but praise God that you bear that name." 1 Peter 4:16. Praise God! History records suffering and death of untold millions wearing that Name.

I will praise God in the blessing, and I will praise God in the suffering! Yet there's more beyond this life because I wear His Name. "The one who is victorious I will make a pillar in the temple of my God. Never again will they leave it. I will write on them the name of my God and the name of the city of my God, the New Jerusalem, which is coming down out of heaven from my God; and I will also write on them my new name." Revelation 3:12. Praise God forever!

March 2 – **Multiple Lessons**

There are so many important lessons we can learn packed into the events recorded in Numbers 11 and 12. God's principles and truths are timeless. Let's look at a few. "Now the people complained about their hardships in the hearing of the Lord, and when he heard them his anger was aroused. Then fire from the Lord burned among them and consumed some of the outskirts of the camp." Numbers 11:1.

Lesson 1: We never accomplish anything good with complaining and wailing against God; it only proves our rejection of the Lord (11:20). I can only wonder what it would be like today if the consequences of our sins were realized immediately as they were in the time of Moses.

Lesson 2: God is merciful; however there are always consequences to our actions in God's timing and God's way (Numbers 11:1, 33; 12:10). "Because of the Lord's great love we are not consumed, for his compassions never fail." Lamentations 3:22. His mercy is always greater than we deserve.

Lesson 3: From the middle of bad, God brings good. God shares the heavy burden on Moses with 70 elders (11:25).

Lesson 4: My paraphrase of 11:23 is this: May I remind you that everything I have said to you up to this point has happened just as I said? Is my arm now too short? "Heaven and earth will pass away, but my words will never pass away." Matthew 24:35.

Lesson 5: Joshua, Moses' successor-in-training, learns a valuable lesson in verse 29.

Lesson 6: God has ways to meet our needs, and it's probably not what we envision (v. 31).

Lesson 7: As we follow and obey God, there is no need to be defensive when attacked. God is our defender (Numbers 12). "Defend my cause and redeem me; preserve my life according to your promise." Psalms 119:154.

March 3 – **Who Are You Listening To?**

Life is full of choices every single day. What's for supper? Do I call that person? Do I stay mad at my spouse? Will I forgive today? Will I do that task I don't enjoy? Who will I listen to today? The twelve spies have just returned from searching out the Promised Land; ten give a negative report; two encourage and proclaim triumph ahead. The majority is *not* always right. The ten spies choose to believe what their eyes see, and the Israelites choose to listen to and believe them. Joshua and Caleb prefer to remember God's Word and victories already won. We choose every day who we listen to and who we believe.

"The Lord said to Moses, 'How long will these people treat me with contempt? How long will they refuse to believe in me, in spite of all the signs I have performed among them?'" Numbers 14:11. "...Yet he does not leave the guilty unpunished..." (14:18). "...No one who has treated me with contempt will ever see it." (14:23). The Israelites believe the word of man over the Word of God, and God calls that contempt. Many lose their lives that day; the rest die over the next forty years and never see God's promise fulfilled.

Who will you listen to today? Where will your thoughts dwell? God gives you permission to choose. You may say that you can't control what you think about; God says you can. "We demolish arguments and every pretension that sets itself up against the knowledge of God, and we take captive every thought to make it obedient to Christ." 2 Corinthians 10:5. "Finally, brothers and sisters, whatever is true, whatever is noble, whatever is right, whatever is pure, whatever is lovely, whatever is admirable – if anything is excellent or praiseworthy – think about such things." Philippians 4:8. Then God gives you strength to do what He asks you to do. "I can do all this through him who gives me strength." (4:13). God doesn't miss a thing!

Commit today to hear God and follow Him; disregard the world's screams competing for your attention and allegiance. Remain in God's Word and remember Who He is and what He's done for you. "Then you will remember to obey all my commands and will be consecrated to your God." Numbers 15:40.

March 4 – **Quick to Forget**

The Israelites seem to not own a short-term memory. How can they so quickly forget the provisions and commandments – the reality – of the One True God? Or do they simply choose to forget? "Isn't it enough that you have brought us up out of a land flowing with milk and honey to kill us in the wilderness? And now you also want to lord it over us?" Numbers 16:13. Egypt was slavery; it was not a land flowing with milk and honey. God chose Moses to lead His people and proves it over and over in signs and wonders never seen before by man. "The next day the whole Israelite community grumbled against Moses and Aaron. 'You have killed the Lord's people,' they said." (16:41). Moses did not open the earth's mouth to swallow the rebellious. And their grumbling and complaining brought swift destruction not so long ago.

Are we so very different than the children of Israel? I think not. Memory is a fascinating ability God has given to man. In psychology, memory is the process in which information is encoded, stored, and retrieved. *Encoding* or registration is the receiving, processing, and combining of received information. *Storage* is the creation of a permanent record of the encoded information. *Retrieval* is the calling back of stored information in response to some cue for use in a process or activity. Where is our disconnect?

God knows we need help in remembering. "Do you still not understand? Don't you remember the five loaves for the five thousand, and how many basketfuls you gathered?" Matthew 16:9. May we always remember Who forgives us, Who saves us, Who answers prayer, Who created this world and us, and Who makes the rules. One way to remember is to be an incessant student of the Word. Another way to remember is through the ordinance of communion. "And he took bread, gave thanks and broke it, and gave it to them, saying, 'This is my body given for you; do this in remembrance of me.'" Luke 22:19.

March 5 – **The Rock**

"Then Moses raised his arm and struck the rock twice with his staff. Water gushed out, and the community and their livestock drank. But the Lord said to Moses and Aaron, 'Because you did not trust in me enough to honor me as holy in the sight of the Israelites, you will not bring this community into the land I give them." Numbers 20:11, 12. There are at least two valuable lessons for us today in these two verses.

First, God tells Moses to speak to the rock; instead, he strikes it. You may ask what is so significant about that; water still comes out. From Exodus 17:6, we learn that the rock has already been struck once. "I will stand there before you by the rock at Horeb. Strike the rock, and water will come out of it for the people to drink..." In God's wisdom, the rock foreshadows Jesus Christ. How is Moses to know that? "and drank the same spiritual drink; for they drank from the spiritual rock that accompanied them, and that rock was Christ." 1 Corinthians 10:4. We don't always understand the ways of God. It is not our responsibility to always understand God; it is our responsibility to always obey Him in what He tells us to do. Jesus Christ was struck (suffered and died) once. He accomplished everything He came to earth to do at His death, burial, and resurrection. "and who have fallen away, to be brought back to repentance. To their loss they are crucifying the

Son of God all over again and subjecting him to public disgrace." Hebrews 6:6.

Secondly, think about this: If Moses disobeyed God one time and had to face the consequence of his sin, who are we to think we can disobey God and get away with it?

March 6 – **A Blessing or a Curse**

"How can I curse those whom God has not cursed? How can I denounce those whom the Lord has not denounced?" Numbers 23:8. "There is no divination against Jacob, no evil omens against Israel. It will now be said of Jacob and of Israel, 'See what God has done!'" (23:23). A blessing instead of a curse flows from Balaam's lips each time he is directed to curse God's people, Israel. Even the promise of great reward and honor can't persuade this heathen diviner to curse Israel, for it would do no good.

I have known Christians who fear being cursed by the ungodly. Hogwash! "Like a fluttering sparrow or a darting swallow, an undeserved curse does not come to rest." Proverbs 26:2. Jesus calls me blessed in His Sermon on the Mount (Matthew 5:3-12). "You, dear children, are from God and have overcome them, because the one who is in you is greater than the one who is in the world." 1 John 4:4. "If anyone does not love the Lord, let that person be cursed! Come, Lord!" 1 Corinthians 16:22.

March 7 – **History Lessons**

Have you ever noticed the extensive history lessons and stories (numerous repeated stories) in God's Word and wondered why? One reason is they serve as examples of God's character, faithfulness, holiness, and righteousness – all of which never change. In a world that is constantly changing at an ever increasing pace, it is comforting to know God never changes – no guesswork here. What about the basic nature of man? Has it ever changed? No. We are all born with a sinful nature, prone to sin throughout our lives, and desperately in need of a Savior. "What has been will be again, what has been done will be done again; there is nothing new under the sun." Ecclesiastes 1:9.

God loves us so much that He reminds us over and over in Scripture to follow Him with our whole heart and to learn from others' past mistakes. "The earth opened its mouth and swallowed them along with Korah, whose followers died when the fire devoured the 250 men. And they served as a warning sign." Numbers 26:10. "But Nadab and Abihu died when they made an offering before the Lord with unauthorized fire." (26:61). God repeats these accounts to make a point; He knows how long it takes us to "get it."

It is to our advantage to learn from God's Word instead of our own personal, and sometimes stupid, mistakes. "You have laid down precepts that are to be fully obeyed." Psalm 119:4. "I have hidden your word in my heart that I might not sin against you." (119:11). Satan works overtime to prevent us from spending time in the Bible; he doesn't want us to learn in God's history class; he wants us to experience failure and sin, because he knows all about God's law of sowing and reaping. Satan wants us to suffer the consequences of our sin. May God help us learn life's lessons from His unchanging Word and those who have gone before us, thus sparing ourselves untold heartache. "But these are written that you may believe that Jesus is the Messiah, the Son of God, and that by believing you may have life in his name." John 20:31.

March 8 – **A Woman's Place**

Zelophehad has five daughters. At this time (approximately B.C. 1375), only sons inherit their father's property. Zelophehad, who dies in the wilderness, would have been proud of his girls as they approach Moses to ask for their father's fair share of the Promised Land. "...The names of the daughters were Mahlah, Noah, Hoglah, Milcah and Tirzah... 'Give us property among our father's relatives.'" Numbers 27:1, 4. Disease, Quiet, Partridge, Counsel, and Delightfulness (as their names translate) are granted their request. "They went to Eleazar the priest, Joshua son of Nun, and the leaders and said, 'The Lord commanded Moses to give us an inheritance among our brothers.' So Joshua gave them an inheritance along with the brothers of their father, according to the Lord's command." Joshua 17:4. This newly enacted law shows the place of dignity and honor that women have in Israel.

Many courageous and godly women are listed in the Bible. Less known women are builders, warriors, judges, landowners, those who travel with and care for the needs of Jesus and His disciples, prophetesses, house pastors, deaconesses, and workers in the church – women such as Sheerah, Shallum's daughters, Jael, Deborah, Acsah, Joanna, Susanna, Phillip's four daughters, Priscilla, Phoebe, Tryphena, Tryphosa, Persis, and Nympha – just to name a few. Women occupy prominent roles in God's Kingdom. "There is neither Jew nor Greek, neither slave nor free, nor is there male and female, for you are all one in Christ Jesus. If you belong to Christ, then you are Abraham's seed, and heirs according to the promise." Galatians 3:28, 29.

March 9 – **A Serious Matter**

"Moses said to the heads of the tribes of Israel: 'This is what the Lord commands: When a man makes a vow to the Lord or takes an oath to obligate himself by a pledge, he must not break his word but must do everything he said.'" Numbers 30:1, 2. God requires people to keep their promises to Him and to others. A vow is something freely undertaken by the individual; God never imposes vows on anyone. A vow is entirely voluntary, but once made, is regarded as compulsory; a binding force not to be taken lightly; and this includes the marriage vow.

Jonah learns the seriousness of the vow lesson the hard way – in the belly of a great fish. "But I, with shouts of grateful praise, will sacrifice to you. What I have vowed I will make good. I will say, 'Salvation comes from the Lord.'" Jonah 2:9. Jesus emphasizes the magnitude of our words in Matthew 12:36. "But I tell you that everyone will have to give account on the day of judgment for every empty word they have spoken."

March 10 – **Why Do the Innocent Suffer?**

"'Because they have not followed me wholeheartedly, not one of those who were twenty years old or more when they came up out of Egypt will see the land I promised on oath to Abraham, Isaac and Jacob – not one except Caleb son of Jephunneh the Kenizzite and Joshua son of Nun, for they followed the Lord wholeheartedly.' The Lord's anger burned against Israel and he made them wander in the wilderness forty years, until the whole generation of those who had done evil in his sight was gone." Numbers 32:11-13. That means that everyone age 19 and younger at the time of the Exodus is spared in this pronouncement of God's judgment. Do you remember Zelophehad and his five daughters? He dies during the forty years in the wilderness; his daughters live (Numbers 27:1-4). "Our father died in the wilderness. He was not among Korah's followers, who banded together against the Lord, but he died for his own sin and left no sons." (v. 3). It is safe to assume that not all of the 603,550 men, age 20 and older, counted in the first census following the Exodus (Numbers 1:46), are in rebellion toward God when they die in the wilderness.

We see it all around us every day: innocent casualties of war; blameless men, women, and children who suffer and die because of the sins of others. Why? We live in a fallen world. When Adam and Eve sinned against God, sin entered the world and with it death. Please read Romans 5:12-21. "Consequently, just as one trespass resulted in condemnation for all people, so also one righteous act resulted in justification and life for all people." (v. 18).

"I have told you these things, so that in me you may have peace. In this world you will have trouble. But take heart! I have overcome the world." John 16:33. This life is not all there is! Hallelujah! God will balance the scales; He will put everything back into perfect order. True life, as God intended it from the beginning of time, better than anything we can possibly imagine, begins in heaven for the child of God. On the other hand, those who do not have a saving relationship with Jesus Christ will enter an eternity of torment and death far worse that our imaginations can ever take us. Our sojourn on earth is the time we're given to make that decision. Our faith in Jesus Christ or our rejection of Him determines our eternal destination. Earthly tragedy can strike anyone at anytime. We are given this moment to draw near to the One True God through His Son Jesus Christ. And His mercy is so huge! We can know His forgiveness and new birth when we turn our hearts to Him and believe in Him and what He did for us on the cross. In Him, we find strength and peace for today and assurance for tomorrow. "He who was seated on the throne said, 'I am making everything new!' Then he said, 'Write this down, for these words are trustworthy and true.'" Revelation 21:5.

March 11 – **His Dwelling Place**

"Do not defile the land where you live and where I dwell, for I, the Lord, dwell among the Israelites." Numbers 35:34. To defile means to make unclean. God commands His people to stay away from anything that would defile the land, because His Presence goes with them. God is holy, and He will not dwell among people who are unholy (defiled, unclean).

"But the things that come out of a person's mouth come from the heart, and these defile them. For out of the heart come evil thoughts – murder, adultery, sexual immorality, theft, false testimony, slander. These are what defile a person; but eating with unwashed hands does not defile them." Matthew 15:18-20. As a born again believer in Jesus Christ, He dwells in my heart. I must guard my heart and keep it pure and clean before Him (Proverbs 4:23). If I allow sin into my heart and life, that sin will create a wedge between me and the Holy Spirit, because sin separates me from God (Isaiah 59:2). "Don't you know that you yourselves are God's temple and that God's Spirit dwells in your midst?" 1 Corinthians 3:16. "so that Christ may dwell in your hearts through faith. And I pray that you, being rooted and established in love, may have power, together with all the Lord's holy people, to grasp how wide and long and high and deep is the love of Christ, and to know this love that surpasses knowledge – that you may be filled to the measure of all the fullness of God." Ephesians 3:17-19. Lord, fill me to overflowing with Yourself!

March 12 – **Who Do You See?**

In chapter one of Deuteronomy, Moses begins to recount Israel's most recent history. Contained in this one chapter is an underlying message for us today. Israel believes two lies from their ultimate enemy, Satan, who lies to us in the very same way. These lies are at opposite ends of the spectrum. If Satan can't defeat us one way, he'll go the other direction. Let's pull back the covers and expose these deceptions for what they are. Does Satan use these tactics on you?

"Then I said to you, 'Do not be terrified; do not be afraid of them. The Lord your God, who is going before you, will fight for you, as he did for you in Egypt, before your very eyes.'" Deuteronomy 1:29, 30. Israel is scared silly! All of a sudden, their eyes come off of God and onto themselves; all they see is their inability and weakness. Of course they are helpless and hopeless in their own ability. When all we see is ourselves and what we bring to the table, we become paralyzed with fear. We can't fight this battle in our own strength; we don't have what it takes to conquer apart from God.

When God rebukes Israel for not trusting Him, they run to the opposite end of the field and embrace pride and arrogance. "So I told you, but you would not listen. You rebelled against the Lord's command and in your arrogance you marched up into the hill country." (v. 43). Both scenarios embody rebellion, sin, eyes directed within, and certain defeat.

Satan will use intimidation and discouragement, and he'll use narcissism and self-importance. Both are lies, and both require taking our eyes off of God and seeing only ourselves and our circumstances. Until we refocus our eyes and heart back to God and trust Him, we will walk in defeat. "I lift up my eyes to the mountains – where does my help come from? My help comes from the Lord, the Maker of heaven and earth." Psalm 121:1, 2. "But thanks be to God! He gives us the victory through our Lord Jesus Christ." 1 Corinthians 15:57. "I can do all this through him who gives me strength." Philippians 4:13.

March 13 – **Bedtime Stories**

My children, neatly tucked in at bedtime: "Mommy, tell us a story about when you were a little girl." History repeats itself. My grandchildren, neatly tucked in at bedtime: "Memaw, tell us a story about when you were a little girl." At times, it's a ploy to stay awake longer; at other times, just because it's fun... and funny! These can be valuable teaching moments with our children and grandchildren. The same God Who watched over us as children, watches over our children and grandchildren today.

"Only be careful, and watch yourselves closely so that you do not forget the things your eyes have seen or let them fade from your heart as long as you live. Teach them to your children and to their children after them." Deuteronomy 4:9. God instructs us to tell our children and grandchildren about Him for two reasons: 1) So *we* don't forget; and 2) Our children *need* to know Him. How well are we doing at handing to the next generation what God has given us? "We will not hide them from their descendants; we will tell the next generation the praiseworthy deeds of the Lord, his power, and the wonders he has done." Psalm 78:4. "His mercy extends to those who fear him, from generation to generation." Luke 1:50.

March 14 – **A Stiff-Necked People**

Have you ever had a stiff neck? From mild soreness to downright painful, a stiff neck makes it difficult to move your head from side to side. Our range of motion and vision are limited. A stiff neck hurts us; it creates problems for us.

"It is not because of your righteousness or your integrity that you are going in to take possession of their land; but on account of the wickedness of these nations, the Lord your God will drive them out before you, to accomplish what he swore to your fathers, to Abraham, Isaac and Jacob. Understand, then, that it is not because of your righteousness that the Lord your God is giving you this good land to possess, for you are a stiff-necked people." Deuteronomy 9:5, 6. God repeats Himself several times to drive home a point to the Israelites. It is not because they are so good, but because the inhabitants of the land are so evil. He doesn't want them to have the wrong perception of themselves; they are stiff-necked and rebellious.

"Stiff-necked" describes the Israelites more accurately than "righteous." It's the same for us. We are often stiff-necked when it comes to following and obeying God. Sometimes we just want our own way when all along God knows best. We must bow our heads and hearts before God and submit our lives to Him. In doing so, the stiffness and stubbornness begin to dissipate. Also, we are in no way righteous apart from Jesus Christ. It is because of Who He is that I am made righteous, not because of who I am. "and be found in him, not having a righteousness of my own that comes from the law, but that which is through faith in Christ – the righteousness that comes from God on the basis of faith." Philippians 3:9. Praise God! He made a way for me through faith in Jesus Christ!

March 15 – **Correctly Handle**

When my brother was a child, he picked up our cat by the tail, and yelled proudly, "Handle!" He quickly found out it was no handle and that he had handled that cat incorrectly. He never did that again!

"See that you do all I command you; do not add to it or take away from it." Deuteronomy 12:32. This is an important truth in God's Word to us that we should heed. God adds a little bit more to this command in the conclusion of His book. "I warn everyone who hears the words of the prophecy of this scroll: If anyone adds anything to them, God will add to that person the plagues described in this scroll. And if anyone takes words away from this scroll of prophecy, God will take away from that person any share in the tree of life and in the Holy City, which are described in this scroll." Revelation 22:18, 19.

Handling God's Word correctly requires three things from us: 1) Recognition of Who He is as God and Creator of the universe; 2) Submission to Him and His authority; and 3) Trust and obedience. He has put in place regulations for us to live by. Who are we to think we know better than God? Do we really think we can make up our own rules as we go through this life, or worse yet, think we are exempt from His sovereignty? Seriously? We must understand there are always consequences to our actions whether good or bad. "Do your best to present yourself to God as one approved, a workman who does not need to be ashamed and who correctly handles the word of truth." 2 Timothy 2:15.

March 16 – **Hardhearted and Tightfisted**

"If anyone is poor among your fellow Israelites in any of the towns of the land the Lord your God is giving you, do not be hardhearted or tightfisted toward them. There will always be poor people in the land. Therefore I command you to be openhanded toward your fellow Israelites who are poor and needy in your land." Deuteronomy 15:7, 11. God commands us to be openhanded, not only to our brothers and sisters in Christ, but to others. How well are you doing?

God is neither hardhearted nor tightfisted with us, and He wants us to be like Him. He is merciful and generous toward us; so we must put on Christ and love as He loves. "The poor you will always have with you, and you can help them any time you want. But you will not always have me." Mark 14:7. There are ample opportunities all around us every day to be Jesus with skin on to somebody. If we don't see these openings, it's because we are blind by our own selfishness, and should ask God to remove the scales from our eyes. He will. "If anyone has material possessions and sees a brother or sister in need but has no pity on them, how can the love of God be in that person?" 1 John 3:17.

March 17 – **Committed Soldiers**

We are at war. There are two armies involved: God's and Satan's. And there is a sideline of people consisting of those who are undecided as to which side they belong. The sideliners have a decision to make – soon. Each can make his own decision; if they delay or refuse to choose, God will take that as a rejection and send them to the enemy's camp. He only recruits people in His army who want to be there.

God gives the Israelites regulations concerning war in Deuteronomy 20:1-9. "When you go to war against your enemies and see horses and chariots and an army greater than yours, do not be afraid of them, because the Lord your God, who brought you up out of Egypt, will be with you." Deuteronomy 20:1. The men in Israel's army must be 100% on board with no distractions. If they have personal, family, or business obligations weighing on their minds, they are released from their service in the army. "Then the officers shall add, 'Is anyone afraid or fainthearted? Let him go home so that his fellow soldiers will not become disheartened too.'" (v. 8). Only high-fives allowed in this army!

King Jesus requires nothing less of those in His army. As a soldier of the cross, I must be all in with no second thoughts. Nothing is more important than following and serving the King of kings and Lord of lords. God demands and deserves my whole heart, full attention, and total commitment. My hand is on the plow, and I will not look back (Luke 9:62).

What or who is competing for your full attention and consumes your thoughts? Something or someone more important that Jesus Christ? I think not! Do you feel torn? Distracted? What are you passionate about? Come back to God. Get off the sidelines. Be a deserter in Satan's army and join the ranks of God's army and serve with purpose. Make your life count!

"Then I saw the beast and the kings of the earth and their armies gathered together to wage war against the rider on the horse and his army." Revelation 19:19. Continue reading in Revelation, and you will discover that King Jesus on the white horse leads His army to eternal victory.

March 18 – **Spring Cleaning**

It's spring and time for some serious spring cleaning. God likes clean. "Designate a place outside the camp where you can go to relieve yourself. As part of your equipment have something to dig with, and when you relieve yourself, dig a hole and cover up your excrement. For the Lord your God moves about in your camp to protect you and to deliver your enemies to you. Your camp must be holy, so that he will not see among you anything indecent and turn away from you." Deuteronomy 23:12-14. God is concerned with hygiene and the prevention of disease in the Israelites' camp, but He cares for more than just physical sanitary conditions.

Let us take a closer look and zoom into our camp – from our nation to our state to our community – to our home and personal life. Regarding the first three, we can pray, get involved and make our voice known, and we should. However, we can exercise more control over our home and personal life and can take action steps to make a difference in these areas.

First, walk through your home with the eyes of Jesus. We pray and ask God to bless our home and family and to fill our home with His Presence; but does He truly feel welcome, or do His eyes see something repulsive? Get rid of the filth, regardless of what culture says is acceptable. "Do not bring a detestable thing into your house…" Deuteronomy 7:26.

What about the campground of your heart? What does God see? Does He see sin hidden in darkness? Repent. Get rid of it. What are you waiting for? If you want everything God has for you and His fullness to dwell mightily in your heart and home, it's past time for some serious spring cleaning! It's time to get rid of the clutter, clean out the junk drawers, under the beds, and that dark secret place in the closet of your heart and home. Then roll out the red carpet and welcome the Holy Spirit in! "From that time on Jesus began to preach, 'Repent, for the kingdom of heaven has come near.'" Matthew 4:17. "that each of you should learn to control your own body in a way that is holy and honorable," 1 Thessalonians 4:4.

March 19 – **Blessings Verses vs. Curses Verses**

Did you notice it too? In today's reading of these two chapters, Deuteronomy 27 and 28, there is a very lopsided account of God's blessings and curses. I counted ten verses of blessing compared to sixty-one verses of curses. God describes the curses for disobeying His commands in greater detail and length than He does explaining His blessings for obedience. Why is that? Is He trying to scare us? It works for me!

"*If* you fully obey the Lord your God and carefully follow all his commands I give you today, the Lord your God will set you high above all the nations on earth. All these blessings will come on you and accompany you *if* you obey the Lord your God." (28:1, 2). "However, *if* you do not obey the Lord your God and do not carefully follow all his commands and decrees I am giving you today, all these curses will come on you and overtake you." (28:15). Notice the "ifs." All of God's promises for blessing and cursing in our lives are conditional based on our actions. Please understand; God's love for us is completely unconditional (as well as undeserved).

Why is it that when we think of God's promises to us, we naturally think of His blessings? We must remember that the promised curses are just as real as the promised blessings. When we look back on the nation of Israel from this side of history, we realize God's promises are true. Many times Israel has reaped the consequences of her disobedience, "until you are destroyed and come to sudden ruin because of the evil you have done in forsaking him." (28:20). God always keeps His promises. "Do not be deceived: God cannot be mocked. A man reaps what he sows." Galatians 6:7.

God desires us to love and obey Him every day. It's a lifestyle, not a temporary fix; and God knows the difference. His blessings to us far out-weigh anything we can give Him. He is such a good God! "Praise be to the God and Father of our Lord Jesus Christ, who has blessed us in the heavenly realms with every spiritual blessing in Christ." Ephesians 1:3.

March 20 – **Faithful Parenting**

Moses has lived a full life, faithfully leading God's people, interceding, teaching, and writing down God's laws for posterity. It hasn't been easy parenting these rebellious, self-centered, and vacillating children. He has exhorted, rebuked, and disciplined; he has given his all. "…Now choose life…For the Lord is your life…" Deuteronomy 30:19, 20. Then God gives Moses sobering news. "And the Lord said to Moses: 'You are going to rest with your ancestors, and these people will soon prostitute themselves to the foreign gods of the land they are entering. They will forsake me and break the covenant I made with them.'" Deuteronomy 31:16. There is nothing more Moses can do. It's heartbreaking.

Christian Mom and Dad, even after doing our best rearing our children to know the Lord, the sad truth is they may still choose to go their own way. It breaks our hearts, because we know destruction is ahead. May it never dissuade us though from the path of fully devoted followers of God. May our faith and trust in God never be shaken. Our Heavenly Father gives His children His best, His Son. Some receive Him; others reject Him. There is nothing more or better God can give us that He has not already given. Let us agree with Joshua: "…But as for me and my household, we will serve the Lord." Joshua 24:15. And may we know the fulfillment of 3 John 1:4. "I have no greater joy than to hear that my children are walking in the truth."

March 21 – **Keep it Current**

One underlying theme throughout Scripture is that we must keep our relationship with God up to date, alive and growing. Salvation is much more than an event; it is a thriving relationship with the King of kings and Lord of lords. God cautions us repeatedly. Perhaps you noticed it in Deuteronomy 8:19: "If you ever forget the Lord your God and follow other gods and worship and bow down to them, I testify against you today that you will surely be destroyed." This implies that the people at one time knew God and followed Him. Or what about Deuteronomy 11:16-17? "Be careful, or you will be enticed to turn away and worship other gods and bow down to them. Then the Lord's anger will burn against you…" This suggests that the people were walking with God. If not, how could they turn away?

"Jeshurun [Israel] grew fat and kicked; filled with food, they became heavy and sleek. They abandoned the God who made them and rejected the Rock their Savior. You deserted the Rock, who fathered you; you forgot the God who gave you birth." Deuteronomy 32:15, 18. How can someone abandon, reject, desert and forget God if he had not previously believed, received, clung to, and known Him? "The Lord saw this and rejected them because he was angered by his sons and daughters." (v. 19).

Just as God gives us the freedom to believe Him and live for Him, He gives us the freedom to lay down our faith and walk away. God doesn't create robots. He won't force us to do anything; it is our decision. He wants us to love and serve Him simply because we want to. Why would anyone stop believing and turn away from God? It doesn't get any better than knowing God and walking in relationship with the One Who loves us so much that He sent His one and only Son to die in our place. "You are the salt of the earth. But if the salt loses its saltiness, how can it be made salty again? It is no longer good for anything, except to be thrown out and trampled underfoot." Matthew 5:13. Keep your life salty and your relationship with Jesus Christ current!

March 22 – **God Says...**

God says to Joshua, "Be strong and courageous, because you will lead these people to inherit the land I swore to their ancestors to give them. Be strong and very courageous. Be careful to obey all the law my servant Moses gave you; do not turn from it to the right or to the left, that you may be successful wherever you go. Keep this Book of the Law always on your lips; meditate on it day and night, so that you may be careful to do everything written in it. Then you will be prosperous and successful. Have I not commanded you? Be strong and courageous. Do not be afraid; do not be discouraged, for the Lord your God will be with you wherever you go." Joshua 1: 6-9.

God says to you and me, "Be strong and courageous, because you will lead. Be strong and very courageous. Be careful to obey My Word; do not turn from it to the right or to the left, that you may be successful wherever you go. Keep this Book always on your lips; meditate on it day and night, so that you may be careful to do everything written in it. Then you will be prosperous and successful. Have I not commanded you? Be strong and courageous. Do not be afraid; do not be discouraged, for the Lord your God will be with you wherever you go."

First is our role: Be strong and courageous (notice God's emphasis on this!); obey the Word; always think about and talk about His Word; do not be scared or discouraged.

Then God will do His part: He will go with me and help me to lead, be successful and prosperous. "Be on your guard; stand firm in the faith; be courageous; be strong." 1 Corinthians 16:13. "So keep up your courage, men, for I have faith in God that it will happen just as he told me." Acts 27:25.

March 23 – **The Wall Collapsed!**

"…the wall collapsed…" Joshua 6:20. Do you know someone who is hiding behind a wall? Maybe you're that someone. Over time, we can build a wall between us and God, brick by brick. We become accustomed to that wall; it's all we see; it's all we know. It provides us with false security and false comfort and keeps God out. We hide behind it. It grows higher and thicker every day, and Satan loves it that way. We don't realize we're in prison, having lost all freedom to be who God created us to be, and held captive by the enemy of our soul. God's people are praying outside of that wall, and the Holy Spirit is trying to break through. From the inside, we're pushing against the wall with all of our strength, trying to keep it in place. What are we doing? "We all fell to the ground, and I heard a voice saying to me in Aramaic, 'Saul, Saul, why do you persecute me? It is hard for you to kick against the goads.'" Acts 26:14.

Rahab, the prostitute, lives inside the Jericho wall. But one day she hears the truth about the God of Israel and believes; at that moment, the wall around her heart crumbles, and she is free. Forgiven and loved by God, she steps over that broken wall that was crushed by the Holy Spirit, and steps into the family of God. God redeems her broken and scarred life and puts her into the lineage of His Son. It happens every day when someone finally steps back from the wall, becomes vulnerable, and allows God in.

When will your wall come down? When will you trust God enough to shatter your walls and give you new life in Him?

"The Spirit of the Sovereign Lord is on me, because the Lord has anointed me to preach good news to the poor. He has sent me to bind up the brokenhearted, to proclaim freedom for the captives and release from darkness for the prisoners," Isaiah 61:1. "By faith the walls of Jericho fell, after the army had marched around them for seven days." Hebrews 11:30.

March 24 – **Lessons to Live By**

Don't you just love the Old Testament stories? They contain so many practical lessons for us, and today's reading is no exception. Allow me to highlight a few examples from Joshua chapters 7-9. Jericho has fallen, and Joshua and the Israelite nation are advancing into enemy territory to claim the Promised Land.

Lesson 1: Pray about everything, because things are not always what they appear! Notice Joshua listens to the "church people" (7:3) before praying about what he should do. Outcome: disaster. He doesn't learn this lesson well, because in 9:14-15 Joshua listens to the enemy in disguise before talking to the Lord. Again, trouble. We should never fully depend on our own wisdom or ability, because God sees and knows so much more than we do about the situation. "And pray in the Spirit on all occasions with all kinds of prayers and requests. With this in mind, be alert and always keep on praying for all the Lord's people." Ephesians 6:18.

Lesson 2: Innocent people often suffer and die because of the sin of others. "When Achan son of Zerah was unfaithful in regard to the devoted things, did not wrath come on the whole community of Israel? He was not the only one who died for his sin." Joshua 22:20. "Then David said to Nathan, 'I have sinned against the Lord.' Nathan replied, 'The Lord has taken away your sin. You are not going to die. Now, therefore, the sword will never depart from your house, because you despised me and took the wife of Uriah the Hittite to be your own.'" 2 Samuel 12: 13, 10.

Lesson 3: Sin progresses on a steady course of devastation. Achan first covets (7:21); then he steals and lies (7:11). At some point, we must humble ourselves, repent, and receive God's forgiveness, or destruction is inevitable. "to open their eyes and turn them from darkness to light, and from the power of Satan to God, so that they may receive forgiveness of sins and a place among those who are sanctified by faith in me." Acts 26:18.

Lesson 4: God always exposes sin for what it is. He never closes His eyes or turns His head away from my sin or your sin. He did that only once when Jesus died on the cross, but never again. "So do not be afraid of them, for there is nothing concealed that will not be disclosed, or hidden that will not be made known." Matthew 10:26.

Lesson 5: Sin doesn't pay; it kills. Achan pays for the new clothes and jewelry with his own life and the lives of his children. Sin is expensive. "What good is it for someone to gain the whole world, yet forfeit their soul?" Mark 8:36.

Old Testament stories are more than historical accounts. They are lessons to live by.

March 25 – **What Only God Can Do**

Joshua is in the heat of battle. He is surrounded by the enemy. It stands to reason; he's in the enemy's territory! But God shows up and does what only He can do. "…the Lord hurled large hailstones down on them…" Joshua 10:11. "So the sun stood still, and the moon stopped, till the nation avenged itself on its enemies…" (10:13). No human hand can accomplish what only God can do. "…Surely the Lord was fighting for Israel!" (10:14).

Even after great victories, Joshua has no time for comfort or complacency. Celebration will have to wait. There are more battles ahead. He must keep the momentum and confront the enemy head-on. Israel's army is comprised of foot soldiers, so the enemy is a formidable foe. He has a job to do – put the enemy out of commission. "Joshua did to them as the Lord had directed: He hamstrung their horses and burned their chariots." Joshua 11:9. He cripples the enemy and ends their advance. "So Joshua took the entire land, just as the Lord had directed Moses, and he gave it as an inheritance to Israel according to their tribal divisions. Then the land had rest from war." (11:23).

Are you in the heat of battle? Do you feel surrounded by the enemy? Trust in God to do what only He can do in your behalf. "Finally, be strong in the Lord and in his mighty power. Put on the full armor of God, so that you can take your stand against the devil's schemes." Ephesians 6:10, 11. And don't take it off! Not until the final battle is won will there be rest for God's soldiers. Be encouraged! Jesus Christ has already defeated our enemy! He wins so we win! "The last enemy to be destroyed is death. For he 'has put everything under his feet.'..." 1 Corinthians 15:26, 27. "I am the Living One; I was dead, and now look, I am alive for ever and ever! And I hold the keys of death and Hades." Revelation 1:18.

March 26 – **A Promise is a Promise**

"Now give me this hill country that the Lord promised me that day...Then Joshua blessed Caleb son of Jephunneh and gave him Hebron as his inheritance." Joshua 14: 12, 13. Joshua and Caleb are quite the celebrities by this time. At 85, no other men in all of Israel are as old as they are. They attract crowds of children wherever they go, because they are the only great grandfathers around! Caleb is still physically fit and his memory sharp. Forty-five years after God made the promise, Caleb is ready to claim it. All this time, he has helped others conquer and inherit their land. Now it is his turn, but God doesn't just hand him the deed to the land; he must go and fight for it – and he does. Hebron is his. A town in the mountains of Judah and designated a city of refuge, Hebron is located about 25 miles from Jerusalem. It contains the traditional burial sites of Abraham and Sarah, Isaac and Rebekah, Jacob and Leah. Later, King David makes it his royal residence.

Never, never give up on the promise God made to you. His Word never fails. Fight for it if you must; God will give you the strength. "The Lord is not slow in keeping his promise, as some understand slowness. Instead he is patient with you, not wanting anyone to perish, but everyone to come to repentance." 2 Peter 3:9. "being fully persuaded that God had power to do what he had promised." Romans 4:21.

March 27 – **Your Inheritance**

What do you think of when you hear the word "inheritance"? Riches? Perhaps you recall the verse that says, "A good person leaves an inheritance for their children's children…" Proverbs 13:22. Perchance you've received an inheritance from a deceased loved one, a gift which did not belong to you originally, something for which you did not work. Inheritances can be challenged, contested in a court of law. Wealth unearned has been known to ultimately destroy lives. An inheritance can be a wonderful blessing or a source of turmoil and estrangement.

"This is the inheritance…" Joshua 15:20. Joshua divides the Promised Land among the tribes of Israel, and the children of Israel go in and take possession, fighting enemies to claim their inheritance. God gives this land to them; it is not theirs in the beginning. It originally belonged to God because He created the land, and He can give it to whomever He wishes.

God's children have an amazing inheritance awaiting them. Someone had to die in order for us to inherit this blessing called heaven, and that Someone is Jesus Christ. This inheritance cannot be contested, and it's better than we could ever imagine. "Now if we are children, then we are heirs – heirs of God and co-heirs with Christ, if indeed we share in his sufferings in order that we may also share in his glory." Romans 8:17. "Then the King will say to those on his right, 'Come, you who are blessed by my Father; take your inheritance, the kingdom prepared for you since the creation of the world.'" Matthew 25:34. "and into an inheritance than can never perish, spoil or fade. This inheritance is kept in heaven for you," 1 Peter 1:4.

March 28 – **Healthy Boundaries**

"Joshua then cast lots for them in Shiloh in the presence of the Lord, and there he distributed the land to the Israelites according to their tribal divisions." Joshua 18:10. God and Joshua are busy allotting the land with its boundaries to each of the tribes of Israel. Each tribe must know where it ends and another begins. We can look at our world and see oceans, rivers, and mountains serving as international and national boundaries. Look at any map and you will notice states, counties, parishes, and provinces distinctly outlined where one ends and another begins. Boundaries are important to God; they help provide order, structure, and a framework in which to live. "Do not move an ancient boundary stone set up by your ancestors." Proverbs 22:28.

God created physical boundaries, but He also created relational boundaries. He instituted them for our protection and well-being. They help us understand where "I" end and "you" begin. As long as we live within these healthy boundaries described in His Word, we can spare ourselves much heartache. The Ten Commandments (Exodus 20:1-17) are examples of God's loving boundaries. Don't go "rogue" on God and ignore, change, step over, or otherwise move the ancient boundary stone. You will only encounter trouble. Jesus summarizes the Ten Commandments in Mark

12:30, 31: "Love the Lord your God with all your heart and with all your soul and with all your mind and with all your strength. The second is this: Love your neighbor as yourself. There is no commandment greater than these."

March 29 – **Our Refuge**

"Then the Lord said to Joshua: 'Tell the Israelites to designate the cities of refuge, as I instructed you through Moses, so that anyone who kills a person accidentally and unintentionally may flee there and find protection from the avenger of blood.'" Joshua 20:1-3. God knows His children will eventually mess up and need a safe place in which to flee, so He plans ahead. Upon entering a city of refuge, one must confess what he has done and prepare to stand trial. God's justice always prevails. These six cities, three on the east side and three on the west side of the Jordan River, provide safe havens for anyone killing another human being without prior intent or premeditation. However, if that person willfully leaves the city of refuge prematurely, he places himself under the death penalty.

Jesus Christ is our Refuge. We run to Him when we're in trouble and find safety and protection. When we go to Him, we confess our sin, and humbly acknowledge our need of Him. He takes us in and covers us with His grace and mercy. Because of His sacrifice on the cross and His grace given freely to us, He receives us, no matter the sin – ignorant, accidental or intentional – He covers us. But we must stay submitted to Him and under His protective care; otherwise we will find ourselves in trouble again. Our Refuge is Someone, not somewhere. "But let all who take refuge in you be glad; let them ever sing for joy. Spread your protection over them, that those who love your name may rejoice in you." Psalm 5:11. "I will remain in the world no longer, but they are still in the world, and I am coming to you. Holy Father, protect them by the power of your name, the name you gave me, so that they may be one as we are one." John 17:11.

March 30 – **That Inner Vacuum**

I have heard it said that God has placed a void in each of our innermost hearts that only He can fill. Nothing else fits. He creates us to worship; it is a natural instinct. What has mankind done since the beginning of time? He tries to fill that place with something or someone in an effort to find satisfaction and peace. Sometimes our god is self, when it's all about me; my personal happiness and comfort at the expense of others – how sad. Only the One True God can satisfy our deepest longing. "But if serving the Lord seems undesirable to you, then choose for yourselves this day whom you will serve, whether the gods your ancestors served beyond the Euphrates, or the gods of the Amorites, in whose land you are living. But as for me and my household, we will serve the Lord." Joshua 24:15.

"He has made everything beautiful in its time. He has also set eternity in the human heart; yet no one can fathom what God has done from beginning to end." Ecclesiastes 3:11. We know there is more to life than just this life, for eternity lives in our hearts. Give God His rightful place in your heart and life, and be filled with Him today. "and to know this love that surpasses knowledge – that you may be filled to the measure of all the fullness of God." Ephesians 3:19.

March 31 – **Just a Little Sin**

Israel does a lot of things right as they take possession of the Promised Land. They obey God on many fronts. Then it happens. "But Manasseh did not drive out the people…Nor did Ephraim drive out the Canaanites...Neither did Zebulun drive out the Canaanites...Nor did Asher drive out those living in...Neither did Naphtali drive out those living in..." Judges 1:27-33. God says, "...Yet you have disobeyed me. Why have you done this?" Judges 2:2. "Whenever Israel went out to fight, the hand of the Lord was against them to defeat them, just as he had sworn to them. They were in great distress." (2:15). Israel fails the test (see Judges 3:5, 6).

So it is with us. The human heart hasn't changed over the centuries. Just like the nation of Israel, we can quickly forget the goodness of God in our lives. Man is prone to evil. Not only that, we create much of the trouble we walk through because of our disobedience to God's clear commands. "Yet man is born to trouble as surely as sparks fly upward." Job 5:7. We need the Savior every day, not just at the moment of our initial conversion experience – but each and every day. Let us not believe this lie from Satan: I'm a good person. I've obeyed God so many times in my life. It's just one little sin. God will continue to bless me. What will it hurt? Besides, I can always ask God for forgiveness.

Don't fail the test (and we all encounter them); distress is the sure reward. When we yield to sin, we plunge thorns in our side and set a snare for our feet (Judges 2:3). It hurts to pull thorns out of flesh and remove feet from the trap. We will suffer wounds that could leave visible scars. It's not worth it. However, God is worthy to receive praise, honor, and glory; He is worthy of our worship and complete obedience. "My dear children, I write this to you so that you will not sin. But if anybody does sin, we have an advocate with the Father – Jesus Christ, the Righteous One." 1 John 2:1.

APRIL

April 1 – **God's Army**

Let's look at two judges, Deborah and Gideon, and two victories. Notice in each victory, three components are involved: God, leadership, and volunteers. "When the princes in Israel take the lead, when the people willingly offer themselves – praise the Lord! The mountains quaked before the Lord, the One of Sinai, before the Lord, the God of Israel. My heart is with Israel's princes, with the willing volunteers among the people. Praise the Lord!" Judges 5:2, 5, 9.

God is in charge. "From the heavens the stars fought…" (5:20). He installs and equips leaders, gives the orders, and goes before them. He also looks for volunteers to actually do the work.

God chooses ordinary, unlikely people to lead His children and calls them princes. He searches for those who will trust Him and depend on His ability and not their own. He speaks to them, teaches them His ways, proves Himself to them and strengthens them to do what He has called them to do. They follow His lead and give Him the glory. "…shout, 'For the Lord and for Gideon.'" Judges 7:18.

God's army is comprised of volunteers, those who "willingly offer themselves." They are "willing volunteers among the people." God sets a high premium on willingness; and sometimes, that is all we have – willingness. He also looks for those who are alert. "Three hundred of them drank from cupped hands, lapping like dogs. All the rest got down on their knees to drink." (7:6). God is culling Gideon's army. Of the 10,000 soldiers left, all but 300 drink water by getting on their knees with face down. The 300 cup water in their hands and bring it to their mouths while watching everything around them, proving themselves vigilant and ready to spring into action at any moment. Those are the volunteers God wants in His army.

We can apply these lessons to church life today. "Be shepherds of God's flock that is under your care, watching over them – not because you must, but because you are willing, as God wants you to be; not pursuing dishonest gain, but eager to serve." 1 Peter 5:2.

April 2 – **The Trumpet and the Light**

A battle is brewing. Gideon leads his 300 men in the dead of night to the enemy's camp (Judges 7:16-22). Their weapons of choice are not the typical weapons of ancient warfare. "Dividing the three hundred men into three companies, he placed trumpets and empty jars in the hands of all of them, with torches inside." Judges 7:16. Whoever heard of waging war against an army of many thousands with a trumpet in one hand and a torch tucked away in an empty clay pot in the other? It's all God's plan; Gideon and his pint-size army are simply obeying God's orders, which prove to be sufficient – as always. It's a dark night. This huge army is sound asleep in the valley below. Suddenly, they're awakened with loud noises and bright lights; panic sets in. There's mass confusion; nobody can see a thing. They start swinging swords at everything that moves – killing each other. Gideon's men? Each one is standing still and watching God work.

When Jesus Christ returns to earth, we will hear a trumpet and see a bright light as well! Those of us who anticipate His return will not be asleep. We won't be confused; we will know what is taking place. "For as lightning that comes from the east is visible even in the west, so will be the coming of the Son of Man." Matthew 24:27. "His lightning lights up the world; the earth sees and trembles." Psalm 97:4. Even the blind will see this great light! "For the Lord himself will come down from heaven, with a loud command, with the voice of the archangel and with the trumpet call of God, and the dead in Christ will rise first." 1 Thessalonians 4:16. Even the deaf will hear this great sound! And God will do what only He can do – raise the dead!

"He who testifies to these things says, 'Yes, I am coming soon.' Amen. Come, Lord Jesus." Revelation 22:20. Are you ready?

April 3 – **Our Mighty Deliverer**

God is so long-suffering with us, and aren't you glad! Even though the Hebrew children know God's history with the nation of Israel, they are often unfaithful. They have a head-knowledge, but their hearts are far from God. No one inherits a personal relationship with God from their parents or grandparents. Israel reconnects with God only in times of crisis and extreme emergencies. "But the Israelites said to the Lord, 'We have sinned. Do with us whatever you think best, but please rescue us now.' Then they got rid of the foreign gods among them and served the Lord. And he could bear Israel's misery no longer." Judges 10:15, 16. God continues to send leaders to rescue Israel. In spite of our sin, fears, failures, and rash vows (Judges 11:30, 31), God cares deeply for us. "The Lord is gracious and righteous; our God is full of compassion." Psalm 116:5.

And while we're here, let's talk about civil war. "Jephthah then called together the men of Gilead and fought against Ephraim… Forty-two thousand Ephraimites were killed at that time." Judges 12:4, 6. Why are we fighting within the church when there are more than enough battles in the world? Satan attempts to destroy us from within, steal our strength and resources, so we have less to employ in the world.

"Then Manoah inquired of the angel of the Lord, 'What is your name, so that we may honor you when your word comes true?' He replied, 'Why do you ask my name? It is beyond understanding.'" Judges 13:17, 18. If this angel's name is beyond understanding, you can be sure there are many things in this life that we will never completely understand. But one thing we know: Our God is the Mighty Deliverer, the One Who rescues us in times of distress when we call upon Him, even in difficulties of our own making. "He is my loving God and my fortress, my stronghold and my deliverer, my shield, in whom I take refuge, who subdues peoples under me." Psalm 144:2. "and in this way all Israel will be saved. As it is written: 'The deliverer will come from Zion; he will turn godlessness away from Jacob.'" Romans 11:26.

April 4 – **The Lion and the Honey**

Samson is a fascinating Bible character. Is the account of his riddle in Judges 14:5-14 only an incredibly entertaining story, or does it carry spiritual significance for us today? We must be careful not to put words in God's mouth, but at the same time, learn everything we possibly can from Scripture. Are there any correlations from this tale for our lives today? Here's a little "sweet food" for thought!

Lions are common in Palestine in Bible days. A young lion is especially fierce and dangerous. God gives Samson a "taste" of His Spirit coming upon him in power, and there's more to come! (Remember how a young David kills a lion and a bear before he kills a giant?) "Some time later, when he went back to marry her, he turned aside to look at the lion's carcass, and in it he saw a swarm of bees and some honey." Judges 14:8. Samson wasn't afraid of the lion; he's certainly not afraid of a few bees now. He eats some of the honey and takes some to his parents. He doesn't tell them where he found the honey, because they probably would not have eaten it. They would have considered it unclean coming from inside the skeleton of a lion – not kosher! Then comes the riddle. I wonder why his thirty companions cannot solve this riddle. Lions and honey are both familiar elements in everyday life, and there's nothing stronger or sweeter. They're obviously not very bright! You know the rest of the story.

Our Lord Jesus conquered Satan, that roaring lion, in His death on the cross and His resurrection from the grave. Because of His victory, believers find strength and new life, enough for themselves and plenty to share with others. "Be alert and of sober mind. Your enemy the devil prowls around like a roaring lion looking for someone to devour." 1 Peter 5:8. Satan can only roar and must ultimately bow to the Lion of Judah!

"Where, O death, is your victory? Where, O death, is your sting?" 1 Corinthians 15:55. Jesus Christ stripped death of its sting for the child of God! There is now no more fear, only sweet peace.

"Now I want you to know, brothers and sisters, that what has happened to me has actually served to advance the gospel." Philippians 1:12. What a powerful statement Paul makes here! He says that something good has come from all his persecution, suffering, and imprisonment. God has brought something wonderful out of evil, and Paul agrees that what he has endured is worth it! What threatened Paul's ruin, God turned to his advantage. Satan is not happy when God gives us honey from his carcass!

April 5 – **How Close is Too Close?**

The Grand Canyon is one of the world's most popular tourist attractions. This incredible natural wonder is breathtakingly beautiful but can also be dangerous. There have been an estimated 600 deaths at the Grand Canyon since the 1870s. Not all the victims fell, but some of them did. The majority of those who fell simply got too close to the edge and toppled over.

Samson walks closer to the proverbial edge as he falls prey to Delilah's tactics. First it is seven fresh thongs (strips of thin leather), then new ropes, then weaving the seven braids of his hair into the fabric on the loom. Do you see the progression? Finally, he positions himself too close to the edge, succumbs to the nagging, and confesses the powerful symbol of his strength. "Then she called, 'Samson, the Philistines are upon you!' He awoke from his sleep and thought, 'I'll go out as before and shake myself free.' But he did not know that the Lord had left him." Judges 16:20. If Samson had chosen to walk more closely to God, could he have accomplished more for God during his lifetime than at his death? "...Thus he killed many more when he died than while he lived." Judges 16:30.

Hophni and Phinehas are priests from the tribe of Levi whom God called to be the spiritual leaders of His people. At some point, they like Samson, forsake God's anointing and follow the evil desires of their hearts. "Therefore the Lord, the God of Israel, declares: 'I promised that members of your family would minister before me forever.' But now the Lord declares: "Far be it from me! Those who honor me I will honor, but those who despise me will be disdained.'" 1 Samuel 2:30.

God paid a high price for my salvation; it is precious to me; may it always be so. I must guard and protect what God has given me through Jesus Christ. God's call and anointing are not to be taken lightly. I cannot gamble with sin and see just how close I can walk to the edge without losing everything. That's just plain stupid! I find in Jesus Christ everything I will ever need in this life and the life to come, eternal life. "His divine power has given us everything we need for a godly life through our knowledge of him who called us by his own glory and goodness." 2 Peter 1:3.

April 6 – **It's Not God's Fault**

"'Lord, God of Israel,' they cried, 'why has this happened to Israel? Why should one tribe be missing from Israel today?'" Judges 21:3. The people should have thought of this before they almost destroyed an entire tribe! Perhaps they should be asking themselves these questions instead: What have we done? Why didn't we think through this before we started killing everything in sight? "The people grieved for Benjamin, because the Lord had made a gap in the tribes of Israel." (v. 15). This is not God's fault. It's so much easier to blame someone else, even if that someone is God, rather than accept personal responsibility for their own actions. The last verse in the book of Judges explains much of the insanity during this time period. "In those days Israel had no king; everyone did as they saw fit." (v. 25).

The apple doesn't fall far from the tree. Do we get caught up in the moment and not think of the ramifications of our actions? It's easy to do. We must remember that every action produces a reaction whether good or bad. Think through it before you do it. Better yet, pray through it before you do it. Who sits on the throne in your heart? Self or God? Be honest with yourself and God; He knows the truth already. Don't blame God; take responsibility for your sin and repent. Learn from it and trust God next time. Life gets crazy when we do as we see fit, and that's not good enough. "For when we were in the realm of the flesh, the sinful passions aroused by the law were at work in us, so that we bore fruit for death." Romans 7:5.

April 7 – **As It Turned Out**

The story of Ruth reminds us that even in a period of great apostasy, there is a godly remnant who continues to love and honor God. Ruth is from Moab, a heathen nation, whose people are forbidden to enter the congregation of the Lord. She demonstrates the truth that acceptance and participation in the family of God are not based on birth or nationality but on faith in, and obedience to, God. Her heart matters more to God than her parentage or upbringing. Along the way, she encounters Naomi whose example and love for God have a profound influence on her life. She loves Naomi and her God.

"'I will do whatever you say,' Ruth answered. So she went down to the threshing floor and did everything her mother-in-law told her to do." Ruth 3:5. She fully trusts Naomi and the God they serve, even though not fully understanding the customs of Israel.

What a coincidence! Have you said that before? Let's look back at Ruth 2:3. "So she went out, entered a field and began to glean behind the harvesters. As it turned out, she was working in a field belonging to Boaz, who was from the clan of Elimelek." In God's economy, there are no coincidences or accidents; nothing happens by chance or randomly. "The Lord makes firm the steps of the one who delights in him;" Psalm 37:23. We read that same verse in the KJV: "The steps of a good man are ordered by the Lord: and he delighteth in his way." Is it just a coincidence that Simon and Andrew are fishing when Jesus walks by? What about the time the Samaritan woman walks to Jacob's well at the same time Jesus is resting there? Is it by chance that blind Bartimaeus is sitting by the roadside begging when Jesus walks within ear-shot? It is no accident that Ruth is an ancestor of Jesus Christ or that her story is recorded in the Bible. It is for our learning. And it is no coincidence that you are alive today and reading this devotional! "The Father loves the Son and has placed everything in his hands." John 3:35.

April 8 – **The Author of Us**

Many of us get bored and bogged down in the genealogies listed in the Bible. We either skip over or read hurriedly through the long lists of "the sons of" to find something more interesting and applicable to our lives. However, we should stop and consider how meticulous God is, how concerned He is about each person He has ever created, and just how unique each one is to Him. When I'm in heaven, will Helah walk up to me and say, "Hello, I'm Helah. You may have read my name in 1 Chronicles 4:5 and 7."

There are many people who enjoy tracing their family trees. We all have one. We all have a spiritual family tree as well. I've often thought about the possibility of tracing my family tree in heaven. I may find gaps in that physical tree, but not in my spiritual family tree! My grandfather led me to the Lord as a child, but who led him, and who pointed that person to Jesus, and so on? Eternity is a long time, so there's plenty of time to investigate!

God gets to choose our parents, when and where we are born. I could have easily been born a thousand years ago in some country on the other side of the world, but God chose now and here for me. And don't you love it when God inserts a diamond (the story of Jabez) in the middle of barren soil? "Jabez was more honorable than his brothers. His mother had named him Jabez, saying, 'I gave birth to him in pain.' Jabez cried out to the God of Israel, 'Oh, that you would bless me and enlarge my territory! Let your hand be with me, and keep me from harm so that I will be free from pain.' And God granted his request." 1 Chronicles 4:9, 10. Jabez sounds like the Hebrew *for pain.* He has no say in choosing his parents or his given name, but he does have something to say about the direction of his heart and life. He looks to God. So, take your time reading through the "less than appealing" chapters; you may find a gold nugget.

"fixing our eyes on Jesus, the pioneer and perfecter of faith. For the joy set before him he endured the cross, scorning its shame, and sat down at the right hand of the throne of God." Hebrews 12:2. "Nothing impure will ever enter it, nor will anyone who does what is shameful or deceitful, but only those whose names are written in the Lamb's book of life." Revelation 21:27. God is the author of our lives, but He invites our input into the final chapter.

April 9 – **A Mother's Prayer**

Hannah prays for Samuel before his birth. We can be sure she continues to pray for him afterwards as well, because although Samuel lives in God's house, he is surrounded by corruption and sin. He needs prayer now more than ever! "…Meanwhile, the boy Samuel grew up in the presence of the Lord." 1 Samuel 2:21. He becomes a mighty prophet of God.

Moses is another example of one who grows up in less than favorable circumstances. His mother, Jochebed, "saw that he was a fine child" (Exodus 2:2). She protects him from death and observes from a distance as her son is raised in the palace of the heathen pharaoh. God uses Moses to lead His people out of Egyptian bondage.

Perhaps you are a mother or grandmother who has known separation from your child. "pray continually," 1 Thessalonians 5:17. That means never stop praying for your child. God hears your prayers. He knows how to answer a mother's prayers. Regardless of the circumstances to which your child is exposed, God has enough keeping power and grace to take care of that child and preserve his or her life for the glory of God. "I am reminded of your sincere faith, which first lived in your grandmother Lois and in your mother Eunice and, I am persuaded, now lives in you also." 2 Timothy 1:5.

April 10 – **Why Wait?**

"When the ark of the Lord had been in Philistine territory seven months, the Philistines called for the priests and the diviners and said, 'What shall we do with the ark of the Lord? Tell us how we should send it back to its place.'" 1 Samuel 6:1, 2. Seven months ago, the Ark of the Covenant was captured in battle and has been in Philistine territory ever since. God is not happy. He overruns the land with rats causing death and destruction. As if that is not enough, God gets really personal and causes tumors in the groin area of all the people, young and old alike. I wonder why it takes the people seven months to realize they need to do something with the ark. Are they unwilling to admit that the all-powerful God of Israel is trying to get their attention? Perhaps they're thinking the problem will go away by itself, and the God of Israel really has nothing to do with this. It reminds me of Pharaoh when he says to Moses that tomorrow is a good day for the plague of frogs to end (Exodus 8:10). Why not today?

Procrastination can get us into serious trouble. Why do we continue to be lost, go our own way and do our own thing, and be miserable? Don't ignore the cry of your heart to draw near to God. God has given us today; tomorrow is His. "As has just been said: 'Today, if you hear his voice, do not harden your hearts as you did in the rebellion.'" Hebrews 3:15. The one thing we should never procrastinate is a right relationship with God. Hell is full of people who thought they had 'tomorrow' to get their lives right with God. Don't be one of them.

Heavenly Father, I come to You today. I'm tired of doing my own thing. I'm hurting. Have mercy on me and forgive me of my sins. Come into my life and make me a new person. I give You my life. I believe in Your Son, Jesus Christ, and that He died for me on the cross. Thank You, Lord. Amen.

"In the same way, I tell you, there is rejoicing in the presence of the angels of God over one sinner who repents." Luke 15:10.

April 11 – **That Didn't Last Long!**

"The Spirit of the Lord will come powerfully upon you, and you will prophesy with them; and you will be changed into a different person. Once these signs are fulfilled, do whatever your hand finds to do, for God is with you." 1 Samuel 10:6, 7. Saul has it all – a changed heart, the empowerment of the Holy Spirit, a strong body, humble attitude, Samuel's guidance and prayers, and the gift of prophecy. However, this change is not unconditional or permanent. Saul has a part to play. "But now your kingdom will not endure; the Lord has sought out a man after his own heart and appointed him ruler of his people, because you have not kept the Lord's command." 1 Samuel 13:14. There's more that separates these two passages of Scripture than 73 verses and a few years. God's presence in Saul's life can only be maintained by obedience to God.

Saul loses it all because of his unfaithfulness to God. "But Samuel replied: 'Does the Lord delight in burnt offerings and sacrifices as much as in obeying the Lord? To obey is better than sacrifice, and to heed is better than the fat of rams.'" 1 Samuel 15:22. No one is exempt; we must all obey the Lord if we want His continued presence and blessings in our lives. "He replied, 'Blessed rather are those who hear the word of God and obey it.'" Luke 11:28.

April 12 – **When It's Convenient**

Let's inspect Saul's heart more closely. "While Saul was talking to the priest, the tumult in the Philistine camp increased more and more. So Saul said to the priest, 'Withdraw your hand.'" 1 Samuel 14:19. Saul is impatient; he doesn't wait for God's answer and so takes matters into his own hands. He speaks before thinking, before seeking God; he makes rash vows. "Then Saul built an altar to the Lord; it was the first time he had done this." (14:35). Does he build the altar to impress others, to make them think he truly is seeking after God? Or is it just a convenient time to insert God into the picture? Saul ultimately does his own thing; he leans to his own understanding. His wisdom and strength are insufficient for the task of leading Israel.

Has God given you a task to accomplish for Him? Rest assured that your personal strength, abilities, intelligence, and charisma are insufficient. You need God's anointing from start to finish. Don't wait for a convenient time to follow God wholeheartedly. Satan strives very hard to make sure there is never a convenient time. "Are you so foolish? After beginning by means of the Spirit, are you now trying to finish by means of the flesh?" Galatians 3:3.

April 13 – **Be On Your Way**

Has your world ever come to a screeching halt? You've been hurt to the very core of your being. Someone has severely disappointed you. All dreams and expectations are completely demolished. It feels like a death. This is not the way it is supposed to be.

Samuel is a faithful and respected prophet in Israel. He is the one the Lord sent to anoint Saul king over Israel (1 Samuel 15:1); they share a special bond, but Saul has deeply disappointed God and Samuel. "The Lord said to Samuel, 'How long will you mourn for Saul, since I have rejected him as king over Israel? Fill your horn with oil and be on your way; I am sending you to Jesse of Bethlehem. I have chosen one of his sons to be king.'" 1 Samuel 16:1. God has made his decision; it's time for Samuel to accept it and move on. God may be through with Saul being King, but He's not through with Samuel. He has work for him to do. Samuel has questions, but He obeys the Lord (vs. 2-4).

Is it time for you to move on with God? You must make the conscious decision to get up from where you are, forgive someone, put one foot in front of the other, and move. Sure, you may have questions, some of which you may never receive answers in this life. Regardless, obey the Lord. He is obviously not through with you yet, because you're still here and you're reading this devotional! "I have considered my ways and have turned my steps to your statutes. I will hasten and not delay to obey your commands." Psalm 119:59, 60. "In everything I did, I showed you that by this kind of hard work we must help the weak, remembering the words the Lord Jesus himself said: 'It is more blessed to give than to receive.'" Acts 20:35.

April 14 – **What Will You Do With the Truth?**

Jonathan recognizes a king in David early in their friendship and knows in his heart that he himself will never be king. "Jonathan took off the robe he was wearing and gave it to David, along with his tunic, and even his sword, his bow and his belt." 1 Samuel 18:4. He submits his heart and life to God's plan. Saul, on the other hand, also sees a king in David, becomes jealous, and resists God's plan. "Saul was afraid of David, because the Lord was with David but had departed from Saul." (v. 12). Saul fights against God's plan, a battle he will lose with his life.

Even though Saul has several true spiritual experiences, he does not continue to walk with God. Both Saul and Jonathan perceive God's choice and will; however, their reactions to God's will are total opposites. Saul is in turmoil; Jonathan has a peaceful heart.

How do you respond to truth, even when it is contrary to your desires? "But if it is from God, you will not be able to stop these men; you will only find yourselves fighting against God." Acts 5:39. "Moreover, we have all had human fathers who disciplined us and we respected them for it. How much more should we submit to the Father of spirits and live!" Hebrews 12:9.

April 15 – **Multi-Talented**

Immunizations are available for just about any illness or disease. That's comforting to know. Wouldn't it be nice if someone could be immunized from troubles in this life simply by accepting Christ as their Savior? Unfortunately, none of us are immune from life's difficulties, Christian or not. The tie-breaker is in knowing that Jesus Christ will walk with us through anything and everything when we know Him as our personal Savior and Lord, Deliverer and Protector.

Psalm 34 is a treasure chest of precious jewels! This Psalm is worthy of deeper exploration than this simple devotional can give it. Set aside time soon for further study and meditation and delve into its riches.

David has just escaped from the hands of Achish, king of Gath, by pretending insanity (1 Samuel 21:10-15). Now we can add acting to David's repertoire of musician, composer, singer, dancer, author, poet, shepherd, leader, giant killer, warrior, architect – you name it – David can do it – a man of many talents! Scripture is clearly unabashed in spotlighting misuse of God's gifts. However, the result of his escape provides us this beautiful and powerful Psalm expressly written for those who fear the Lord.

"The righteous person may have many troubles, but the Lord delivers him from them all;" Psalm 34:19. "Endure hardship as discipline; God is treating you as his children. For what children are not disciplined by their father?" Hebrews 12:7. "Blessed are those who are persecuted because of righteousness, for theirs is the kingdom of heaven." Matthew 5:10. When God's purpose for permitting our suffering is accomplished, He will either supernaturally intervene, or He will take us to our heavenly home. Either way, we win!

"he protects all his bones, not one of them will be broken." Psalm 34:20. This is a vivid picture for complete preservation. It is literally fulfilled in the experience of Christ (John 19:33).

"Taste and see that the Lord is good; blessed is the one who takes refuge in him." Psalm 34:8.

April 16 – **Migration**

Jeremiah 8:7 is an interesting verse. "Even the stork in the sky knows her appointed seasons, and the dove, the swift and the thrush observe the time of their migration. But my people do not know the requirements of the Lord." What does this reference to migration have to do with David? In today's reading of three Psalms penned by David, he shares the constant danger that encases him at every step. "I am in the midst of lions; I am forced to dwell among ravenous beasts – men whose teeth are spears and arrows, whose tongues are sharp swords." Psalm 57:4.

David's emotions are all over the map. Can you relate? There is something very healing about being able to express one's emotions, and David does that uninhibited. David is a man's man, a warrior king; he's no wimp. He doesn't stuff, hide, ignore, or pretend his emotions do not exist. He acknowledges them. He takes them out and looks at them; then he returns safely home. Read again the last verse in each of these Psalms. "Be exalted, O God, above the heavens; let your glory be over all the earth." Psalm 57:11. "Set me free from my prison, that I may praise your name. Then the righteous will gather about me because of your goodness to me." Psalm 142:7. "For what you have done I will always praise you in the presence of your faithful people. And I will hope in your name, for your name is good." Psalm 52:9.

We will have those times in life when we experience the extreme gamut of emotions, and that's okay, just so we always return home to the safe arms of Jesus. He understands. Like David, we can praise the Lord at all times. "'Return home and tell how much God has done for you.' So the man went away and told all over town how much Jesus had done for him." Luke 8:39.

April 17 – **Wrestling**

David flees for his life while Saul hunts him like an animal. He doesn't understand everything that is happening to him. "How long must I wrestle with my thoughts and day after day have sorrow in my heart? How long will my enemy triumph over me?" Psalm 13:2.

Have you ever asked God, "How long?" or struggled with your thoughts? Been there; done that! I've wrestled with my thoughts, emotions, situations in life, and God's Word all at the same time, trying to make sense of it all. I've discovered that thoughts come and go; emotions can change with the wind; and my perception of a situation may be wrong. But God's Word? It never changes; it is solid; it is 100% true always. So I've become an everyday life-long student of the Word. I allow it to saturate my heart and renew my mind. I hold it tightly and will never let it go. I believe what the Bible says and strive to live like I believe it.

What does David do when he's wrestling? He leans into God's Word and does what he knows to do. "But I trust in your unfailing love; my heart rejoices in your salvation. I will sing the Lord's praise, for he has been good to me." Psalm 13:5, 6. David worships God at all times. "I will sacrifice a freewill offering to you; I will praise your name, O Lord, for it is good." Psalm 54:6. God's Word, alive in David, keeps him from killing Saul. He leaves vindication to God where it rightfully belongs (1 Samuel 24:15).

Remember Paul and Silas, thrown into prison for walking out their faith in God. "About midnight Paul and Silas were praying and singing hymns to God, and the other prisoners were listening to them." Acts 16:25.

April 18 – **God Needs No Help**

David has his chance, and he blows it! That would be the world's conclusion. Saul and his men are still pursuing David and his men. One night, Saul's camp is asleep. David and Abishai walk into the enemy camp with sleeping soldiers all around to find Saul. There he is, sound asleep, his men asleep around him, and his spear stuck in the ground near his head. David and Abishai are whispering loudly to each other over the snoring (1 Samuel 26:8-11). It looks like the perfect set-up, and Abishai wants to pin Saul to the ground. "But David said to Abishai, 'Don't destroy him! Who can lay a hand on the Lord's anointed and be guiltless?'" 1 Samuel 26:9.

Satan is making it easy for David to take revenge and thus displease God. If David should kill King Saul, the sleeping soldiers would probably awaken, and David would lose his life as well. Satan knows the Messiah will most likely come from David's line; his plan is to destroy David. God put the soldiers into a deep sleep (v. 12) just in case David should kill Saul. God's using this situation as another test for David. Will he do the right thing? He does. He leaves justice in the hands of God. He probably thinks of Jonathan too. After all, Saul is the father of his best friend. And let us not ignore God's great mercy extended to Saul at this time. God is not willing that any should perish (even Saul) but wants everyone to repent (2 Peter 3:9). If only he would truly repent!

David takes Saul's spear and water jug, and then calls out to Saul's commander, Abner. After Saul wakes up and realizes what just happened, he calls out to David, "Is that your voice, David my son?" (v. 17). Suddenly David is "my son" when Saul realizes he could be dead at that moment! "...Why is my lord pursuing his servant? What have I done, and what wrong am I guilty of?" (v. 18). The answer to both questions is nothing. The truth is Saul is far from God and consumed with jealousy.

We may, at times, be tempted to do God a favor and take justice into our own hands, because we grow impatient. When we do, we mess things up royally! Justice belongs to God, and He does not need our help (Romans 12:19). "Here is my servant whom I have chosen, the one I love, in whom I delight; I will put my Spirit on him, and he will proclaim justice to the nations." Matthew 12:18. "The Lord rewards everyone for their righteousness and faithfulness..." 1 Samuel 26:23.

April 19 – **Protect the Home Front**

David and his 600 men leave their wives, children, and homes unprotected as they traverse the countryside fighting battles. Ziklag is an easy target for the Amalekite raiders. "When David and his men reached Ziklag, they found it destroyed by fire and their wives and sons and daughters taken captive." 1 Samuel 30:3. The men weep; David finds strength in the Lord. "and David inquired of the Lord, 'Shall I pursue this raiding party? Will I overtake them?' 'Pursue them' he answered. 'You will certainly overtake them and succeed in the rescue.'" (v. 8). David and his fighting men are fortunate in that they recover everyone and everything they lost.

Let this be an eye-opener to us! If you are a spouse and a parent, God has given you the responsibility to take care of your family – first! We can get so busy pursuing more possessions, more recognition, more worldly security, even working more for God, and neglect those most precious to us. Don't leave your family exposed and vulnerable to the enemy's attacks, because Satan will go after your marriage and family. Protect and provide for your family, because you may not experience the same favorable outcome as David and his men. "Anyone who does not provide for his relatives, and especially for their own household, has denied the faith and is worse than an unbeliever." 1 Timothy 5:8.

April 20 – **Courage with Humility**

"…Then the Israelites retreated, but Eleazar stood his ground and struck down the Philistines till his hand grew tired and froze to the sword. The Lord brought about a great victory that day. The troops returned to Eleazar, but only to strip the dead." 2 Samuel 23:9, 10. This is a fascinating story of courage mixed with humility. Eleazar is one of King David's mighty men. In the midst of intense battle, his colleagues desert him. It doesn't matter; he knows what he must do. He stands firmly planted, surrounded by the enemy, fighting with all his might, gripping his sword to the point that his fingers and hand must be pried off his weapon. Eleazar understands that it is the Lord Who won that victory, so he stays away from the spotlight. Even when his buddies return after the fact to claim their share of the plunder, Eleazar doesn't object. The battle is won, God gets the glory, and that's all that counts.

"Take the helmet of salvation and the sword of the Spirit, which is the word of God." Ephesians 6:17. Do I hold so tightly to God's Word, even during those times of extreme pressure and uncertainty, that absolutely nothing can pry His Word out of my heart and hand? May it be so! If God's Word, that holy sword of the Spirit, is all I have, it is more than enough.

Dear Lord, help me to be an Eleazar in your army, firmly holding Your Word, being courageous yet humble, deflecting all praise to you, and sharing your blessings with others.

April 21 – **Man's Wrath**

Man's wrath has produced countless acts of treachery and bloodshed through the years. It accomplishes nothing except more of the same. Look again at today's reading. Abner is commander of what's left of Saul's army, and Joab is commander of David's men. Much rivalry and jealousy now exist between these proven warrior leaders. Ish-Bosheth, Saul's son, is feeling threatened and accuses Abner of invading his deceased father's harem, which is customary for new kings to do when they seize the kingship. "Abner was very angry because of what Ish-Bosheth said. So he answered, 'Am I a dog's head – on Judah's side?...'" 2 Samuel 3:8. When Joab discovers that King David had a business meeting with Abner, he confronts David in a jealous rage trying to convince him that Abner's intention is deception. When Joab fails to persuade David that Abner is a spy, he sends a message (unknown to David) to Abner to return for further conference. Joab murders Abner. More bloodshed ensues with the murder of Ish-Bosheth by two bounty hunters whom David promptly executes. All of this mayhem illustrates the fact that God's perfect will for Israel did not include a human king (1 Samuel 8:5-7, 19-22).

We will do well to heed and apply the admonition given us in James 1:19, 20. "My dear brothers and sisters, take note of this: Everyone should be quick to listen, slow to speak and slow to become angry, because human anger does not produce the righteousness that God desires." This is obvious in light of today's reading!

April 22 – **Puzzle Pieces**

When was the last time you put together a thousand piece puzzle? Some pieces come together quickly – others not so quickly. That partial picture may decorate your breakfast table for a month before the last piece completes the image. Let's say your life is a thousand piece puzzle, but you don't have the box top to show you what your complete life looks like. You may think you know what the finished product of your life looks like, but God is in possession of your box top. He knows when He put the first piece down on the table (your birth), and He knows when the final piece will fit into place. He knows when and where the other 998 pieces go. You see, He holds the pieces of your picture in His hands.

"In the course of time, David inquired of the Lord…" 2 Samuel 2:1. "When all the elders of Israel had come to King David at Hebron, he made a covenant with them at Hebron before the Lord, and they anointed David king over Israel, as the Lord had promised through Samuel." 1 Chronicles 11:3. Approximately twenty years pass from the time Samuel secretly anoints a youth named David king over Israel until he actually becomes king over all of Israel. Perhaps David wonders many times when that promised piece will find its rightful place in his life. All the while, God holds the puzzle pieces to Saul's life and everyone else, many of whom intersect with David's life. Only God can keep all that straight!

So it is with you and me. Jesus says, "I am the Alpha and the Omega, the First and the Last, the Beginning and the End." Revelation 22:13. He is also everything in between! As a child of God, we can trust Him with our puzzle. When that day comes, and He puts the last piece in place, glossed with His grace, we will look at that picture and exclaim, "Wow! Picture perfect!"

April 23 – **A True Leader**

1 Chronicles chapters 15 and 16 contain choice leadership skills we can glean from the life of King David. Let's take a closer look.

1. He appoints leaders, those clearly selected by God. "He appointed some of the Levites to minister before the ark of the Lord…" (16:4).
2. He empowers them. "You are the heads of the Levitical families…" (15:12).
3. He instructs them. "David told the leaders… (15:16).
4. He demonstrates what he wants. "That day David first appointed Asaph and his associates to give praise to the Lord in this manner:" (16:7).

Finally, David does the most essential leadership component of all – he trusts them. He leaves them and lets them do the work. "David left Asaph and his associates before the ark of the covenant of the Lord to minister there regularly, according to each day's requirements. He also left Obed-Edom and his sixty-eight associates to minister with them…David left Zadok the priest and his fellow priests before the tabernacle of the Lord at the high place in Gibeon." (16:37-39).

David relaxes. "Then all the people left, each for their own home, and David returned home to bless his family." (16:43).

"After this the Lord appointed seventy-two others and sent them two by two ahead of him to every town and place where he was about to go." Luke 10:1.

April 24 – **God Just Keeps Blessing**

"After David was settled in his palace, he said to Nathan the prophet, 'Here I am, living in a house of cedar, while the ark of the covenant of the Lord is under a tent.'" 1 Chronicles 17:1. David realizes how very blessed he is. He is indisputably the King of Israel; his enemies are subdued; there is peace all around; he has a beautiful home, and life is good. He desires to bless God; perhaps God would enjoy a nice home too. God's response: "'…I declare to you that the Lord will build a house for you.'" (v. 10). Obviously, God is not through blessing David.

"Then King David went in and sat before the Lord, and he said: 'Who am I, Lord God, and what is my family, that you have brought me this far?...For you know your servant.'" 1 Chronicles 17:16, 18. Humbled and awestruck, David knows God knows all about him – his many faults and failures – and yet God still loves him and desires to bless him more! Incomprehensible!

God always gives us so much more than we deserve or can ever give Him. There is nothing we can give Him that He does not already own. "for every animal of the forest is mine, and the cattle on a thousand hills." Psalm 50:10. "And he is not served by human hands, as if he needed anything. Rather, he himself gives everyone life and breath and everything else." Acts 17:25. God knows all there is to know about me, and He still loves me! He gives to us not because of who we are but because of Who He is. He is a giving God. And His blessings endure far beyond this life! Praise His Holy Name!

April 25 – **Kindness**

Kindness given is not always kindness received. Regardless of the response from the other, God calls us to show kindness to all. After all, it is a fruit of the Spirit (Galatians 5:22).

King David is intentional about two acts of kindness. In both instances, he thinks about it, speaks it, and then acts upon it. "David asked, 'Is there anyone still left of the house of Saul to whom I can show kindness for Jonathan's sake?'" 2 Samuel 9:1. He is told about Mephibosheth, son of Jonathan, who is lame in both feet, so he sends for him. Mephibosheth is terrified to face King David and bows before him. It is customary when new kings take power to destroy all survivors of the previous dynasty. But that is not King David's intention. He restores all the land that belonged to his grandfather and offers Mephibosheth a place at his table for the rest of his life. He is humbled by the king's kindness; expecting death, he receives rich blessing instead. "Mephibosheth bowed down and said, 'What is your servant, that you should notice a dead dog like me?'" (9:8). Those are familiar words to King David (1 Samuel 24:14).

In the next chapter, David attempts to show kindness to Hanun in the event of his father's death, King Nahash of the Ammonites (2 Samuel 10:1-19). This time, King David's act of kindness is not well received. Hanun's commanders persuade him to believe that this is no act of kindness on David's part, but an attempt to spy out the land for overthrow. He rejects the kindness and humiliates the envoys. King David prepares for war, and Hanun is soundly defeated.

God extends His kindness to all. "Or do you show contempt for the riches of his kindness, forbearance and patience, not realizing that God's kindness is intended to lead you to repentance?" Romans 2:4. What will be your response? 1) To humble yourself before the King, admitting your unworthiness, repent, graciously receive His kindness, and forever feast at His table; or 2) Reject His kindness, fight against Him, and suffer defeat and humiliation. The choice is yours.

April 26 – **Pure Praise**

One thing King David learns from the whole experience with Bathsheba is that God requires truth and faithfulness from us. "Yet you desired faithfulness even in the womb; you taught me wisdom in that secret place." Psalm 51:6. God's Holy Spirit reaches deep within our soul searching for truth. We can somewhat succeed in displaying surface truth to ourselves and the world. But He longs for more from us. We must invite and allow Him to step into the inner chambers of our heart with His spotlight and point out the encrusted sin clinging to its walls. Then we must confess God's accuracy and repent of sometimes forgotten and embedded wrongdoing. How sweet is forgiveness as it rushes in and washes out the ugliness! It is then that God is free to teach us wisdom, and we're free to receive it, "in the inmost place."

"Praise the Lord, O my soul; all my inmost being, praise his holy name." Psalm 103:1. Praise in its purest form comes from recognizing Who God is, and what He has done for us and in us that we cannot do ourselves. When David is deeply and truly cleansed by God's Holy Presence, torrents of pure praise gush forth. As God exposes and cleanses the deepest recesses of my heart, I will also praise His Holy Name. "For in my inner being I delight in God's law." Romans 7:22. "Praise be to the God and Father of our Lord Jesus Christ! In his great mercy he has given us new birth into a living hope through the resurrection of Jesus Christ from the dead." 1 Peter 1:3.

April 27 – **All in the Family**

Oh, how we need God in our families! We can sure find ourselves in precarious predicaments when we stray from God's plan. A few of King David's family problems are shared in 2 Samuel 13 for the whole world to see, as well as teach us a few lessons on family dynamics. Yes, this chapter traces the fulfillment of the judgment pronounced against David's house. However, I can't help but wonder that better results may have happened if David had handled a few things differently. As they say (whoever they are): Hindsight is 20/20.

First of all, let's keep in mind that there is nothing "fun" about dysfunction. Amnon, David's oldest son in line for the throne, is obsessed with his half-sister, Tamar. His cousin, Jonadab, who is only mentioned in this chapter, is a conniving busybody "what's in it for me" kind of guy, and encourages Amnon to fulfill his demented lust. "Then Amnon hated her with intense hatred. In fact, he hated her more than he had loved her. Amnon said to her, 'Get up and get out!'" 2 Samuel 13:15. (Did they have bi-polar back then?)

"When King David heard all this, he was furious." (13:21). David is king, but he is also a father. There is no record of him addressing this issue with his son. Two years later, Absalom murders his brother, Amnon, for what he did to his sister, Tamar. Scheming Jonadab goes to placate the king and make himself look good. Absalom flees and David mourns for his sons. It goes from bad to worse.

Dysfunction in the family can be traced back to Adam and Eve. Bitterness and resentment in the human heart breeds hatred and produces tragic results. The antidote is forgiveness. We can't force someone to forgive us and reconcile if they choose not to. However, we can forgive, release all bitterness and resentment, ask God to heal our heart, pray blessing on the other, and give it all to God. And never ever stop praying and believing (1 Thessalonians 5:17 and 1 Corinthians 13:7). God is more than able to take care of the situation. Life is too short. We have too much to do for God to carry this weight. There are souls to reach for the Kingdom.

Listen to God's Word. "Then, after desire has conceived, it gives birth to sin; and sin, when it is full-grown, gives birth to death." James 1:15. "If it is possible, as far as it depends on you, live at peace with everyone." Romans 12:18.

April 28 – **Eye for Eye?**

David spends many years fleeing from rival armies, his king, and now his son. "Arise, Lord! Deliver me, my God! Strike all my enemies on the jaw; break the teeth of the wicked." Psalm 3:7. I think I have prayed that prayer a few times! David lives under the law and an, "eye for eye, tooth for tooth, hand for hand, foot for foot," (Exodus 21:24). I'm not sure David ever prays blessing over his enemies. However, today we live under grace and a new order. Read the words of Jesus in Matthew 5:38-48. "You have heard that it was said, 'Eye for eye, and tooth for tooth.' But I tell you, do not resist an evil person. If anyone slaps you on the right cheek, turn to them the other cheek also…But I tell you, love your enemies and pray for those who persecute you," Matthew 5:38, 39, 44.

Shimei adds insult to injury by cursing David as he walks along the road. Without batting an eye, King David could easily call for Shimei's immediate execution. "David then said to Abishai and all his officials, 'My son, my own flesh and blood, is trying to kill me. How much more, then, this Benjamite! Leave him alone; let him curse, for the Lord has told him to. It may be that the Lord will look upon my misery and restore to me his covenant blessing instead of his curse today.'" 2 Samuel 16:11, 12. He's thinking like Jesus! He reinforces the truth that God is a just God. "For the Lord is righteous, he loves justice; the upright will see his face." Psalm 11:7. "Your righteousness is like the highest mountains, your justice like the great deep..." Psalm 36:6. It's immeasurable! Yet, David never forgets Shimei and passes his judgment on to Solomon before his death.

The world we live in is unjust, but God always administers justice and sets the record straight. He doesn't need me to tell Him how to do His job. He is more concerned about the posture of my heart. Do I truly forgive those who wrong me? Am I careful not to wrong another? Do I pray blessing instead of wrath upon my enemies? *Lord, instill in me a heart that is pleasing to You.*

April 29 – **Obeisance**

It is the day of Absalom's death, and King David is anxiously waiting for news of the battle and the welfare of his son (2 Samuel

18:19-33). He is sitting between the inner and outer gates, and the watchman is on the roof. Back on the front lines, Commander Joab dispatches a runner to take King David the report that the battle is over and Absalom is dead. Ahimaaz asks to run with the news as well. He is the son and successor of Zadok the high priest. Joab gives his permission. Ahimaaz outruns the Cushite.

The watchman spots a runner, then another. "Then the watchman said, 'It seems to me that the first one runs like Ahimaaz son of Zadok.' 'He's a good man,' the king said. 'He comes with good news.'" 2 Samuel 18:27. Ahimaaz gives obeisance to the king, bowing down before him with his face to the ground, and soon realizes that the news of his son's death is not what the king wants to hear. "The king asked, 'Is the young man Absalom safe?' Ahimaaz answered, 'I saw great confusion just as Joab was about to send the king's servant and me, your servant, but I don't know what it was.'" (v. 29). He chooses not to be the bearer of painful tidings to the king. The Cushite runner arrives shortly and blurts out the news that Absalom is dead. The king immediately goes into mourning. All Absalom's faults are forgotten in the welling up of parental love. He grieves the loss of his son magnified by the fact that he dies while in the act of rebellion and sin.

Obeisance is the act of expressing deep respect or submission before a superior. The word is used nine times in the KJV, but is rendered "bowing" or "bowed down" in the NIV. Examples are in the story of Joseph's dream about his brothers bowing before him (Genesis 37:7 and 43:28). The Magi give obeisance to the newborn King by bowing and worshiping him (Matthew 2:11). Jairus falls at Jesus' feet in desperation, humble respect and submission. "Then a man named Jairus a synagogue leader, came and fell at Jesus' feet, pleading with him to come to his house because his only daughter, a girl of about twelve, was dying..." Luke 8:41, 42.

There is no one more worthy of our obeisance than our Lord Jesus Christ. When was the last time you humbled yourself before Him in body and heart?

April 30 – **A Mother's Love**

Rizpah. Ever heard of her? She's a mother of grown sons and perhaps a grandmother. A mother's love for her children is one of the strongest powers on earth and no where better expressed than in the life of Rizpah (2 Samuel 21:1-14).

The land has experienced famine for three years all because King Saul had broken a vow (a serious transgression) and massacred the Gibeonites. King David takes seven descendants of Saul, men implicated in the slaughter (blood-stained house), and hands them over to the Gibeonites who crucify them. Five of the men are sons of Merab, King Saul's daughter, and two are the sons of his concubine, Rizpah. David grants the request, because according to the law (Numbers 35:33) bloodshed pollutes the land and can only be atoned for by the blood of the criminal. The bodies are left hanging for six months. "Rizpah daughter of Aiah took sackcloth and spread it out for herself on a rock. From the beginning of the harvest till the rain poured down from the heavens on the bodies, she did not let the birds touch them by day or the wild animals by night." 2 Samuel 21:10. David finally notices Rizpah and is moved by her example. He goes and takes the bones of Saul and his son Jonathan from the citizens of Jabesh Gilead, and along with the bones of the seven, gives them a proper burial.

What would make a woman do what Rizpah does? A mother's love for her children, created by God and implanted in a mother's heart. Jesus knows all about a mother's love, because he had one who stayed with him through his suffering, death, resurrection, and beyond. "Near the cross of Jesus stood his mother…" John 19:25.

Knowing a mother's love may not be your experience. Sadly, we live in a fallen world, and Satan steals everything he can from us. That's why I'm so thankful for Isaiah 49:15: "Can a mother forget the baby at her breast and have no compassion on the child she has borne? Though she may forget, I will not forget you!"

MAY

May 1 – **Justice**

God makes it abundantly clear to David – again – that he is not to avenge himself. David is ready to destroy Nabal and his household when Abigail intercepts him and convinces him that his plan is not a good one. David listens to her wise counsel. Not long afterwards, Nabal dies. "When David heard that Nabal was dead, he said, 'Praise be to the Lord, who has upheld my cause against Nabal for treating me with contempt. He has kept his servant from doing wrong and has brought Nabal's wrongdoing down on his own head.' Then David sent word to Abigail, asking her to become his wife." 1 Samuel 25:39. "He is the God who avenges me, who subdues nations under me," Psalm 18:47.

"He reached down from on high and took hold of me; he drew me out of deep waters. You, Lord, keep my lamp burning; my God turns my darkness into light." Psalm 18:16, 28. Many times, David feels like he is drowning, but God reaches down and rescues him. At other times, it's as if he is engulfed in darkness; then God turns on His light. Like David, we must learn to wait on God and trust Him and not take matters into our own hands. God answers David's prayers quickly in the situation with Nabal. However, it takes many years for God to unfold His plan in Saul's case. In both instances, God's justice is accomplished. "And will not God bring about justice for his chosen ones, who cry out to him day and night? Will he keep putting them off?" Luke 18:7. I choose to trust God and His written Word and to wait on Him.

May 2 – **A True Sacrifice**

"But King David replied to Araunah, 'No, I insist on paying the full price. I will not take for the Lord what is yours, or sacrifice a burnt offering that costs me nothing.'...He called on the Lord, and the Lord answered him with fire from heaven on the altar of burnt offering." 1 Chronicles 21:24, 26. The angel of the Lord is about to destroy Jerusalem, but God relents and commands David to build an altar. He obeys, and the angel puts his sword back into its sheath. David understands that a sacrifice costs somebody something; it's not for show. The true value of our gifts to God is measured by the sacrifice and cost involved.

God sacrificed His Son for our salvation. It cost Him His most valuable possession in all of heaven. Christianity that costs us nothing is worth nothing. Fasting is a form of sacrifice and combined with prayer is a mighty force that attracts God's attention. We joke about fasting Brussels sprouts, but it's no fast if it's easy; and fasting without prayer is just a diet. Sacrifice is dying to self to gain more of Christ. Paul says in 1 Corinthians 15:31, "I face death every day..." How serious am I about denying myself so that Christ may live in me more fully? I admit that I still have much to learn about sacrifice. "Therefore, I urge you, brothers and sisters, in view of God's mercy, to offer your bodies as a living sacrifice, holy and pleasing to God – this is your true and proper worship." Romans 12:1. I want the words of John the Baptist to be my daily prayer: "He must become greater; I must become less." John 3:30.

May 3 – **Sing Praise!**

King David is a man of many God-given abilities; among those are leadership and music. As the aged king, David makes abundant preparation for the transition of kingship to his son, Solomon. David is a leader who thinks and works beyond his own generation. He also embodies a tremendous love for music, praise and worship to God. We know him as "the hero of Israel's songs" in 2 Samuel 23:1. He helps insure that music, voice and instrumental, are always interwoven into the fabric of worship in the temple. "…four thousand are to praise the Lord with the musical instruments I have provided for that purpose. They were also to stand every morning to thank and praise the Lord. They were to do the same in the evening." 1 Chronicles 23:5, 30. What an incredible orchestra and choir that must have been!

David appoints Levites to lead in praise and worship, those whom God has chosen to minister, those for whom ministry is deep-rooted. He outlines precise directives for music in the temple. Music, singing, and musical instruments are first mentioned in the same breath in Genesis 31:27. This shining thread weaves itself all the way through the Bible to Revelation 19:1. "After this I heard what sounded like the roar of a great multitude in heaven shouting: 'Hallelujah! Salvation and glory and power belong to our God.'" God also makes it quite clear in Scripture that those of us who are not particularly gifted in singing have a place in His choir. Seven times in the Psalms, the KJV refers to making a joyful noise to the Lord. That's me; joyful and noisy! The NIV describes the noise as a shout. I shout better than I sing! (Psalm 66:1, 81:1, 95:1-2, 98:4, 98:6, 100:1).

Here's one more thought from today's reading. I find the name Happizzez in 1 Chronicles 24:15 quite fascinating. This is the only place in all of Scripture he is mentioned. The name is rendered Aphses in the KJV. Happizzez is a personal name meaning "the shattered one" or "disperse." Like Jabez, however,

Happizzez refuses to live up to his given name. Instead, he brings people together and leads them into the presence of the Holy God, worshiping and praising His Holy Name. He's happy!

"Sing for joy, you heavens, for the Lord has done this; shout aloud, you earth beneath. Burst into song, you mountains, you forests and all your trees, for the Lord has redeemed Jacob, he displays his glory in Israel." Isaiah 44:23.

May 4 – **Great Advice**

A parent may leave a rich inheritance, materially and spiritually, to a child, but there are a couple of things children must acquire on their own, and they involve decisions. I cannot decide anything for my adult child. I can leave a rich spiritual heritage, a clear path of faithfully loving and serving God, but my child gets to decide to make it his own or not. King David is advanced in years and prepares to transition the throne to his son, Solomon. He does everything he knows to do; now it's up to Solomon. "And you, my son Solomon, acknowledge the God of your father, and serve him with wholehearted devotion and with a willing mind, for the Lord searches every heart and understands every desire and every thought. If you seek him, he will be found by you; but if you forsake him, he will reject you forever." 1 Chronicles 28:9.

Solomon must acknowledge God, serve Him, seek Him, and remain faithful; no one else can do these things for him. And these aren't just one time decisions; they must happen every day for a lifetime. It's the same for us.

- "...Love the Lord your God with all your heart and with all your soul and with all your strength and with all your mind..." Luke 10:27.
- "Jesus knew their thoughts..." Matthew 12:25.

- "Ask and it will be given to you; seek and you will find; knock and the door will be opened to you." Matthew 7:7.
- "See to it, brothers and sisters, that none of you has a sinful, unbelieving heart that turns away from the living God." Hebrews 3:12.

May 5 – **Jesus is King!**

How many times must King David say it? The people either don't remember, don't want to remember, or just don't "get it"! Solomon will be king and sit on David's throne. "My lord the king, the eyes of all Israel are on you, to learn from you who will sit on the throne of my lord the king after him." 1 Kings 1:20. So he says it again, this time to Bathsheba. "I will surely carry out this very day what I swore to you by the Lord, the God of Israel: Solomon your son shall be king after me, and he will sit on my throne in my place." (v. 30).

Do I hear God clearly today? There are so many voices in the world today clamoring for my attention. I must stay in tune with God's voice, keep the volume turned up, and listen – read His Word and really listen to Him. "My sheep listen to my voice; I know them, and they follow me." John 10:27. I want to always hear God's voice distinctly over the clutter.

God's message is clear and unchanging. His Son, Jesus Christ, is forever King of kings and Lord of lords and sits on the throne. I don't ever want to forget that truth. I must grow in my walk with the Lord every day. He sits on the throne of my heart. Throughout Holy Scripture, Jesus is King! "They will wage war against the Lamb, but the Lamb will triumph over them because he is Lord of lords and King of kings – and with him will be his called, chosen and faithful followers." Revelation 17:14.

May 6 – **A Prevalent Theme**

Almighty God wants to bless little old me! So then, why doesn't He just go ahead and do it? I'm saved; I said that prayer a long time ago. What more does God want from me? "and observe what the Lord your God requires: Walk in obedience to him, and keep his decrees and commands, his laws and regulations, as written in the Law of Moses. Do this so that you may prosper in all you do and wherever you go" 1 Kings 2:3. This is a prevailing theme in Scripture. David, while speaking to his son, Solomon, conveys to us the heart of God.

Entitlement is a common notion in our minds today. I deserve to be happy and blessed! I have a right to the good things in life! In reality, I deserve God's judgment more than anything. It is solely because of His love, mercy, and grace that I'm even saved from my sins. Now what? He wants me to know Him and obey Him. Obedience and blessing are connected. Therefore, I must know His Word and what He says to me today. I must read it for myself and apply His Word to my life – every day. Am I doing that?

God calls each of us to a life of obedience. He is our Creator; He is God of the universe. Jesus Christ is King of kings and Lord of lords; He alone is worthy of our lives dedicated to Him. We are guilty many times of making this Christian life too easy. We need to stoke the fire inside and be red hot for Jesus! "So, because you are lukewarm – neither hot nor cold – I am about to spit you out of my mouth." Revelation 3:16. God's blessings are not automatically automatic; they are conditional on us doing our part.

Is God calling you to walk more closely to Him? Don't turn away from Him. Humble yourself today before Him, repent, and recommit your life to Him – to love, follow, obey, and serve Him with everything you are and have. From the Law of Moses to the New Covenant, God desires obedience so He can bless. "Jesus replied, 'Anyone who loves me will obey my teaching. My Father will love them, and we will come to them and make our home with them.'" John 14:23.

May 7 – **Without Excuse**

"The heavens declare the glory of God; the skies proclaim the work of his hands. Day after day they pour forth speech; night after night they reveal knowledge. They have no speech, they use no words; no sound is heard from them. Yet their voice goes out into all the earth, their words to the ends of the world." Psalm 19:1-4. "For since the creation of the world God's invisible qualities – his eternal power and divine nature – have been clearly seen, being understood from what has been made, so that people are without excuse." Romans 1:20.

Man, whenever or wherever he may live on this earth, can acquire knowledge of God through His creation. The heavens and skies, day and night, all declare there is a God. His power and nature are clearly seen in what He has made.

If this is true, and it is, then why do we send missionaries to every dot on the map? Why go to all that trouble and expense if man can find God in creation? It's simple: God commands it. "He said to them, 'Go into all the world and preach the good news to all creation.'" Mark 16:15. We are compelled to share the Living Word through the spoken and written Word of God. Everyone everywhere has the right to hear, see, and know the story of God's great saving love through His Son Jesus Christ. God gave you that blessing. What are you doing to reach others with that same message?

May 8 – **Kindergarten**

Many years ago, my husband and I taught a kindergarten Sunday school class. Two things I observed about five year olds: They are eager to learn, and they believe everything you say. Age five must be the easiest age to teach! As we grow older, we tend to lose some of this eagerness and acceptance and often replace them with lethargy and distrust.

"Show me your ways, Lord, teach me your paths. Guide me in your truth and teach me, for you are God my Savior, and my hope is in you all day long." Psalm 25:4, 5. King David asks God to teach and guide him. In so doing, he expresses that he is teachable and that he trusts the Divine Leader to lead him in the right direction. As long as we live, we must remain teachable in order to grow spiritually, and we must know and trust the One we follow.

Being teachable is essential to entrance into God's Kingdom. "And he said: 'Truly I tell you, unless you change and become like little children, you will never enter the kingdom of heaven.'" Matthew 18:3. Once in the Kingdom, who do we follow and where will he lead us? "They were on their way up to Jerusalem, with Jesus leading the way, and the disciples were astonished, while those who followed were afraid. Again he took the Twelve aside and told them what was going to happen to him." Mark 10:32. As a child of God, I follow Jesus Christ, and He leads me to the cross. We can learn a lot from a five year old!

May 9 – **Forgiveness**

David's sins of adultery and murder leave his conscience dead for nearly a year until Nathan, the prophet, comes to him. "When I kept silent, my bones wasted away through my groaning all day long. For day and night your hand was heavy on me; my strength was sapped as in the heat of summer. Then I acknowledged my sin to you and did not cover up my iniquity. I said, 'I will confess my transgressions to the Lord' – and you forgave the guilt of my sin." Psalm 32:3-5. Notice that David keeps silent about his sins. Does he think he can continue to hide and ignore his sins and God will automatically forgive and forget? After all, he is a man after God's own heart and King of Israel. However, in his unrepentant state, God's heavy hand is upon David, and his body becomes sick and feels the distress of conviction. Finally, he acknowledges and confesses his sins to God, and God forgives him. Although he and his family reap the consequences for many years, David is restored back into right relationship with God.

"Therefore confess your sins to each other and pray for each other so that you may be healed. The prayer of a righteous person is powerful and effective." James 5:16. If we don't confess our sin, we forfeit the healing of body, soul, and spirit God has for us. It's imperative that we confess our sin first to God, receive forgiveness, and then confess to those we've wronged. Wonderful healing and freedom comes with forgiveness! Don't wait any longer; be restored! The greatest sinner can find pardon if he truly repents.

May 10 – **Will You Inherit the Land?**

I remember as a child running through my father's and grandfather's gardens, tall with corn, relishing life, fragrance, and sunshine. Today, I enjoy the green grass and roses in my back yard. It's only a back yard, but I love this tiny piece of land God has given me. Read Psalm 37 again. What do these have in common: those who hope in the Lord, the meek, those the Lord blesses, the righteous, and those who keep His way? You're right; they will inherit the land.

Land is important to God. He created it on the third day. He made the Promised Land flowing with milk and honey and gave it to His chosen people, the children of Israel. We get the food we eat from the land. God connects the physical and spiritual laws of sowing and reaping. The land praises its Creator. "Let the rivers clap their hands, let the mountains sing together for joy;" Psalm 98:8.

God has created another land for those who love Him. I have an inheritance awaiting me! "Your eyes will see the king in his beauty and view a land that stretches afar." Isaiah 33:17. "Then the angel showed me the river of the water of life, as clear as crystal, flowing from the throne of God and of the Lamb down the middle of the great street of the city. On each side of the river stood the tree of life, bearing twelve crops of fruit, yielding its fruit every month. And the leaves of the tree are for the healing of the nations." Revelation 22:1, 2.

May 11 – **The Brevity of Life**

It's taking forever to grow up! I remember thinking and believing that when I was a child. Then when I became a mother of preschoolers, I thought those long and busy days would never end. Was I ever wrong! The older I get, the more I believe that time really does fly.

"You have made my days a mere handbreadth; the span of my years is as nothing before you. Everyone is but a breath, even those who seem secure." Psalm 39:5. Truer words were never spoken! Many people are living well into their 90s, and some reach the century mark. However, compared to eternity, this life at its longest is a mere breath, a single grain of sand on all the beaches of the world. The brevity of life and the reality of eternity come into even sharper focus when someone you're close to and love very much dies. In death's aftermath, our thoughts gradually shift more to life after death. We think differently.

God has given each of us only a short time on earth. We can choose to spend it on self and living for the world, or we can live our lives for God, reaching others for Christ, making an eternal difference so that others may be saved. It's our choice. Only what we do for God and others will endure eternally; everything else will burn. "Why, you do not even know what will happen tomorrow. What is your life? You are a mist that appears for a little while and then vanishes." James 4:14.

May 12 – **Rags to Riches**

"Surely the lowborn are but a breath, the highborn are but a lie. If weighed on a balance, they are nothing; together they are only a breath…though your riches increase, do not set your heart on them…and, 'You reward everyone according to what they have done.'" Psalm 62:9, 10, 12.

"There was a rich man who was dressed in purple and fine linen and lived in luxury every day. At his gate was laid a beggar named Lazarus, covered with sores and longing to eat what fell from the rich man's table. Even the dogs came and licked his sores. The time came when the beggar died and the angels carried him to Abraham's side. The rich man also died and was buried. In Hades, where he was in torment, he looked up and saw Abraham far away, with Lazarus by his side." Luke 16:19-23.

One's earthly riches and outward appearance matter not to God. He's concerned with what we do with what He gives us. And don't forget – everything belongs to God anyway. We are only stewards of His gifts. God looks through the fine clothes or rags to the heart of man. He sees our innermost being and searches for His reflection. Based on what He finds there determines our eternal destination.

Dear God, I pray that what is important to you will be important to me. May You find Jesus Christ alive and well in my heart.

May 13 – **Be Careful!**

I'm reaching into the archives for this one! *Oh be careful little eyes what you see; Oh be careful little eyes what you see; For the Father up above is looking down with love; So be careful little eyes what you see.* Second verse: *Oh be careful little ears what you hear...* Third verse: *Oh be careful little feet where you go…*

"I will be careful to lead a blameless life – when will you come to me? I will conduct the affairs of my house with a blameless heart. I will not look with approval on anything that is vile…no one who speaks falsely will stand in my presence." Psalm 101:2, 3, 7. King David is fully aware that what he sees, hears, and where his feet take him will affect his relationship with God; so he sets boundaries for himself, to protect that which he values and does not want to lose.

We must learn from King David, because Satan has even more opportunities today to lure us far away from God. We need to make that children's church song our personal slogan. Our conscious effort to put in place safe and healthy guardrails will protect us, our marriages, and our families. God will give us strength to do what He asks us to do if we look to Him. "May he strengthen your hearts so that you will be blameless and holy in the presence of our God and Father when our Lord Jesus comes with all his holy ones." 1 Thessalonians 3:13.

May 14 – **Now is a Good Time!**

If you're waiting for just the right time, you may miss it! Any time and all the time is a good time to praise the Lord! David says, "Praise the Lord, all his works everywhere in his dominion. Praise the Lord, my soul." Psalms 103:22. "I will extol the Lord at all times; his praise will always be on my lips." Psalm 34:1. So, when is a good time to praise the Lord? When…

- I'm alone or in a crowd
- At home or in church
- In the morning, afternoon, evening, or at night
- Things are going great or not
- I'm well or I'm sick
- I'm happy or sad
- I'm in pain or not
- I mourn or I'm filled with joy
- People like me or they don't
- I wake up or go to sleep
- I understand or not
- I'm coming or going
- God says Yes or says No or says Wait
- In the maternity ward or the cemetery
- In war or peace
- In confusion or clarity
- I'm moving or still
- I'm lying down, sitting, standing, walking or running
- Friends surround me or when they don't
- In the city or in the country
- At work or at play
- In the sunshine or rain
- People agree with me or not
- I'm with friends, the not so friendly, or enemies
- I'm on earth or in heaven
- In victory or defeat
- I'm rich or poor
- I feel like praising or not
- I'm hungry or not

- I'm young or old
- I'm hot or cold
- Someone remembers my birthday or not

Did I miss one? The point is this: It is always a good time to praise the Lord! We can praise Him loudly or in the quiet of our heart. Sometimes it takes practice, practice, and more practice to make praise a habit. He is worthy of our praise, now and always. "And again, 'Praise the Lord, all you Gentiles; let all the peoples extol him.'" Romans 15:11. Praise the Lord! NOW!

May 15 – **Above All Things**

"I will bow down toward your holy temple and will praise your name for your unfailing love and your faithfulness, for you have so exalted your solemn decree that it surpasses your fame." Psalm 138:2. David is praising God's Name and His Word above everything. There is nothing greater in all creation than God's Name and Word. "Such knowledge is too wonderful for me, too lofty for me to attain." Psalm 139:6.

As a child of the Living God, it breaks my heart when I hear God's name used in vain. "You shall not misuse the name of the Lord your God, for the Lord will not hold anyone guiltless who misuses his name." Exodus 20:7. There is no lovelier name than Jesus Christ. He is the One Who died for me. And what can I say about the precious Word of God? It is my daily Bread; it teaches me the ways of God; it is powerful in its working in me. "For you have been born again, not of perishable seed, but of imperishable, through the living and enduring word of God." 1 Peter 1:23. May I never become desensitized to that Name above all names or the Word that's sharper than any two-edged sword. May nothing in my life ever take precedence above His Name or His Word. "He is dressed in a robe dipped in blood, and his name is the Word of God." Revelation 19:13.

May 16 – **It's Who He Is**

"You can take that to the bank!" That's an expression we've all heard and probably said a few times. It means this is real; it's not counterfeit; it's true; you can count on it. God's faithfulness is a repeated theme in Psalm 89. "Who is like you, Lord God Almighty? You, Lord, are mighty, and your faithfulness surrounds you." (v. 8). The answer to the question this verse asks is clearly "no one." Faithfulness is one of God's attributes; it's Who He is. To be faithful is to be true to one's word and promises, reliable, trustworthy. Faithfulness surrounds Him wherever He goes.

He remains faithful even when I am not. There have been times in my life when I've deserved and received His discipline (v. 30-34), but He still loves me faithfully. "if we are faithless, he remains faithful, for he cannot disown himself." 2 Timothy 2:13. People will betray us – say one thing and do another. Someone we trust will let us down. If truth be told, we may have walked in those same shoes. But God never lets us down. "Be strong and courageous. Do not be afraid or terrified because of them, for the Lord your God goes with you; he will never leave you nor forsake you." Deuteronomy 31:6. When we put our confidence in man, there's a good chance we're setting ourselves up for disappointment. It's crucial we keep our eyes fixed on God and our confidence in Him and His Holy Word that is true forever. "The one who calls you is faithful and he will do it." 1 Thessalonians 5:24.

May 17 – **Glory Ahead!**

Asaph is a musician, prophet, and poet in the days of Kings David and Solomon. Listen to his words in Psalm 73:24: "You guide me with your counsel, and afterward you will take me into glory." This life is full of trials and tribulations, disappointments and struggles, but God guides us through the rough terrain with His counsel. When we have and heed His counsel, we can make it through anything successfully! Life also has its joys and victories, sunshine and laughter – all provided by Him. Praise the Lord! Wherever you are today in this life – there is a better day coming! Don't give up!

How do we safely maneuver through this obstacle course called life? Read again what the Teacher says in Ecclesiastes 12:13: "Now all has been heard; here is the conclusion of the matter: Fear God and keep his commandments, for this is the duty of all mankind." Focus more on God and His Word and less on the problem.

"...and afterward you will take me into glory." Asaph knows! The Apostle Paul knows it too. "For to me, to live is Christ and to die is gain." Philippians 1:21. What a great motto to live by! Death is simply the end of our earthly mission and the beginning of a better life in the presence of Jesus Christ – a life far more real than this brief walk on planet earth! "I consider that our present sufferings are not worth comparing with the glory that will be revealed in us." Romans 8:18.

May 18 – **The Next Generation**

King David appoints a fellow musician and poet named Asaph to preside over the sacred choral services. Psalm 78 is one of his writings which tells of God's power and wonders but also highlights the history of Israel so that future generations might be warned against a repetition of past failures. "...we will tell the next generation the praiseworthy deeds of the Lord,...so the next generation would know them..." Psalm 78: 4, 6. Godly leaders are truly concerned about the next generation.

Do you have a next generation living in your home or next door? As Christ-followers, one of our responsibilities is to share Jesus Christ with the next generation. So how are you doing? When was the last time you told a younger person – or a child – what Jesus has done in your life and what He means to you? Will your personal history help someone avoid a pitfall you made? Will your exuberance and joy shift to another?

Only God knows when the next generation is the last generation as we know it. Here's a truth: Younger eyes are watching you. Like it or not – realize it or not – you are transferring something to the next generation. Is it Godly?

The next generation is always extremely important to God. Jesus shows us in Mark 10:13-14. "People were bringing little children to Jesus for him to place his hands on them, but the disciples rebuked them. When Jesus saw this, he was indignant. He said to them, 'Let the little children come to me, and do not hinder them, for the kingdom of God belongs to such as these.'"

May 19 – **Our Saving Judge**

"The Israelites did evil in the eyes of the Lord; they forgot the Lord their God and served the Baals and the Asherahs. But when they cried out to the Lord, he raised up for them a deliverer, Othniel son of Kenaz, Caleb's younger brother, who saved them." Judges 3:7, 9. "Again the Israelites did evil in the eyes of the Lord, now that Ehud was dead. Now Deborah, a prophet, the wife of Lappidoth, was leading Israel at that time." Judges 4:1, 4. The history of Israel demonstrates the fickleness of people as well as the faithfulness of God to a people who deserve His wrath more than

His mercy. Time and time again, God raises up judges to deliver His wayward children from the enemy. God promised Israel long ago that the Messiah would come through Abraham's lineage. He watches over His Word to fulfill it (see Jeremiah 1:12).

We live in a fallen world. He didn't have to send His Son to save the world from sin, but He did. We don't deserve God's grace and mercy, but He offers it to us anyway. There are times we fail and disappoint God, but He still loves us. Left to our own plans, we will eventually encounter certain destruction. "So I gave them over to their stubborn hearts to follow their own devices." Psalm 81:12. "In the same way your Father in heaven is not willing that any of these little ones should perish." Matthew 18:14. Cry out to God today; He is the Holy and Righteous Judge. He will deliver you.

May 20 – **Benaiah**

Picture with me a young boy with an extreme imagination – slaying dragons, fighting giants, a mighty warrior! He takes the lid off of a pot in his mother's kitchen, picks up a stick, and pretends he is fighting enemies and wild beasts. You may know a little boy like Benaiah.

Benaiah is the son of Jehoiada, a priest, and a contemporary of David. But he does not follow his father into the priesthood; instead, he pursues his dream – a life of adventure for God. You may remember him from 2 Samuel 23:20 and 1 Chronicles 11:22: "He also went down into a pit on a snowy day and killed a lion." His name means "made by the Lord," and he's mentioned at least 22 times in the Old Testament. A popular name, there are eleven other Benaiahs in Scripture.

Benaiah works hard and proves himself a man of courage and integrity, always in the middle of the activity of God. From brave warrior, to King David's personal bodyguard, to Commander in

Chief, Benaiah is obviously not out for personal gain. He serves God and King David faithfully even though David commits adultery and murder; he follows the cause more than the man. He is still on staff when Solomon is born and watches him grow up. He is loyal to King David through Absalom's rebellion and then again to King Solomon through Adonijah's insurgence. "The king put Benaiah son of Jehoiada over the army in Joab's position…The kingdom was now established in Solomon's hands." 1 Kings 2:35, 46. We even read of Benaiah's son, Ammizabad, in 1 Chronicles 27:6 where father and son work together in the army. Benaiah fades into anonymity.

A possible New Testament counterpart to Benaiah is Barnabas (son of encouragement) who ministers alongside the Apostle Paul. He recognizes potential and the call of God in the life of Saul of Tarsus before others, and serves God wholeheartedly even though overshadowed by Paul's growing and powerful ministry. "Then Barnabas went to Tarsus to look for Saul, and when he found him, he brought him to Antioch. So for a whole year Barnabas and Saul met with the church and taught great numbers of people…" Acts 11:25, 26.

We can learn many important life lessons from Bible characters, not only from the King Davids and King Solomons, but from the Benaiahs as well.

May 21 – **A Sight to Behold!**

The temple Solomon built for the Presence of God must have been the most magnificent building ever constructed by man. "…He overlaid the inside with pure gold…He adorned the temple with precious stones." 2 Chronicles 3:4, 6. Yet, it was temporary; nothing exists of the original structure today.

God's Word tells me I am now the temple of the Lord, because His Holy Spirit lives in me (1 Corinthians 6:19). However, this body or tent as the Apostle Paul describes it in 2 Corinthians 5:1 & 4, is momentary as well.

One day, in the not too distant future, I will step into that glorious city and behold sights that have never entered my imagination. My jaw will drop; I'll fall to my knees, and with every breath, praise the One Who died for me. "The wall was made of jasper, and the city of pure gold, as pure as glass. The foundations of the city walls were decorated with every kind of precious stone...The twelve gates were twelve pearls, each gate made of a single pearl. The great street of the city was of gold, as pure as transparent glass. I did not see a temple in the city, because the Lord God Almighty and the Lamb are its temple." Revelation 21:18-22. This will be my forever home. I will see indescribable beauty; I will look into and touch the radiant faces of loved ones. But the most wonderful sight these eyes will ever see is when I behold the face of my Lord and Savior Jesus Christ. Praise His Holy Name!

May 22 – **Your Skill**

What do you love to do, and you're good at it? Where does your skill come from? Jesus learns the skill and trade of carpentry from His earthly father, Joseph (Matthew 13:55 and Mark 6:3). James and John learn fishing from their father, Zebedee (Matthew 4:21). Some people seem to be super talented and gifted by God to do what they do – and they are. One thing is clear; God has given each of us gifts and abilities to do the work He has called us to do. "for God's gifts and his call are irrevocable." Romans 11:29. It's good when we discover and develop our gifts early in life and use them for God's glory. As you know, people can also use their God-given talents and strengths for evil. "A silversmith named Demetrius, who made silver shrines of Artemis, brought in a lot of business for the craftsmen there." Acts 19:24.

Nothing more is known about Huram that what we find in Scripture. "King Solomon sent to Tyre and brought Huram, whose mother was a widow from the tribe of Naphtali and whose father was from Tyre and a skilled craftsman in bronze. Huram was filled with wisdom, with understanding and with knowledge to do all kinds of bronze work. He came to King Solomon and did all the work assigned to him." 1 Kings 7:13, 14. Huram is half Israelite, so perhaps King Solomon feels a claim to him. Therefore, he sends for him and brings him to Jerusalem. Huram obviously must have a good reputation in his work. Only God can fill him with wisdom and understanding and knowledge to do all kinds of bronze work. Nothing has ever been built like the temple King Solomon is building for the Lord. It will take a very special somebody who can also teach many others to do the work according to exact specifications. Huram is faithful to the task. "…So Huram finished the work he had undertaken for King Solomon in the temple of God:" 2 Chronicles 4:11.

Are you an employer looking for just the right one(s) to fill positions in your company or ministry? You're looking for that certain skill set. The God Who gives gifts to men, the One Who equips and enables, is the same God Who causes paths to cross. "Do you see someone skilled in their work? They will serve before kings; they will not serve before officials of low rank." Proverbs 22:29.

"Now may the God of peace, who through the blood of the eternal covenant brought back from the dead our Lord Jesus, that great Shepherd of the sheep, equip you with everything good for doing his will, and may he work in us what is pleasing to him, through Jesus Christ, to whom be glory for ever and ever. Amen." Hebrews 13:20, 21.

May 23 – **God's Line of Blessing**

Draw a straight line in your mind or on a piece of paper. On the left beginning point, write God's Promise; on the right ending point, write Fulfillment. "You have kept your promise to your servant David my father; with your mouth you have promised and with your hand you have fulfilled it – as it is today." 1 Kings 8:24. King Solomon obeys God's guidelines; he stays on track and witnesses God fulfill His promise.

A racehorse trainer puts blinders on his horse to keep the horse focused straight ahead. He knows if the horse looks behind or to the side, he will become distracted and veer off course, possibly causing injury or disqualification. "Let your eyes look straight ahead, fix your gaze directly before you." Proverbs 4:25. When Peter attempts to walk on the water to Jesus (Matthew 14:30), he gets distracted by the storm, takes his eyes off of Jesus, and begins to sink. Thankfully, the Lord is near and rescues the 'wavering' Peter. "I press on toward the goal to win the prize for which God has called me heavenward in Christ Jesus." Philippians 3:14.

Where are you on God's line of blessing – from promise to fulfillment? Have you unintentionally removed yourself and strayed off course? Do you need to refocus on Jesus Christ and fall back in line with His blessing? There is only one direction for our faith: forward.

Heavenly Father, forgive me for allowing the world to distract me from following You. I want to get back in line with Your Word and Your blessing. Help me set up guardrails and boundaries that will make it difficult to stray from the path You have for me. Thank You, Lord. In Jesus' Name. Amen.

May 24 – **An 'Ify' Heart**

The temple is complete; a promise is fulfilled. God, King Solomon, and the people of Israel are satisfied and joyful. "The Lord said to him: 'I have heard the prayer and plea you have made before me; I have consecrated this temple, which you have built, by putting my Name there forever. My eyes and my heart will always be there. As for you, if you walk before me faithfully with integrity of heart and uprightness, as David your father did, and do all I command and observe my decrees and laws, I will establish your royal throne over Israel forever...'" 1 Kings 9:3-5. Notice that God refers to his own heart as well as Solomon's heart. God's "heart will always be there." Solomon's heart is 'ify'; "if you walk before me faithfully with integrity of heart and uprightness." In other words, a man's heart can go either way at any time.

God knows my heart and the inclinations of my heart. "would not God have discovered it, since he knows the secrets of my heart?" Psalm 44:21. "God, who knows the heart, showed that he accepted them by giving the Holy Spirit to them, just as he did to us." Acts 15:8. I don't want an 'ify' heart! I want a steadfast heart (Psalm 57:7)! Make that a steadfast heart *and* a steadfast spirit! "Create in me a pure heart, O God, and renew a steadfast spirit within me." Psalm 51:10.

O Lord, only You can do that in my heart. I give you my heart today.

May 25 – **Get Off Your High Horse!**

Just in case you haven't learned this from personal experience, Satan is subtle and patient. He is a master of deception and can be extremely patient in working his plan. Satan has a challenge before him in King Solomon. Just because Solomon is the richest and wisest human king of all time, does Satan back away from Solomon and think – why bother? No, he doesn't. Satan goes back to Deuteronomy 17:14-17 where God warns future kings not to acquire great numbers of horses from Egypt, large amounts of gold and silver, or many wives who will lead their heart astray.

Just because Solomon is the richest and wisest human king of all time, does he think he is safe from Satan's attacks, that he's smarter than Satan, that he can handle anything Satan may throw at him? Possibly. Maybe he thinks he is entitled to excess. "Solomon accumulated chariots and horses; he had fourteen hundred chariots and twelve thousand horses...The king made silver and gold as common in Jerusalem as stones...Solomon's horses were imported from Egypt..." 2 Chronicles 1:14-16. We will read later in 1 Kings 11:1-6 how his 700 wives and 300 concubines slowly turn his heart away from God. Satan patiently does his dirty work in Solomon's heart over the years, because the king ignores God's warnings and lets his guard down. We learn again that God's Word is always true.

If King Solomon can fall away from God, who are we to think we will never fall or turn away from God? No one is immune from the enemy's devices. God's Word and warnings apply to all of us. So get off your high horse! "For everything in the world – the lust of the flesh, the lust of the eyes, and the pride of life – comes not from the Father but from the world." 1 John 2:16.

May 26 – **Solomon vs. Jesus**

Solomon is by far the richest and wisest earthly king who has ever walked the face of the earth (2 Chronicles 1:11, 12). "During Solomon's lifetime Judah and Israel, from Dan to Beersheba, lived in safety, everyone under their own vine and under their own fig tree. God gave Solomon wisdom and very great insight, and a breadth of understanding as measureless as the sand on the seashore." 1 Kings 4:25, 29. Solomon reigns for 40 years. It is a very blessed time to be alive. "From Dan to Beersheba" is a common expression which means all of Israel territory. There is peace and prosperity everywhere, and everyone is happy (1 Kings 4:20). In addition to supernatural wisdom, God gives Solomon great understanding and knowledge in what we now recognize as science.

Psalm 72 is generally believed to have been written as a prayer by King David for his son's coronation. However, several of the verses will only see their complete fulfillment in the reign of Jesus Christ (vs. 8, 11, 17). The glory of King Solomon is the closest comparison we have to the glory of Jesus Christ and His Kingdom, but even then, there is really no comparison (1 Corinthians 2:9). Solomon's reign is a success in every way except spiritually, because of his slide into idolatry from which the nation never fully recovers. Therefore, his reign is judged a failure.

"The Queen of the South will rise at the judgment with the people of this generation and condemn them, for she came from the ends of the earth to listen to Solomon's wisdom; and now something greater than Solomon is here." Luke 11:31. "Your kingdom is an everlasting kingdom and your dominion endures through all generations. The Lord is trustworthy in all he promises and faithful in all he does." Psalm 145:13.

May 27 – **My Mistake**

In kindergarten, little Annie makes a few mistakes. She learns that two plus two does not equal five; she also learns that 'hapy' does not spell happy. Annie learns from her innocent mistakes, but she also takes home a lower grade.

The world tells me I can learn from my mistakes. Maybe so. But unpleasant consequences follow mistakes. The law tells me I should not text and drive at the same time. It's good advice; why not take it and learn from the carelessness of others? For life's lessons, the best teacher is not my mistake; it's the Word of God.

When I fully believe and trust what the Bible says to me, take it to heart, act upon it, live it – then I can avoid much heartache and the consequences of mistakes. Or should I say the consequences of sin? God knows where the line is between an innocent mistake and sin. Sometimes I do too, but I choose to turn a deaf ear to God and listen to the world. God does not regard sin as a mistake, disease, or freedom of choice. Sin is sin, and it separates us from Him (Isaiah 59:2).

I gain wisdom and strength when I believe and apply God's Word. I can learn from the true life experiences of the people in the pages of the Bible. That is the reason God includes their stories. I choose the Bible as my primary teacher, not my mistakes. The Book of Proverbs is an excellent place to start. I have learned over the years to read Proverbs slowly and let the words sink in and take root in my heart. "Listen, my sons, to a father's instruction; pay attention and gain understanding. Wisdom will save you from the ways of wicked men, from men whose words are perverse," Proverbs 4:1; 2:12. "I do not write to you because you do not know the truth, but because you do know it and because no lie comes from the truth." 1 John 2:21.

May 28 – **Regret**

Today's reading, Proverbs chapters 5-7, gives us some serious straight talk about sin, all kinds of sin, from laziness to murder. However, in all three chapters, King Solomon offers strong words of wisdom concerning adultery and fornication. "Whew, that was close," you say. "I don't do those things." That's great, but do you indulge in pornography, because it's a very close relative to adultery and fornication with the same family name of Sin? "But a man who commits adultery has no sense; whoever does so destroys himself." Proverbs 6:32.

"Can a man scoop fire into his lap without his clothes being burned? Can a man walk on hot coals without his feet being scorched?" Proverbs 6:27, 28. The answer to both of those questions is an emphatic No. Do you really think no one sees or knows what you do in secret? Do you believe your sin of pornography is not hurting anyone? Have you really swallowed the enemy's lies – hook, line, and sinker? "For your ways are in full view of the Lord, and he examines all your paths. The evil deeds of the wicked ensnare them; the cords of their sins hold them fast." Proverbs 5:21, 22.

You have better things to do with your time: read the Bible, pray, spend time with your family, mow the lawn, go fishing, bake a cake – sleep. Don't let these next verses describe you. "At the end of your life you will groan, when your flesh and body are spent. You will say, 'How I hated discipline! How my heart spurned correction! I would not obey my teachers or turn my ear to my instructors.'" Proverbs 5:11-13. I implore you; don't live with those regrets.

Pornography is an insidious trap of Satan. But there is hope, and His name is Jesus. Only God and the power of His Word can set the captive free. If you've been there and done that, own it; it's your sin. Fall at the feet of Jesus today. He will set you free. "The Spirit of the Lord is on me, because he has anointed me to proclaim good news to the poor. He has sent me to proclaim freedom for the prisoners and recovery of sight for the blind, to set the oppressed free." Luke 4:18.

May 29 – **Jesus in Proverbs**

Proverbs chapter eight is an amazing description of Jesus Christ, replete with many New Testament parallels. Jesus is the very embodiment of wisdom, so He is the One speaking to us here. Verse 17 is a key verse: "I love those who love me, and those who seek me find me." "For everyone who asks receives; the one who seeks finds; and to the one who knocks, the door will be opened." Matthew 7:8.

Take a few extra minutes and read again Proverbs eight, and then read the corresponding verses in the New Testament.

- Verses 1-5 remind me of the parable of the lost sheep found in Luke 15:3-6.
- Verses 6-10. Now read Luke 24:13-35 which is the story of Jesus appearing to two of His followers on the road to Emmaus. Pay special attention to verses 27 and 32.
- Verses 11-16 speak of knowledge, power, and rulers. See Colossians 2:3, Matthew 28:18, and Colossians 1:16.
- Verses 18-21. This is a taste of heaven! Philippians 4:19 and Revelation 5:12.
- Verses 22-31 point to creation in Genesis chapter one but also to John 1:1-4.
- Verses 32-35 – Hear His voice today! James 1:25 and Revelation 3:20.
- Verse 36 leaves us with this warning: "But those who fail to find me harm themselves; all who hate me love death." "Whoever believes in the Son has eternal life, but whoever rejects the Son will not see life, for God's wrath remains on them." John 3:36.

Place your faith in Jesus Christ today and your heart in His hands. His love for you is forever!

May 30 – **Win a Soul for Christ!**

Our daughter, Jamie, lived and worked among the people of Northern Asia. Oh, how she loved the people in her city! She went because of God's call on her life and her love for those who have never heard about Jesus or not had an adequate witness of the Gospel. Winning the lost is not an overnight achievement in that part of the world. It's painstakingly slow, but worth it, even if just one comes to faith in Jesus Christ. She patiently built relationships. She knew how much God loves people and is not willing that any should perish. She knew God gave the precious gift of His Son for people everywhere. She planted seeds, watered them with tears and prayers, and saw a handful come to Christ. Jamie is in heaven now, but the seeds she planted continue to grow and produce fruit as God gives the increase. Only God knows where those seeds are growing now and how many souls will be saved because of Jamie's love. She's waiting for them in heaven.

"The fruit of the righteous is a tree of life, and the one who is wise saves lives." Proverbs 11:30. That Scripture almost sounds like it should be in the New Testament. What is King Solomon thinking when he writes, "and the one who is wise saves lives"? Does he win souls for God? Long before the time of Jesus, Solomon believes in eternity. His faith looks forward to the Messiah. People needed to know and believe back then that the Messiah would be born. Our faith looks back to Christ on the cross *and* forward to His second coming.

"What good will it be for someone to gain the whole world, yet forfeit their soul? Or what can anyone give in exchange for their soul?" Matthew 16:26. Whether we realize it or not, our soul is the most valuable possession we have. It is the only thing we have that will last forever – in either heaven or hell. Solomon knew that truth; Jamie understood it. He who wins souls is wise. Are you wise?

May 31 – **Avoid the Bump – or Worse**

I consider myself to have a healthy fear of God; therefore, I refuse to participate in seemingly innocent activities that our culture says are okay. For instance, I avoid video/phone/internet games. I have a relatively competitive disposition, and I know I can easily be swayed and end up wasting hours at something that will profit me zero. I have better things to do with my time and energy, like spend it with Jesus, family, growing in Christ, and helping others do the same. Also, I made the decision a long time ago, that my lips would never touch any form of alcohol. I can do without it just fine, thank you. Why should I give the enemy an opportunity to take me captive years down the road? If I'm going to be addicted to anything, let it be to the Lord Jesus Christ and God's Word and His work!

I respect my weaknesses and compromising tendencies; therefore, I try not to think more highly of myself than I should, thus knocking down those subtle lies of Satan that I can handle it. I'm not perfect and never have been. I've been jerked upside down by the ankle in Satan's snares a few times in my life, and only by the grace of God, dropped on my head, escaping with only a bump and embarrassment. It's better and smarter to recognize and walk around that snare than take a chance, because it will require far more of my personal resources to get free than to avoid it altogether. I've lived long enough to know that I must stay tight with the Lord to steer clear of Satan's veiled traps. "The fear of the Lord is a fountain of life, turning a person from the snares of death." Proverbs 14:27.

"No one serving as a soldier gets entangled in civilian affairs – but rather tries to please his commanding officer." 2 Timothy 2:4.

JUNE

June 1 – **Bubble or Babble**

I grew up in the woods of Deep East Texas. As a child with nothing better to do with my time, I would walk what seemed like several miles along the old Katy railroad line to a spring and drink from the cool fresh water bubbling out of the ground. I remember the peacefulness and quiet of the forest and the soft gurgling of the fresh clear water rising from underground.

"The words of the mouth are deep waters, but the fountain of wisdom is a rushing stream." Proverbs 18:4. The Bible has much to say about the words that come out of my mouth. "With the tongue we praise our Lord and Father, and with it we curse human beings, who have been made in God's likeness. Out of the same mouth come praise and cursing. My brothers and sisters, this should not be. Can both fresh water and salt water flow from the same spring?" James 3:9-11.

My brook can either bubble or babble. An example of a refreshing, life-replenishing, bubbling brook is found in Proverbs 16:24: "Gracious words are a honeycomb, sweet to the soul and healing to the bones." One definition of babble is to talk unwisely or foolishly. A perfect example is found in Proverbs 18:13: "To answer before listening – that is folly and shame." Ouch!

"The tongue has the power of life and death, and those who love it will eat its fruit." Proverbs 18:21. I am personally responsible for the words that come out of my mouth. With God's help, I can bubble instead of babble.

June 2 – **Generosity**

Some of the poorest people of the world are some of the most generous. It doesn't matter how much or how little you have. What matters is: what you do with what you have. "The generous will themselves be blessed, for they share their food with the poor." Proverbs 22:9. Those in this Scripture have their eyes directed outwardly. They are looking for someone with whom they can share. The verse doesn't say if they are rich or poor. I've watched those in a third world country share the very little food they had with others. At that moment, I thought of my full pantry and freezer back home and felt shame that I haven't given more. By the way, one doesn't have to go far from home to discover those who have little to eat. Our problem is that our eyes are always focused on me and mine.

The poor and needy have a very special place in the heart of our Lord. He notices them and our response to them. He notices the widow's offering in Mark 12:44. "They all gave out of their wealth; but she, out of her poverty, put in everything – all she had to live on." We can be sure God blesses her for her generosity. It's here that we must guard our heart; we give because it is the right thing to do, not in order to get a blessing.

Parents, lead your children by example. Let them witness you giving to the Lord and others. Start today; share what you have with someone less fortunate. And leave the blessing part to God.

June 3 – **Money Tips**

Remember that King Solomon is the richest and wisest man who has ever lived. He's no E. F. Hutton, but we should still listen when he talks about money. He offers several good tips in today's reading that hit us right in the wallet.

#1: Do not co-sign for someone if you want to keep your bed (Proverbs 22:26, 27).

#2: Do not wear yourself out to get rich, because they will fly away and you'll be stranded (Proverbs 23:4, 5).

#3: Don't go into debt. Establish your business first, and then buy a house. Have an income coming in! "Put your outdoor work in order and get your fields ready; after that, build your house." Proverbs 24:27.

#4: Go to work! Laziness will get you nowhere (Proverbs 24:33, 34).

There is a good prayer in Proverbs 30:8, 9. Do you dare make it your own? Just give me my daily bread, Lord. That's all I need.

"But godliness with contentment is great gain. For we brought nothing into the world, and we can take nothing out of it. But if we have food and clothing, we will be content with that." 1 Timothy 6:6-8.

June 4 – **A Fox Named Neglect**

Why is it that the barber's son always needs a haircut, the plumber always has a leaky kitchen faucet, and the landscaper's yard needs mowing? Do we get so busy with work and life and other people that we forget the ones most important to us? It's easy to do. "...my own vineyard I had to neglect." Song of Songs 1:6.

Perhaps one of those little foxes is named Neglect. "Catch for us the foxes, the little foxes that ruin the vineyards, our vineyards that are in bloom." Song of Songs 2:15. "Your wife will be like a fruitful vine within your house; your children will be like olive shoots around your table." Psalm 128:3. Don't short-circuit God's blessings in your life by overextending yourself to the detriment of your family. We must maintain our priorities and balance in all things. "Woe to you, teachers of the law and Pharisees, you hypocrites! You give a tenth of your spices – mint, dill and cumin. But you have neglected the more important matters of the law – justice, mercy and faithfulness. You should have practiced the latter, without neglecting the former." Matthew 23:23.

"(If anyone does not know how to manage his own family, how can he take care of God's church?)" 1 Timothy 3:5. Don't neglect your family and home wherein your first calling lies.

June 5 – **No Trespassing**

Today an atheist dies. An elderly gentleman and very intelligent by the world's standard, he suddenly meets the One Whom he has challenged, fought against, denied existed, and has tried to prove to everyone that there is no such thing as God or His Son Jesus Christ. The "No Trespassing" sign falls from his heart, and now he faces "The Truth." "I'm so sorry, Lord. Have mercy." But it's too late. "I never knew you. Away from me, you evildoer!" (Matthew 7:23).

This life is the one and only chance we have to reconcile with God. After our final heart beat, there are no more opportunities. And yet, if Mr. Atheist had humbled himself before God in the final moments of his life and put his faith in Jesus Christ as his Savior, he would have been saved. "For, 'Everyone who calls on the name of the Lord will be saved.'" Romans 10:13. But how do we know if we will possess the mental faculties needed to make such a decision in those last moments of life? We don't. That is why God says that today is the day of salvation (2 Corinthians 6:2).

Is it possible to put a No Trespassing sign on our heart after we have known God? King Solomon proves it is possible, for God will never stay where He is not welcome. He will not share His throne with an idol. "As Solomon grew old, his wives turned his heart after other gods, and his heart was not fully devoted to the Lord his God, as the heart of David his father had been." 1 Kings 11:4. The Lord becomes angry with Solomon (v. 9), and He raises up adversaries against him (vs. 14, 23, 26). Solomon tries to kill Jeroboam (v. 40). Scripture doesn't tell us if Solomon ever becomes fully devoted to God again.

Our heart is what matters to God. When God looks at us, does He see His Son, Jesus Christ, living in our heart or a No Trespassing sign posted over our heart? "And, 'But my righteous one will live by faith. And I take no pleasure in the one who shrinks back.' But we do not belong to those who shrink back and are destroyed, but to those who have faith and are saved." Hebrews 10:38, 39.

Jesus, today is the day. I come to You. I throw away the No Trespassing sign over my heart. Please come into my heart and my life. Forgive me of my many sins. Cleanse me with Your blood that you poured out for me on the cross. I believe in You. I give You my life. Help me live for You every day for the rest of my life. I love You, Lord. Thank You for Your great mercy and Your forgiveness. Thank You for saving me. Amen.

June 6 – **Braided Together**

I officiated a beautiful outdoor spring wedding of a young couple where they used a three cord strand to symbolize their love for each other and the Lord. The gold strand represents the divinity and holiness of God; the purple symbolizes the husband's role as the royal Bridegroom, and the white signifies the purity of the Bride of Christ. Together they braided their lives into one with the Lord. "Though one may be overpowered, two can defend themselves. A cord of three strands is not quickly broken." Ecclesiastes 4:12.

A healthy Godly marriage is like that cord of three strands. When a Christian husband and wife include the Lord in every thread of their marriage, holding tightly to each other, the union will remain strong. If the cord ever loosens, it's not because of God; He wants to be involved and active in our marriage. Any relaxing of the strength of the marriage bond is the fault of the husband and/or wife. If we continue to let go of God, the strength of our marriage will diminish. Then when a crisis or shaking comes along, our marriage will unravel – all because the three strands do not remain tightly woven together.

Love is active. We express our love for each other through words, attitude, and demonstration. With God at the center of our marriage and home, we braid our lives around Him. He is in the middle of everything we do. We love and serve Him, pray together, read our Bibles, attend church, obey Him, train our children by example to know Him, and share His love with others. Carelessness, self-centeredness, and neglect cause love to loosen and weaken. When we remove Him from the middle of the braid, our marriage, lives, and family can quickly unravel and leave us hanging by a thread. However, God is always close by, waiting for us to look His direction and invite Him back into His rightful place. He will put His arms around us, forgive, heal, strengthen, and enable us to move forward. Oh, praise His Holy Name!

"Love is patient, love is kind. It does not envy, it does not boast, it is not proud. It does not dishonor others, it is not self-seeking, it is not easily angered, it keeps no record of wrongs. Love does not delight in evil but rejoices with the truth. It always protects, always trusts, always hopes, always perseveres." 1 Corinthians 13:4-7.

June 7 – **Read the Word Today!**

God's Word is extremely important to Him. He has watched over it to preserve and perform it for many generations. Millions have risked their lives and shed their blood for the Truth in its pages. One day you will stand before God, the Creator of the universe, and He will demand an account of your life. What will you say?

Imagine with me for a moment. The day has come; you've stepped into heaven. God looks at you and says, "Welcome!" You bow before Him in honor and worship and a heart overflowing with thankfulness. Eventually He says to you: "What did you think of My Book?" Will you fumble for words? "Uh, I really liked it, especially John 3:16. For God so loved the world that…" "Yes, but how many times did you read it? I gave you a whole lifetime." "Uh…" "Stand over there. I'll get back to you. Next."

"Whatever your hand finds to do, do it with all your might, for in the realm of the dead, where you are going, there is neither working nor planning nor knowledge nor wisdom. Moreover, no one knows when their hour will come…" Ecclesiastes 9:10, 12. This passage tells us that today is all we have. We need to be about the Father's business today, not procrastinating another minute. Have you ever seen a roundtuit? They are apparently very elusive. We say, "One day, when I get around to it, I will read my Bible completely through. I also plan to do this for God and that for God…" These are famous last words of many a child of God!

"As long as it is day, we must do the works of him who sent me. Night is coming, when no one can work." John 9:4. What will you do for God today?

June 8 – **Seems Right or Seems Good**

Rehoboam is now king over a united Israel following the death of his father, King Solomon. Being the son of the wisest man who ever lived doesn't seem to have given an advantage to Rehoboam. Does he even read any of his father's proverbs? Apparently wisdom is not inherited. "There is a way that appears to be right, but in the end it leads to death." Proverbs 14:12.

This warns us not to lean on our own understanding alone; we should pray about everything, read God's Word to get the mind of Christ, and get wise counsel from more than one person. I might just be wrong if I neglect to consult God or others.

Rehoboam has an extremely important decision to make and doesn't particularly like the advice given to him by the elders who served his father. So, he calls in his cronies, young men who grew up with him. Just because someone agrees with my already 'made-up-my-mind' opinion, doesn't make it right. "The king answered the people harshly. Rejecting the advice given him by the elders, he followed the advice of the young men…So Israel has been in rebellion against the house of David to this day." 1 Kings 12:13, 14, 19. Things do not go well for Rehoboam.

The early church leaders learn to seek God's counsel before embarking on first-time ventures. "It seemed good to the Holy Spirit and to us…" Acts 15:28. What leadership lessons can we learn today? Don't surround yourself with only people like you. Different perspectives can stretch and challenge us and cause us to see options unnoticed before. Above all, make certain "it seems good to the Holy Spirit."

June 9 – **Your Epitaph**

At the funeral of a dear woman of God, it was said of her, "She will be remembered for her love for Jesus, her prayers for her family, how she enjoyed reading her Bible, and her broad beatific smile." I admit it; I had to look up beatific in the dictionary. It simply means showing great joy. What a beautiful word! What a splendid way to be remembered by loved ones and friends!

Asa is remembered as one of the good kings of Judah. "…Asa's heart was fully committed to the Lord all his life." 1 Kings 15:14 and 2 Chronicles 15:17. I hope and pray the same can be said about me when I tell this world goodbye. Now look at the extreme contrast recorded about a later King of Judah, Jehoram: "...He passed away, to no one's regret..." 2 Chronicles 21:20. How sad is that!

How do you want people to remember you? You and I will not live forever on this earth; the day will come when we will depart this life. "Just as people are destined to die once, and after that to face judgment," Hebrews 9:27. Begin today to leave a godly legacy and a beatific smile.

June 10 – **What Happened?**

In our reading yesterday, we saw where Scripture records that "Asa's heart was fully committed to the Lord all his life." And then we read today that Asa stops relying on the Lord and trusts human resources, he rejects God's warning, he becomes extremely angry and imprisons the prophet Hanani, and he brutally oppresses some of the people (2 Chronicles 16:7-10). "In the thirty-ninth year of his reign Asa was afflicted with a disease in his feet. Though his disease was severe, even in his illness he did not seek help from the Lord, but only from the physicians." 2 Chronicles 16:12. What happens to Asa?

First of all, the Bible never tells us that Asa *never* fails or makes a mistake. In fact, God's Word is brutally honest with the sins of its heroes. I, for one, am relieved, because I can relate better to these individuals. "For David had done what was right in the eyes of the Lord and had not failed to keep any of the Lord's commands all the days of his life – except in the case of Uriah the Hittite." 1 Kings 15:5. Even King David, a man after God's own heart, fails God. No sugar-coating here! In other words – for the most part, overall – David and Asa are Godly kings – and that's how we remember them.

Secondly, Asa is an example to all believers that it is indeed possible to fall away from faithfulness to God even after serving

God successfully for many years. We cannot let our guard down. God never overlooks sin, no matter who commits it; He always deals with people and their sins, yet stands by ready to forgive and restore when one repents.

Yes, we will be tested, and at times we may fail. But He is quick to forgive when we are quick to repent. Praise God! "To the one who is victorious, I will give the right to sit with me on my throne, just as I was victorious and sat down with my Father on his throne." Revelation 3:21.

June 11 – **A Gentle Whisper**

I have learned over the years that God prefers to speak to me in those quiet times I make to spend with Him and His Word. I hear His gentle whisper to my heart as I pray, read, and meditate on Him. However, when I neglect to carve out those times dedicated to Him, He will get louder and more demonstrative and do whatever it takes to get my attention. Personally, I prefer the peaceful and quiet times; I think He does too.

God interrupts the Prophet Elijah's pity party. "When Elijah heard it, he pulled his cloak over his face and went out and stood at the mouth of the cave." 1 Kings 19:13. God wants to correct Elijah's erroneous thinking. First and foremost, Elijah is not the only one left who still worships God; God has seven thousand faithful believers in Israel. Also, God still has work for Elijah to do, so he better get moving. Have you ever experienced a "poor me" Elijah moment?

Finding quiet time alone in the presence of God can be a challenge. Satan makes sure of that! He certainly doesn't want you spending quiet time with God in prayer and reading your Bible, because he knows that is where you will find strength and encouragement. "He says, 'Be still, and know that I am God; I will be exalted among the nations, I will be exalted in the earth.'" Psalm 46:10.

We know that Jesus intentionally made quiet time with His Heavenly Father while on earth (Mark 1:35). All of us make time for those things we consider valuable and important. Have you ever heard the expression, "Silence is golden"? Being still and quiet before God is holy whether you're on earth or in heaven. "When he opened the seventh seal, there was silence in heaven for about half an hour." Revelation 8:1.

June 12 – **Among the People**

Things are not always as they appear. There's an unassuming crowd gathered, because King Ahab has proclaimed a day of fasting (1 Kings 21:8-14). Naboth is seated in a prominent place, when all of a sudden, hushed whispers surge through the throng. Naboth has cursed God and the king! He is hurriedly taken outside and stoned to death! Among the people (vs. 9, 12), there's more murmuring: "Well, that is what God commands – anyone who curses God will be stoned." They're oblivious. If anyone does suspect anything underhanded, no one is brave enough to confront. The crowd disperses, none the wiser.

Most of the time, we are part of the credulous crowd – easily deceived. It all looks holy and innocent enough. That's because, without the supernatural discernment of the Holy Spirit, we observe only the superficial. However, God sees at a deeper level. He knows the thoughts and motives of the heart – good or evil. "Immediately Jesus knew in his spirit that this was what they were thinking in their hearts, and he said to them, 'Why are you thinking these things?'" Mark 2:8.

Before we leave 1 Kings 21, here's something else worth noting. "(There was never anyone like Ahab, who sold himself to do evil in the eyes of the Lord, urged on by Jezebel his wife.

He behaved in the vilest manner by going after idols, like the Amorites the Lord drove out before Israel.)" (vs. 25, 26). Ahab is bad to the bone! Yet when he hears God's judgment spoken to him by Elijah the prophet, he humbles himself before God – and God notices. As a result, God changes His mind about the timing of His judgment. Ahab receives God's mercy. True humility and repentance (and God knows the difference between true and false) are powerful in their working. What is God speaking to your heart today?

June 13 – **Rejoice Again and Again!**

Jehoshaphat is another good king of Judah. I thank God for 2 Chronicles chapter 20, for it is rich in truth for us today. When a vast enemy army approaches, Jehoshaphat seeks the Lord and proclaims a fast for all of Judah. The people follow their leader and seek help from God. He reminds God of His promises to the children of Israel. "Our God, will you not judge them? For we have no power to face this vast army that is attacking us. We do not know what to do, but our eyes are on you." (v. 12). Have you ever felt like that or said that to God? I know I have.

God responds to Jehoshaphat's prayer. "...Do not be afraid or discouraged because of this vast army. For the battle is not yours, but God's." (v. 15). God then gives Jehoshaphat specific instructions. His response is to bow before God and worship Him. "After consulting the people, Jehoshaphat appointed men to sing to the Lord and to praise him for the splendor of his holiness as they went out at the head of the army, saying: 'Give thanks to the Lord, for his love endures forever.' As they began to sing and praise, the Lord set ambushes against the men of Ammon and Moab and Mount Seir who were invading Judah, and they were defeated." (vs. 21, 22). Praise moves the hands of God. "Then, led by Jehoshaphat, all the men of Judah and Jerusalem returned joyfully to Jerusalem, for the Lord had given them cause to rejoice over their enemies." (v. 27).

"Rejoice in the Lord always. I will say it again: Rejoice!" Philippians 4:4. When you're under attack – rejoice! When you're outnumbered – rejoice! When you don't know what to do – rejoice! When it makes no sense to the human mind – rejoice! When it looks like certain defeat without God's intervention – rejoice! Send praise ahead in faith for what God will do! Praise before there's cause to rejoice, and God will give you cause to rejoice! God expects praise before, during, and after the battle – no matter how long it takes! Rejoice again and again!

June 14 – **An Excellent Teacher**

My husband has worked in sales for many years. One day he decided to visit another store in the same company and observe their top salesman at work, hoping to gain new insights that would put money in his own pocket. His colleague was very helpful, taking time to teach by example, answer questions, and share his knowledge from years of experience with that product. My husband quickly put into practice the information he gleaned from his friend. As a result, his first month of sales exceeded that of his teacher! This may be a minor case in point, but it does prove one thing: One definition of an excellent teacher is one whose students accomplish more than he does.

Look at Elisha. "But Jehoshaphat asked, 'Is there no prophet of the Lord here, through whom we may inquire of the Lord?' An officer of the king of Israel answered, 'Elisha son of Shaphat is here. He used to pour water on the hands of Elijah.'" 2 Kings 3:11. Simply put, Elisha is the Prophet Elijah's servant who does not let Elijah out of his sight! He sticks like glue to Elijah, learns everything he can, and wants a double portion of the spirit that is on Elijah – and he receives it. Scripture records that Elisha does twice as many miracles as Elijah.

Jesus is the Master Teacher who gives us His promise. "Very truly I tell you, whoever believes in me will do the works I have been doing, and they will do even greater things than these, because I am going to the Father." John 14:12. Stay close to Jesus, learn all you can, be filled with His Holy Spirit, and serve God like crazy!

June 15 – **Determination**

Have you ever encountered a strong-willed child? Maybe you have one or you were one! It's not always a bad thing. Raising a strong-willed child can be challenging and exhausting at times. They know what they want, and they are determined to get it!

Elisha is very determined. He knows what he wants, and he refuses to let Elijah out of his sight until he receives it. He knows God is about to take Elijah to heaven, and he wants a double portion of Elijah's spirit more than anything. "As surely as the Lord lives and as you live, I will not leave you." Elisha says this three times to Elijah (2 Kings 2:2, 4, 6). The Lord takes Elijah to heaven in a whirlwind, and Elisha picks up his cloak. "…The spirit of Elijah is resting on Elisha…" 2 Kings 2:15.

Elisha meets a woman who prepares a room for him and his servant and provides meals for them whenever they come to Shunem. For her kindness, Elisha tells her God will give her and her husband a son. Several years later, the boy dies. She hurries to find Elisha. "But the child's mother said, 'As surely as the Lord lives and as you live, I will not leave you.' So he got up and followed her." 2 Kings 4:30. That sounds familiar! She is determined; she knows what she wants. Elisha prays for the boy, and God restores his life.

"Then Jesus told his disciples a parable to show them that they should always pray and not give up." Luke 18:1. He tells them the story of the persistent widow who keeps going to the judge for justice against her adversary. She is wearing him out with her perseverance! He grants her request.

Elisha's determination pays off, for it is God's will for his life. He receives a double portion of God's Spirit after Elijah goes to heaven. This reminds me of the words of Jesus in John 14:12: "Very truly I tell you, whoever believes in me will do the works I have been doing, and they will do even greater things than these, because I am going to the Father." Jesus gives us His Holy Spirit to empower us to do His work. Don't give up! Pursue God and everything He has for you.

June 16 – **Divine Supplies**

God knows how to meet the needs of His children, and most of the time, in ways we do not expect. I think God likes to surprise us! For instance, He feeds the Israelites in the wilderness with bread from heaven and gives them water to drink from a rock. A raven brings the Prophet Elijah bread to eat. Jesus takes a couple fish and a few loaves and feeds several thousand people – twice. God supplies money to pay Peter's taxes from a fish's mouth.

Samaria is under siege, and the people are starving until God turns the enemy's camp into a shopping mall. "The men who had leprosy reached the edge of the camp, entered one of the tents and ate and drank. Then they took silver, gold and clothes, and went off and hid them. They returned and entered another tent and took some things from it and hid them also…'Let's go at once and report this to the royal palace.'" 2 Kings 7:8, 9.

Job speaks of the riches of the wicked. "Though he heaps up silver like dust and clothes like piles of clay, what he lays up the righteous will wear, and the innocent will divide his silver." Job 27:16, 17. "...but a sinner's wealth is stored up for the righteous." Proverbs 13:22. Lest you begin to think you're entitled to your rich heathen neighbor's BMW, may I remind you of Paul's words to Timothy? "For the love of money is a root of all kinds of evil. Some people, eager for money, have wandered from the faith and pierced themselves with many griefs." 1 Timothy 6:10.

Yes, God has unlimited resources to meet the needs of His children. In the days of the Old Testament, often He used plunder from the enemy's camp. Today, the main ingredients are faith, obedience, and trust in Him. "And my God will meet all your needs according to the riches of his glory in Christ Jesus." Philippians 4:19.

June 17 – **Busy But Wrong**

Jehu is a very busy man (2 Kings 9:1-10:31), carrying out the commands of God on his life. He is ambitious, prudent, calculating, and passionless, quick to decide on a plan of action, and equally ready in execution. "The Lord said to Jehu, 'Because you have done well in accomplishing what is right in my eyes and have done to the house of Ahab all I had in mind to do, your descendants will sit on the throne of Israel to the fourth generation.' Yet Jehu was not careful to keep the law of the Lord, the God of Israel with all his heart. He did not turn away from the sins of Jeroboam, which he had caused Israel to commit." 2 Kings 10:30, 31. Jehu moves to rid Israel of Baal worship, yet he continues to worship the golden calves at Bethel and Dan (v. 29). He accomplishes great purposes, but he is not great or good in himself.

We can oppose sin yet receive the same into our lives. We can preach, stand, and fight against the sin of alcohol, drugs, sexual immorality, dishonesty, pornography, abortion, hate, you name it, and yet receive the same into our lives. This is just wrong! May God open our eyes before it's too late! "Can a man scoop fire into his lap without his clothes being burned?" Proverbs 6:27. Burned? Is he talking about hell? Possibly, if there is no confession and repentance.

When all is said and done, an obedient heart and life outrank obedient actions. We don't enter heaven because of our good works. "For it is by grace you have been saved, through faith – and this is not from yourselves, it is the gift of God – not by works, so that no one can boast." Ephesians 2:8, 9. Don't be so busy "doing" the work of God that you neglect "being" a child of God.

Good deeds should follow our faith; they go together. We cannot have one without the other and please God. James in referring to Abraham says this: "You see that his faith and his actions were working together, and his faith was made complete by what he did." James 2:22.

O Lord, may my heart and life agree, and may I please You in everything I am and do.

June 18 – **Family Extremes**

We see it all in today's reading – extreme wickedness and extreme righteousness in the same family. Perhaps you know a family like this.

Athaliah is one wicked woman! What do you expect? She is the daughter of Ahab and Jezebel. "When Athaliah the mother of Ahaziah saw that her son was dead, she proceeded to destroy the whole royal family of the house of Judah. But Jehosheba, the daughter of King Jehoram, took Joash son of Ahaziah and stole him away from among the royal princes who were about to be murdered and put him and his nurse in a bedroom…He remained hidden with them at the temple of God for six years while Athaliah ruled the land." 2 Chronicles 22:10-12. It's likely

Athaliah murders some of her own children and grandchildren. Jehosheba, on the other hand, is a daughter, sister, and aunt to three of Judah's kings, and she is married to the High Priest, Jehoiada. There is something special about that baby boy, Joash, so she takes her life in her hands and rescues Joash from certain death. Athaliah seeks to destroy the family; Jehosheba and Jehoiada work to preserve it.

Athaliah rules Judah for six long years. "When the righteous thrive, the people rejoice; when the wicked rule, the people groan." Proverbs 29:2. It was not a good time for the people of Judah.

Joash is anointed King of Judah at the age of seven. "Joash did what was right in the eyes of the Lord all the years Jehoiada the priest instructed him." 2 Kings 12:2. One of the first things he does is repair the temple that is his literal home from age one to seven. Then Jehoiada dies, and King Joash quickly turns away from God and the nation digresses into apostasy (2 Chronicles 24:17-22). He orders the murder of Jehoiada's son, Zechariah his cousin, because he confronts Joash with a message from the Lord, the same Zechariah mentioned in Luke 11:51. "from the blood of Abel to the blood of Zechariah, who was killed between the altar and the sanctuary. Yes, I tell you, this generation will be held responsible for it all."

Two things are certain: 1) We need God in our families; and 2) We will not finish this race successfully on the faith of a faithful uncle. My faith must be my own. "They went out from us, but they did not really belong to us…" 1 John 2:19.

June 19 – **Jack's Story**

An interesting thing happens to Jack today. (I don't know his real name, so I'll just call him Jack.) Jack was dead this morning. (Stay with me.) But on the way to the cemetery, the grave diggers are frightened when they spot Moabite raiders heading their direction. So what do they do? They toss poor Jack into the closest tomb – a used tomb I might add. Now that's just downright disrespectful! Crunch! Jack lands on top of someone's bones! And not just anyone's bones! They are the bones of the Prophet Elisha! Can you guess what happens next? You got it! Jack comes back to life, stands up, and runs out of the tomb! He almost catches up with his friends, the grave diggers. "Hey, wait for me!" But when they turn around and see Jack running toward them and waving his arms, they kick it into high gear and leave Jack in a cloud of dust! Well, maybe that's not exactly the way it happens.

"Elisha died and was buried. Now Moabite raiders used to enter the country every spring. Once while some Israelites were burying a man, suddenly they saw a band of raiders; so they threw the man's body into Elisha's tomb. When the body touched Elisha's bones, the man came to life and stood up on his feet." 2 Kings 13:20, 21.

Are you impacting others for Jesus Christ today? God wants us to live our lives in such a way that others will be attracted to Jesus when they see Him alive in us. However, your influence doesn't have to die with you. A Godly person's influence can continue after death and be a source of spiritual life for others. What are you doing today that will live on and bless others long after you're in heaven? What spiritual investments are you making in the lives of others who will outlive you? "Very truly I tell you, unless a kernel of wheat falls to the ground and dies, it remains only a single seed. But if it dies, it produces many seeds." John 12:24.

June 20 – **Jonah's Ride**

Jonah is one of God's prophets, but on this occasion, he is completely unwilling to do what God calls him to do and that is to preach to Nineveh. Jonah doesn't like Nineveh; he wants to see God's wrath poured out on the city, not His mercy. So he runs from God (not smart). He boards a ship that is going in the opposite direction. God blows in a violent storm. Far below the ship is a rather large sea creature, also called by God to keep his eye on that ship and for a tasty tidbit soon to come in his direction. He sees it. Gulp. Not so tasty after all, but mission accomplished, and thus begins Jonah's incredible ride to the roots of the mountains, but this is no joy-ride. It's pitch black, the second-hand air is stale, and it's mushy and slimy all around. The growls coming from the walls of this submarine are deafening. The fish's stomach is working hard to digest its latest meal. Jonah wants back on dry land, but there are no control panels in this submarine; in fact, it has a mind of its own. "When my life was ebbing away, I remembered you, Lord, and my prayer rose to you, to your holy temple." Jonah 2:7.

Meanwhile, back at command central, the largest case of indigestion ever recorded is underway. Could it be something he ate? Why doesn't he just puke at 10,000 feet below sea level? Because the Commander of this vessel gives the order to swim to a certain shore. Out comes the reluctant prophet, slightly bleached from the acid in the fish's belly, but thankful to see the sun, breathe fresh air, and feel the dry sand between his toes. Reluctant no more, he high-tails it to Nineveh!

The story of Jonah demonstrates that it is not a good idea to run from God. "Where can I go from your Spirit? Where can I flee from your presence?" Psalm 139:7. Nowhere, for God is everywhere. God sees and God hears when we cry out to Him. God's love for us is wide and long and high and deep (Ephesians 3:18). That covers everything and everywhere. Stop running from and start running to God today. "But Jesus took him by the hand and lifted him to his feet, and he stood up." Mark 9:27. "Humble yourselves before the Lord, and he will lift you up." James 4:10.

June 21 – **God's Remnant**

One may purchase a fabric remnant from any store that sells fabric and sewing supplies. The remnant is a small piece neatly pinned or rolled and rubber-banded together. That remnant at one time belonged to a larger bolt of fabric, but now it is all that remains of the original bolt. Many different colors, textures, and shapes of remnants exist. In the right hands, remnants of fabric can be created into beautifully patterned heirlooms.

"This is what the Lord says: 'As a shepherd rescues from the lion's mouth only two leg bones or a piece of an ear, so will the Israelites living in Samaria be rescued, with only the head of a bed and a piece of fabric from a couch.'" Amos 3:12. "Hate evil, love good; maintain justice in the courts. Perhaps the Lord God Almighty will have mercy on the remnant of Joseph." Amos 5:15. God has always had and will always have a Godly remnant. During times of severe judgment and persecution when enemy nations have sought to completely eliminate Israel from the face of the earth, God has preserved His faithful remnant, and He always will. It is because of the faithfulness of a few among many that His Word has survived over the centuries. Thank God for the remnant!

At the end of time as we know it, God will have a holy patchwork of people pieced together from all nations around the globe – those who have kept their faith in Him – and create a work of art, a masterpiece – His Bride. "So too, at the present time there is a remnant chosen by grace." Romans 11:5.

June 22 – **Famine**

Israel has despised and rejected God's Word sent to them by the prophets so many times that God finally gives them what they want: silence. God's judgment rests on us when He gives us over to our own sinful desires and then leaves us to our own devices. That is not a good place to be. Famine is a consequence of God's judgment, but more serious than a famine of food and water is a famine of His Word. "'The days are coming,' declares the Sovereign Lord, 'when I will send a famine through the land – not a famine of food or a thirst for water, but a famine of hearing the words of the Lord. People will stagger from sea to sea and wander from north to east, searching for the word of the Lord, but they will not find it.'" Amos 8:11, 12. We notice in the pages of the Bible from Malachi to Matthew a 400 year absence of God's Word.

Food and water are essential for this temporary man to live. God's Word is necessary and inimitable for man's soul to live. We must have eternal food to feed our eternal soul. There is no substitute for the Word of God. Without it and the life it brings, man is doomed to hell. "Simon Peter answered him, 'Lord, to whom shall we go? You have the words of eternal life.'" John 6:68.

June 23 – **Don't Lose Your Faith**

Even though King Ahaz of Judah has a Godly grandfather, father, and son, he is a wicked king. Judah is being threatened by enemy invasion when God sends the Prophet Isaiah with a word of encouragement to Ahaz. Judah's enemies will not succeed this time, because God obviously has another plan to go along with his supernatural mercy. Notice the introduction and conclusion of this Word from the Lord. "Be careful, keep calm and don't be afraid. Do not lose heart...If you do not stand firm in your faith, you will not stand at all." Isaiah 7:4, 9.

This is a good word for us today. Wherever you are at this moment, whatever you're going through – don't lose your faith in God. Whatever happens, whatever you do, don't lose your faith. Even though the enemy surrounds you, you're in trouble over your head, and you don't see a way out – don't lose your faith.

Perhaps you haven't been an obedient follower of Jesus Christ; maybe you've strayed off course. Faith is your life-line back into right relationship with God. He will walk with you through your darkest night and your deepest valley. If you throw away your faith, you're a goner.

"And without faith it is impossible to please God, because anyone who comes to him must believe that he exists and that he rewards those who earnestly seek him." Hebrews 11:6.

June 24 – **Hope in the Midst of Devastation**

As a child, I loved watching Superman on TV. I was so impressed with his strength, his ability to fly, and his x-ray vision. He could see right through someone! (As a matter of fact, Superman is still my favorite super hero.)

"…He will not judge by what he sees with his eyes, or decide by what he hears with his ears;" Isaiah 11:3. The Prophet Isaiah refers here to the coming Messiah. Everywhere the nations of Israel and Judah look, they see doom and gloom, darkness and foreboding – brought on because of their sins and idol worship. God is preparing judgment, and He will use the surrounding nations to carry it out. He sees beyond their pretense and hypocrisy and sees their dark cold hearts.

As bad as it is, when it seems it cannot get any worse, God offers man hope in the midst of devastation, His promise of a future restoration. "The people walking in darkness have seen a great light; on those living in the land of deep darkness a light has dawned." Isaiah 9:2. (See also Matthew 4:16.) Isaiah's generation passed away centuries before Jesus Christ was born. Nevertheless, God's promise came to pass. This assures us that His promises yet to be fulfilled will indeed be fulfilled in His perfect time. Better than x-ray vision, God's eyes see my heart, but they also see the future and into eternity. What a mighty God we serve!

Jesus Christ is the Hope we hold onto. Yes, there is darkness all around us. Yes, God's judgment will come upon the world. But all is not lost when we have the Light and the Hope of the world, Jesus Christ, living within us. So be patient, child of God, and rest in His love and sovereignty today. "Be joyful in hope, patient in affliction, faithful in prayer." Romans 12:12.

June 25 – **Ah Hah!**

Have you had an "ah hah" moment recently? That is when you finally get it, you finally understand something that's been missing; it clicks. A teacher can usually see it on the face of a student when, at last, it all makes sense; it's the "light bulb over the head turning on" moment. Teachers love when that happens!

We've heard it said that a picture is worth a thousand words. That's the life of the Prophet Hosea. God uses Hosea to speak His words, but He also uses his life as a living demonstration. God desires the people to understand what He is saying to them. Some still don't get it, or they refuse to believe it. "When the Lord began to speak through Hosea, the Lord said to him, 'Go, marry a promiscuous woman and have children with her, for like an adulterous wife this land is guilty of unfaithfulness to the Lord.'" Hosea 1:2.

Jesus does more than just talk about God and His Kingdom; He demonstrates the power of God with healings, miracles, and his death and resurrection. He paints mental pictures with His parables; He forgives sin. God uses His creation to speak to mankind, and His Holy Spirit deals with man's heart. Sadly, some people still choose not to believe. God does everything He can to help people come to faith in Christ; but one thing He will not do is force someone to believe in Him. God's Kingdom is populated with people who want to be there.

Two men walking along the road to Emmaus were joined by a third man as they discussed the events of the past few days. The conversation continues as they reach their destination when all three decide to have dinner together. "Then their eyes were opened and they recognized him, and he disappeared from their sight." Luke 24:31. An "ah hah" moment of significant proportion!

June 26 – **Mercy Triumphs Over Judgment**

God presents His case against Israel by outlining their many sins in Hosea chapters 4-8. This nation definitely deserves God's judgment. But then again, so do I. In the middle of all the stark but true testimony against them, God inserts His heart. Hear Him. "Come, let us return to the Lord..." (6:1). "…I long to redeem them…" (7:13). "…How long will they be incapable of purity?" (8:5). He says the same to me today.

I could defend myself and argue that I'm not as bad as they are. I haven't committed all those sins against God like they did. I'm better than they are. No I'm not. Jesus Christ bore my sin on the cross too.

Even though our sins are many and deserve God's judgment, His mercy is greater still. "…Mercy triumphs over judgment." James 2:13. Praise God! God wants more than anything to trade with me: I give Him my sins, and He gives me His mercy. I come out way ahead in this deal! "But because of his great love for us, God, who is rich in mercy, made us alive with Christ even when we were dead in transgressions…" Ephesians 2:4, 5.

June 27 – **Righteous or Rebellious**

One thing we should keep in mind as we read the Old Testament, especially the prophets, is that God speaks to individuals in the same way He speaks to nations and cities. What is true of one is true of the other. Approach God's Word each day with this prayer: Lord, what do You want to say to me today? Open my eyes to see, my ears to hear, and my heart to understand. "Open my eyes that I may see wonderful things in your law." Psalm 119:18. God will answer the sincere prayer of your heart.

God's words through Hosea to Israel serve to teach and warn us today. God has not changed in His dealings with man. He still judges the sins of nations and individuals. Have you ever asked yourself the question, "Why is all this bad stuff happening to me?" "But you have planted wickedness, you have reaped evil, you have eaten the fruit of deception. Because you have depended on your own strength…" Hosea 10:13. "Whoever sows to please their flesh, from the flesh will reap destruction; whoever sows to please the Spirit, from the Spirit will reap eternal life." Galatians 6:8. You may say, "But I repented years ago! I thought God forgave me!" He did. The fact remains: We reap what we sow, sometimes years later. Sowing and reaping – It's a natural and spiritual law. However, in the middle of a briar patch, God creates a smooth trail. He can still bring something good out of something bad. Look for it!

Break up the unplowed ground of your heart; plant good seed; it is time to seek the Lord (Hosea 10:12). Tomorrow's harvest will be new and improved. God concludes the book of Hosea with 14:9. "Who is wise? Let them realize these things. Who is discerning? Let them understand. The ways of the Lord are right; the righteous walk in them, but the rebellious stumble in them."

June 28 – **Sufficiency in God**

"The bed is too short to stretch out on, the blanket too narrow to wrap around you." Isaiah 28:20. Isaiah offers us an interesting picture to illustrate the truth that when we put our trust in anyone or anything other than the One True God, it will never be enough. Every other source of confidence will fail our expectations; they are inadequate to protect and provide. Israel, in their suffering, is looking to false gods and other nations to help them. No one and no thing will ever compare to our God; He is sufficient to meet every need in our lives.

Israel is experiencing distress and turmoil because of their sin and refusal to turn back to God. "The Israelites secretly did things against the Lord their God that were not right..." 2 Kings 17:9. They think their sin is secret, but there is no such thing as secret sin to God. He knows all. Yet God still offers His wayward children salvation. "'Come now, let us settle the matter,' says the Lord. 'Though your sins are like scarlet, they shall be as white as snow; though they are red as crimson, they shall be like wool.'" Isaiah 1:18.

God offers us salvation through the precious blood of His Son, Jesus Christ. "and repentance for the forgiveness of sins will be preached in his name to all nations, beginning at Jerusalem." Luke 24:47. When we ask Jesus to cover our sins with His blood, He does. When God the Father looks for our sins through the blood of Jesus, He sees white as snow! Hallelujah!

Dear God, I've tried everything, and I'm miserable. My sins are no secret to You. I come to You now and ask you to forgive me; apply the blood of Jesus to my heart; cleanse me as white as snow. I give my life to You. Thank You, Lord. Amen.

June 29 – **Palliation of Sin**

Isaiah warns Judah of impending judgment because of their many sins for which they refuse to acknowledge or repent. God asks the question, "What more could have been done for my vineyard than I have done for it?" Isaiah 5:4. The answer is nothing. He has no other choice but to send judgment.

"Woe to those who call evil good and good evil...they parade their sin like Sodom..." Isaiah 5:20; 3:9. "who freely strut about when what is vile is honored by the human race." Psalm 12:8. God's Word remains the same throughout eternity (Hebrews 13:8). Sexual immorality, homosexuality, and murder (abortion) will always be sins in God's Book. He has never relaxed His standards and definitions of holiness and wickedness. Our society today, on the other hand, embraces palliation of sin. In other words, the sins are not so bad; they are not even considered sin any more. God has not changed His mind about sin and their consequences. He will always hate sin and love the sinner. He is not willing that any should perish but that all would come to faith in Jesus Christ and His finished work on the cross. He offers hope and freedom from bondage to sin. We should be more concerned with what God thinks about us, than what those around us think.

Romans 1:26-32 gives a crystal clear description of today's world and ends with these words in verse 32. "Although they know God's righteous decree that those who do such things deserve death, they not only continue to do these very things but also approve of those who practice them." May God have mercy on us.

June 30 – **Always More to Learn**

"Oh, that's what that means! Praise God!" exclaims several sitting in a small group in heaven on the side of a verdant hill with Bibles in their laps, laughing, and high-fiving each other. I believe we will continue learning and growing in our knowledge of God and His Word after we arrive in heaven. His Word is so awesome and powerful that our finite minds are unable to grasp every truth in its entirety here on earth.

Isaiah prophesies how God will bring judgment on Israel and Judah using the evil nation of Babylon. He will then judge Babylon with total annihilation but have compassion on Jacob. God moves people and nations around on His chess board to accomplish His will in the earth. Many prophecies in the Bible have more than one designation. "See, the day of the Lord is coming – a cruel day, with wrath and fierce anger – to make the land desolate and destroy the sinners within it." Isaiah 13:9. Isaiah speaks of Jacob's near future but also foretells the distant future in the end times. "But the day of the Lord will come like a thief. The heavens will disappear with a roar; the elements will be destroyed by fire, and the earth and everything done in it will be laid bare." 2 Peter 3:10. We see in Isaiah 14:12-17 a triple reference to Satan, the king of Babylon, as well as the anti-christ in the last days.

The Holy Bible will forever be the living written Word of God, breathing life into those who heed its truths. It is where we find God's plan for mankind and hope in the midst of chaos (Isaiah 16:4, 5). There is no such thing as hope in the enemy's camp. Cling to God's Word and never let it go.

JULY

July 1 – **Old Testament Revival**

One of the definitions of revival is the process of bringing someone back to life. This implies that at one time someone had been alive but had died. King Hezekiah is well aware what Assyria has done to the children of Israel, and he knows that only God can deliver Judah from their hands. He goes to work. According to the first Scripture in our reading today, 2 Chronicles 29:3, King Hezekiah of Judah wastes no time in restoring worship in the temple and leading the people back to the God of their forefathers. Notice the last Scripture in today's passage, 2 Chronicles 31:21, which tells us that Hezekiah "sought his God and worked wholeheartedly. And so he prospered."

There are two important lessons we can learn from this time period in Judah's history. First, Hezekiah sends out the invitation for people to come to Jerusalem and return to the Lord (30:6-9). Not everyone accepts this invitation, however, and the couriers are scorned and ridiculed (v. 10). Nevertheless, some humble themselves and go to Jerusalem (v. 11). Doesn't this remind you of the story in Luke 14:15-24 when those invited make excuses why they can't come to the banquet? "Then the master told his servant, 'Go out to the roads and country lanes and compel them to come in, so that my house will be full.'" Luke 14:23. So don't quit inviting people to church or to know Christ as Savior just because someone says no. Be encouraged; keep inviting; someone will come to the Lord because of your invitation.

Secondly, those who go to Jerusalem at Hezekiah's invitation and reconnect with God experience the joy and blessing of God. They immediately become generous givers. "...They brought a great amount, a tithe of everything." 2 Chronicles 31:5. "In the midst of a very severe trial, their overflowing joy and their extreme poverty welled up in rich generosity. For I testify that they gave as much as they were able, and even beyond their ability. Entirely on their own," 2 Corinthians 8:2, 3.

Lord, revive me! Help me to be a better inviter and giver!

July 2 – **Give Me Some of Those Burning Coals!**

I must admit that Proverbs 25:21, 22 has always puzzled me. Let's look at it closely. "If your enemy is hungry, give him food to eat; if he is thirsty, give him water to drink. In doing this, you will heap burning coals on his head, and the Lord will reward you." I understand what verse 21 is saying, because the New Testament also teaches us to pray for and be good to our enemies. We may not like it, and it may be extremely difficult to do at times, but this is what the Lord expects us to do. Romans 12:17-21 reminds us of this same passage of Scripture. "Do not repay anyone evil for evil. Be careful to do what is right in the eyes of everyone." (v. 17). So what about these burning coals?

Burning coals on someone's head sounds painful. Surely God will not reward us for harming someone. Doesn't God's Word teach us that vengeance belongs to Him alone? To understand the meaning of this passage, we must go back to the time and culture in which these Scriptures were written. When a person's fire went out at home, he or she would go to a neighbor and get some live coals to rekindle the fire. They were usually carried in a pan on the head. God asks us to show kindness and meet the needs of everyone, even our enemies. And don't wait to be asked; offer first. Intense heat is also used to soften and melt metal. Kindness can soften and melt the hardest of hearts. So we heap coals on our enemy's head, not to hurt him, but to help him. God approves and will bless us whether our enemy repents or not. We are not responsible for the results; we just obey the Lord. God takes care of the rest. "Do not be overcome by evil, but overcome evil with good." Romans 12:21.

Heavenly Father, give me the strength to obey You.

July 3 – **Super Woman**

"A wife of noble character who can find?..." Proverbs 31:10. I have several questions about the Proverbs 31 woman. Does such a super woman exist? Is Lemuel's mother describing herself? Does she even come close to this description? Does King Lemuel die a bachelor, always searching for and never finding this ideal woman? (Maybe his mother doesn't want him to get married.) First of all, we don't know anything about Lemuel. Some Bible commentators identify him with Solomon; others think he is Hezekiah. Still others suggest he may be some neighboring petty Arabian prince.

Perhaps the attributes of this "wife of noble character" are goals for which women should strive. Let's look at some of these. If you're a wife and mother, how are you doing?

- She takes good care of her husband and makes him look first-class.
- She is not lazy by any stretch of the imagination.
- She is a savvy business woman and a financial genius, shrewd and strategic.
- She is an excellent cook, and her house is always immaculate.

- She sews clothes for everyone in her family and even sews her own bedspreads.
- She sews more than she needs and sells them to make a profit.
- She gets little sleep taking care of everybody around her.
- She is industrious and has a sense of humor to boot.
- She is physically strong and a hard worker.
- She stays on top of everything and never procrastinates.
- She stays awake at night until everything on her list for that day is checked off.
- She is generous to the poor and needy, and has a true servant's heart.
- She is wise beyond words and articulate in everything she says (never tongue-tied).
- She is the best mother ever.
- Again, she makes her husband look good.

After looking at this list, I am more convinced than ever that this woman does not exist on planet earth. Can I just pick out two or three of these traits and work on them? That should keep me busy for a while.

Two things this woman apparently does not possess in abundance are charm and beauty (v. 30). This could be the problem with today's woman. We are more concerned about those two things and devote more energy, time, and finances than we should, endeavoring to perfect those in our lives, and we leave the other things hanging. It's time for a reality check.

Actually, the Proverbs 31 woman is sprinkled all over the New Testament and not so neatly packaged into one chapter as it is here. It teaches us how to love our husbands, respect and assist them, embrace purity, submit to our husbands, develop a gentle and quiet spirit, be a good mother, and even a great homemaker. "Wives, submit yourselves to your own husbands as you do to the Lord." Ephesians 5:22. When we do this, it is seen by God as obedience to Christ.

July 4 – **David, Warrior King**

So, now you're a Christian. Praise God! No more problems. WRONG! Okay, you've been around for a while; you're a seasoned Christian. You're fulfilling God's plan for your life, and things are going great. Now, no more problems. WRONG AGAIN! Where do these strange ideas come from? Not from the Bible.

David, King of Israel, is God's man of the hour. Scripture records his many military victories as he and his army conquer surrounding nations. "Our help is in the name of the Lord, the Maker of heaven and earth." Psalm 124:8. However, evidence exists that along with his string of victories, God inserts a small defeat or two. It is during those times that David is forced to regroup, reevaluate, and refocus. "I do not trust in my bow, my sword does not bring me victory; but you give us victory over our enemies, you put our adversaries to shame." Psalm 44:6, 7.

"Consider it pure joy, my brothers and sisters, whenever you face trials of many kinds," James 1:2. James writes this letter to believers assuring them they will face many different trials in their lifetime. And he tells them to be joyful in the middle of it! Yes, we will experience victories in this life, and we will also suffer loss. God uses all of it to "mature and complete" us (James 1:4). He knows our tendency to get over-confident and self-satisfied (sometimes we're totally oblivious), so He throws in a defeat – for our good, to wake us up, and make us more dependent upon Him. Hopefully, it will cause us to stop and take inventory and get this derailed train back on track.

"Give us aid against the enemy, for human help is worthless." Psalm 108:12. David does not trust himself or other men. He knows victory comes from the Lord. "I have told you these things, so that in me you may have peace. In this world you will have trouble. But take heart! I have overcome the world." John 16:33.

July 5 – **His Dwelling Place**

I love church! I love worshiping God with other believers and being in the holy presence of the Lord. Psalm 84 speaks of Solomon's temple in Jerusalem. I also believe it refers to gathering with our brothers and sisters in Christ today to hear the preaching and teaching of God's Word with signs and wonders following and to sing praises to our God. It has a third reference as well – heaven. This Psalm is worth reading through three times with each of those dwelling places in mind.

"How lovely is your dwelling place, Lord Almighty! My soul yearns, even faints, for the courts of the Lord; my heart and my flesh cry out for the living God." Psalm 84:1, 2. When we're desperate for God, He gives us His promise. "Blessed are those who hunger and thirst for righteousness, for they will be filled." Matthew 5:6. When we're no longer hungry or thirsty for the things of God, it is a clear sign we are dying.

Dear God, increase my hunger and thirst for Your presence. More of You, Lord, is my prayer.

July 6 – **He is My Refuge**

My husband and I were parents of small children on our way to Disney World the first time we all flew in an airplane. To put it mildly, I was terrified – of flying – not Disney World. Being the Bible thumper I am, I carried my Bible on board, put it on my lap, turned to Psalm 91 (already marked), and kept it open there throughout the trip. I read that Psalm over and over and over, making sure God knew I was serious.

Only God knows how many times my thoughts and prayers have turned to that beautiful and calming Psalm throughout the years. It was also a favorite of my husband's grandmother who asked him to read it to her one more time just hours before she went to heaven.

Why is Psalm 91 a favorite to so many believers? There are lots of reasons; here are just a few. He is my refuge (v. 2) where I find safety and protection. Because I trust Him, He keeps me secure in times of physical and spiritual danger. He is with me, so I don't have to be afraid of anything happening around me. I remember hearing a story many years ago of a new believer who had just left a church service where the preacher spoke on this Psalm. She was accosted by several men who were up to no good. All she could remember from Psalm 91 was the word feathers. She began to yell "feathers" repeatedly (after all, it is the word of God), and her abductors left her alone. You may smile, but it's the power of God's Word at work.

"For he will command his angels concerning you to guard you in all your ways; they will lift you up in their hands, so that you will not strike your foot against a stone." (vs. 11, 12). You may recall Satan uses this passage of Scripture when he tempts Jesus in the wilderness (Matthew 4:6 and Luke 4:10, 11). Jesus fires back with more Word. This is incentive for me to learn and know the full counsel of God's Word.

There's one more thing we need to understand from Psalm 91. We must continue to dwell in the shelter of the Most High (v. 1) and remain under His wings. At any time, we can choose to step out from under His protection, but then we're on our own – not a good place to be. As long as we love Him and stay under His domain, God gives us precious promises in verses 14-16. "I will be with him in trouble." Notice, God does not say we will never have trouble, but He will be with us in trouble. That makes all the difference in the world.

July 7 – **What's There to be Glad About?**

I am so thankful God included the Book of Psalms in our Bible. Every emotion known to mankind (and womankind) can be found in that book – from deep sorrow to exuberant joy, from emptiness to fulfillment, from depression to a mountain-top high – and everything in between. Some days I may not even know how I feel; Psalms helps clarify. Have you ever been so confused that you don't know what you want or need? Read Psalms. If you don't read somewhere a Scripture or passage that describes where you are emotionally, then you're not paying attention. Read through all 150 Psalms again. Yes, take the time and do it. Nothing will ever and should ever take the place of God's Word in your life. Read it again.

"The Lord reigns, let the earth be glad; let the distant shores rejoice." Psalm 97:1. We are on the earth, so let's be glad, because the Lord reigns; He is in control. God desires everyone everywhere to know Him and be glad. "Declare his glory among the nations, his marvelous deeds among all peoples." Psalm 96:3. So tell somebody! Your neighbor down the street and the people across the ocean need to know the Lord and what He has done for them, so they can be glad. Everyone deserves a chance to hear about the goodness of the Lord.

When you talk to someone about the Lord, encourage them to read the Bible. When they say they don't know where to begin, suggest the Psalms. I can always find myself or my situation described in the Psalms. I have many reasons to be glad today – and so do you. "The people read it and were glad for its encouraging message." Acts 15:31.

July 8 – **My Conscious Effort**

I consider myself a fairly accomplished multitasker. I can wash dishes in the dishwasher, wash clothes in the washer, dry clothes in the dryer, bake a casserole in the oven, vacuum the floor, and talk to my friend on the phone all at the same time. But when it comes to praising and worshiping God, my mind and heart should be fully engaged in the adulation. Sure, I can sing praises to God while I mop the kitchen floor or mow the backyard as long as my heart and mind are singing to Him as well, and I'm not thinking about that conversation with my neighbor or mentally forming my grocery list.

Do you ever stand and sing in church, mindlessly allowing words and melody overflow your mouth? Perhaps you even raise your hands in worship, but all the while wondering what the person directly behind you thinks about your hair, or if your shirt is tucked in properly, or thinking about what you will do that afternoon, or if people think you're holy? I'm guilty. I make a conscious effort to worship and praise God with my whole being. I don't want to multitask when it comes to worshiping my God. Also up for consideration: The goal is not entertainment or individual aggrandizement, but worship and praise to our God.

Read Psalm 104 again. The Psalmist extols the majesty and power of God in all creation. Think about each phrase. Our God is so BIG! The natural response to such a God – our God – is praise! "I will sing to the Lord all my life; I will sing praise to my God as long as I live. May my meditation be pleasing to him, as I rejoice in the Lord." Psalm 104:33, 34. Did you hear it? May my thoughts please Him as I sing! "speaking to one another with psalms, hymns, and songs from the Spirit. Sing and make music from your heart to the Lord," Ephesians 5:19.

July 9 – **Red Flags**

When our daughters were young teens, my husband and I taught them the concept of the red flag. A red light or a red STOP sign means STOP. That sounds simple enough. When I position the red flag on my mailbox up, I hope the mail carrier will notice it and STOP at my mailbox and get my out-going mail. When the Holy Spirit sends up a red flag in our spirit, He is warning us to STOP, turn around and go back; there is danger ahead. It's a feeling we get, a check in our spirit. It is always in our best interest to pay attention to the Holy Spirit. He is attempting to protect us and steer us in the right direction. We decide to heed or ignore the Spirit. If we continually ignore His red flags, we soon don't notice them anymore and eventually find ourselves in a precarious predicament that could have been avoided.

"Blessed are those who act justly, who always do what is right." Psalm 106:3. The Apostle Paul listens to the Holy Spirit when the Spirit forbids him to go into Asia (Acts 16:6-10). We never learn the reason why, and that is okay; God always knows what He is doing whether we understand it or not.

God loves you. Be sensitive to the Holy Spirit and obey His leading. The next time you sense a Holy Spirit red flag, that check in your Spirit, STOP. Don't over-analyze the situation; just obey the Lord. He is watching over you for good. Trust Him. "For we are taking pains to do what is right, not only in the eyes of the Lord but also in the eyes of man." 2 Corinthians 8:21.

July 10 – **A Whisper**

A mother can hold a frightened crying baby and soothe him with her whispers of tender loving care. Her gentle touch, arms enfolded around him, holding him close, brings peace and calm.

Our Heavenly Father desires to do the same for His children who are experiencing storms. His touch makes all the difference. "He stilled the storm to a whisper; the waves of the sea were hushed." Psalm 107:29. "He got up, rebuked the wind and said to the waves, 'Quiet! Be still!' Then the wind died down and it was completely calm." Mark 4:39.

"Who is like the Lord our God, the One who sits enthroned on high, who stoops down to look on the heavens and the earth?" Psalm 113:5, 6. Here's an understatement for you: God is big. The truth is there is no one like our God. He is so big that He must stoop down to look on the heavens and the earth! There is nothing He cannot do.

Your storm may be inner turmoil. It may be relational, financial, physical, or anything else. Jesus is our Peacemaker. He is big enough and loving enough to take care of you today. Ask Him.

July 11 – **Precious**

Just a few hours before our beautiful daughter, Jamie, went to heaven, she saw and talked to someone in her room. While in the pangs of death, she opened her eyes, smiled really big, looked to the corner of her room behind her and said, "It won't be long now!" She could see someone clearly, someone waiting to escort her to her new home with the Lord. Jamie died of breast cancer at the age of 36 in our home. I was beside her bed when she left us. Her little face, just moments before, writhing in agony – now relaxed, peaceful, quiet, lovely, precious. She was with Him.

Jamie was a missionary to Northern Asia, a faithful servant of the Most High God. "Precious in the sight of the Lord is the death of his faithful servants." Psalm 116:15. Why is that? Because God knows we will rest from our labors. He will wipe away all our tears. The complete fulfillment of every promise in His Word is now a reality for all eternity. There's no better place to be. Shortly before Jamie died, we talked about heaven. I told her, "When I get to heaven, I want to see Jesus first, but I want to see you standing right beside Him!" She chuckled softly, "I'll try, Momma."

"We are confident, I say, and would prefer to be away from the body and at home with the Lord." 2 Corinthians 5:8.

July 12 – **The Early Bird Gets the Word!**

I love a good ham bone. When my family eats all the ham it can stand for several days, I don't throw the bone away. There is a lot of good meat and flavor around the bone, so I save it for the next week. Then I put it in a crock pot with a little water, turn it on low, and let it simmer for about 24 hours. Next, I let it cool, throw away the bones, and save all the good meat. In the meantime, I soak dried baby lima beans overnight. Early in the morning, I parboil the beans, drain the water, and add the beans to the crock pot and let it simmer on low all day, blending the flavors. When my family walks through the door at the end of the day, the aroma permeates the house, and mouths salivate. I cook a pot of rice, and we're ready to sit down and enjoy a delicious meal that's healthy and satisfying. My family knows I care about them, because I take the time to plan ahead; and I feel confident that I'm giving the ones I love a nourishing, stick-to-your-ribs meal.

"I rise before dawn and cry for help; I have put my hope in your word." Psalm 119:147. "Oh, how I love your law! I meditate on it all day long." (v. 97). I desire to feed my class or congregation a nourishing meal of God's Word. To do so, I must prepare early in the week, giving the Word time to simmer in my spirit. When it's time to eat, I want those whom God loves to enjoy the meal, savor every morsel, inhale the sweet smell of a well-prepared feast of God's Word, and leave the table with a good taste in their mouths. There are far too many spiritual skeletons walking around today, even in our churches. We all grow tired of fast food and microwaveable meals; we hunger and thirst for that which really satisfies – the Word. Our families and others whom God places in our care know when we hurriedly throw a meal together. "Very early in the morning, while it was still dark, Jesus got up, left the house and went off to a solitary place, where he prayed." Mark 1:35. Rest assured; the Word rises early in the morning! So be the early bird. You know what they say: The early bird gets the Word!

July 13 – **Joy Will Come!**

Do you know that mourning and sadness have an expiration date? But many times, we help ourselves to generous amounts of expired doses, way beyond the recommended shelf life. Like sour milk and rancid bacon, stuck in grief and sorrow is bad for you. Yes, we all experience loss and have times of extreme grief and emotional lows, but God intends for mourning and sadness to last only for a season. Granted, these seasons have different lengths for different people. No two losses are the same. But there comes a time when we must decide we don't want to be stuck anymore, and we want to live again. God promises us that joy is on the way. "Those who sow with tears will reap with songs of joy. Those who go out weeping, carrying seed to sow, will return with songs of joy, carrying sheaves with them." Psalm 126:5, 6.

Perhaps you have lost someone you love dearly. Maybe you're experiencing an extended trial or illness. Remember, God has joy prepared for you. So, how do you get from point A to point B? How do you get unstuck from grief and sadness? Choose to move forward. Put one foot in front of the other, and do the next thing. Build or re-build relationships; express your emotions to God and others qualified to listen; serve others in your community; begin a new sport, hobby, or activity. Smile more. Do something first and trust God to come alongside you. Your joy will come back!

"I have told you this so that my joy may be in you and that your joy may be complete." John 15:11.

July 14 – **Stars and Sand**

We can learn a lot about God's character in His dealings with the nation of Israel. God chooses Abraham and His descendants as His special people. He makes Israel His dwelling place throughout the generations and gives them many promises. The children of Israel disappoint God, forsake Him, and disobey His revealed Word time and time again. However, they have never and will never be able to make God's Word null and void. He makes a way to keep His promises.

"The Lord swore an oath to David, a sure oath he will not revoke: 'One of your own descendants I will place on your throne. If your sons keep my covenant and the statutes I teach them, then their sons will sit on your throne for ever and ever.'" Psalm 132:11, 12. It doesn't take long for David's descendants to forget God. His own son, Solomon, starts the downward spiral. Over the centuries, God disciplines and Israel repents; God forgives and restores; the cycle repeats itself many times. When it seems Israel strays so far away from Him, when it seems all is lost and hopeless, God sends His Son to earth to accomplish what is impossible for man to do. He is the Holy One, the Spotless Lamb. Through Jesus Christ, God's Word is fulfilled. Read Psalm 130 again. "He himself will redeem Israel from all their sins." Psalm 130:8.

As believers and followers of Jesus Christ, we are part of Abraham's seed, the stars and sand that God talks about in Genesis 22:17. God grafts us into His family tree as mentioned in Romans chapter 11. "If you belong to Christ, then you are Abraham's seed, and heirs according to the promise." Galatians 3:29. As our

Heavenly Father, He disciplines us when we need it and lavishes His love upon us when we don't deserve it, because that is what a loving father does. He will never stop loving us, because He has chosen us as His own.

July 15 – **The Problem with Understanding**

"Do you understand what I'm saying? Do I make myself perfectly clear? Any questions?" I've said those words a time or two or three, etc. to my children when they were young. I was either trying to correct, discipline or protect them. "But Mom, you don't understand." "I understand more than you know." As incomprehensible as it was for them, I was a child once upon a time.

Humans have a problem with understanding God. We want to understand Him and His ways; that's the problem. We can't fully grasp His working in our lives, because our understanding is terribly limited. His is not. "Great is our Lord and mighty in power; his understanding has no limit." Psalm 147:5. "who by his understanding made the heavens, His love endures forever." Psalm 136:5. Isaiah tells us that no one can fathom his understanding (Isaiah 40:28).

Until I have personally walked in someone's shoes, until I have been there and done that, it's challenging for me to understand another's grief or confusion or pain. The best I can do is listen, pray, care, empathize, and be a friend. However, Jesus has walked in our shoes. God became a man. He is the Creator of us, and He understands us like no one else.

Even at the age of twelve, Jesus' understanding is unparalleled. "Everyone who heard him was amazed at his understanding and his answers." Luke 2:47. I've said it once, and I'm sure I'll say it again: I may never fully understand this side of eternity all the why's and how's about God and His ways, and I'm okay with that, because I know He loves me, and I know I can trust Him totally. Think about this: If we could understand everything there is to know about our God, He would not be a very big God.

July 16 – **He Holds the Key**

Shebna is an officer in Hezekiah's court, probably put in office by Ahaz. He is most likely a foreigner since there is no mention of his father; he is self-seeking and an enemy of Judah. God replaces him with Eliakim son of Hilkiah, a good man, who will faithfully serve as treasurer and prime-minister of state. He is given the key to the temple and will open and close the doors as needed. "I will place on his shoulder the key to the house of David; what he opens no one can shut, and what he shuts no one can open." Isaiah 22:22. Eliakim is here pictured as a type of Christ.

All power in heaven and earth has been given to Jesus Christ. His authority in the kingdom of heaven and in the ordering of all affairs of that kingdom is supreme, absolute, and given to Him by the Father forever. "To the angel of the church in Philadelphia write: These are the words of him who is holy and true, who holds the key of David. What he opens no one can shut, and what he shuts no one can open." Revelation 3:7.

Jesus holds the key to government and authority in and over the church. (See Isaiah 9:6.) When He opens a door on earth for his works or his servants, none can shut it; and when he shuts a door against whatever would hurt or defile, none can open it. Christ decides who is and who is not to be admitted to the heavenly palace. He opens and shuts the prison door. He holds the keys to hell and death (Revelation 1:18). Our God is the final authority, and He is in control. We serve an awesome God!

July 17 – **Tears in Heaven**

Do you know someone who can cry at the drop of a hat? You may know others who never cry, or at least you never see them cry. We cry when we're in pain and when we're in distress emotionally. We cry when we're happy and when our tickle box is turned upside down; we cry when we're sad and our heart is broken. We cry when our eyes are irritated or a small particle invades our eye space. Tears are a healthy part of our eyes.

God created our eyes with the ability to make tears for several reasons. Lubrication is one reason; cleansing is another, so is emotional release. Tears triggered by emotions have a different chemical make-up than those for lubrication. Emotional tears contain protein-based hormones which can serve as natural pain-killers, making an individual feel better. So that's why I feel better after a good cry! It's one of God's ways to help us through times of grief, pain, and emotional anguish. So don't stifle the tears; it can be part of the healing process.

"he will swallow up death forever. The Sovereign Lord will wipe away the tears from all faces..." Isaiah 25:8. "He will wipe every tear from their eyes. There will be no more death or mourning or crying or pain, for the old order of things has passed away." Revelation 21:4. Notice what these verses do not say. They do not say there will be no tears in heaven; they tell us the Lord will wipe away the tears. When I step into heaven and I don't find someone I loved on earth there waiting for me, will a tear form in my eye? If it does, Jesus will walk up to me and gently wipe it away. As time goes by and I realize someone I expected to be there does not arrive, will another tear glisten in my eye? If it does, Jesus will again lovingly wipe it away with His touch. There is no pain or emotional stress in heaven, so those tears are no longer needed. The abundance of everlasting joy, delight, peace, love, glory, eternal life, and radiant light and presence of God the Father and Jesus Christ, King of Kings and Lord of Lords, will quickly outshine and overwhelm any iota of former sadness. We will thank the Lord for His truth and justice and rejoice in His new "order of things."

July 18 – **Walking Orders**

"Whether you turn to the right or to the left, your ears will hear a voice behind you, saying, 'This is the way; walk in it.'" Isaiah 30:21. From whom do you get your walking orders? Many Christians today go from place to place to hear this speaker or that speaker, hoping to hear a word from the Lord. We have our sights set way too low if we're looking to man. Perhaps we're just too busy or too lazy to get alone with God on a daily basis and take the time needed to hear His voice. Perhaps we're afraid of what He might show us about ourselves. Regardless, in this life we need God's daily guidance; in the pages of the Bible is where we find that direction. Pastors, teachers, evangelists, and other men and women of God are His gifts to the church to aid us in spiritual growth. Praise God for them! But don't totally rely on others to feed your spiritual man; spend one on one time with God and His Word; hear directly from His Holy Spirit. Chances are, your time spent alone with God will become sweeter to you as time goes by. "The law from your mouth is more precious to me than thousands of pieces of silver and gold." Psalm 119:72.

How blessed we are to have the freedom to pick up the Holy Bible at any time and begin to read. Most people in this world are not so privileged. God has something He wants to teach you every day; He has something He wants you to do each day for Him. Receive your daily walking orders from your Heavenly Father. "So I say, walk by the Spirit, and you will not gratify the desires of the flesh." Galatians 5:16.

July 19 – **Search and Rescue**

We have search and rescue teams in our nation trained in ground search, mountain, urban, combat and air-sea search and rescue. A search and rescue team can be called in to assist anytime someone is missing or in distress and imminent danger. The good shepherd is a search and rescue team of one when he goes to look for the lost sheep until he finds it (Luke 15:4). "In distress and imminent danger" describes each of us before Jesus Christ found us. The one lost in sin and without Christ is in danger at every turn in the hands of Satan. The lost sheep finds comfort, safety, healing, provision, love, and forgiveness in the hands of the Savior. Jesus saves us from our sins; He saves us from ourselves. He rescues us from the iron grip of Satan in this world, and He rescues us from hell in the next.

"and those the Lord has rescued will return. They will enter Zion with singing; everlasting joy will crown their heads. Gladness and joy will overtake them, and sorrow and sighing will flee away." Isaiah 35:10. "The Lord will rescue me from every evil attack and will bring me safely to his heavenly kingdom. To him be glory for ever and ever. Amen." 2 Timothy 4:18.

Jesus, I'm lost. I don't know what to do. There is danger all around me. I'm scared. Please rescue me; save me. Forgive me. Hold me close.

July 20 – **Where Does Sin Go?**

The Bible teaches us that when we repent of our sins and ask God to forgive us, He forgives us. This is a blessed truth of Scripture which I have personally experienced. It's a beautiful thing when the weight of sin is lifted from our lives. Praise God for this provision of forgiveness He makes available to us through the precious blood of Jesus Christ.

When Jesus forgives us, where does the sin go? "Who is a God like you, who pardons sin and forgives the transgression of the remnant of his inheritance? You do not stay angry forever but delight to show mercy. You will again have compassion on us; you will tread our sins underfoot and hurl all our iniquities into the depths of the sea." Micah 7:18, 19. This passage declares He puts our sins under his feet and also throws them into the deep sea. There's more!

- He removes them as far as the east is from the west (Psalm 103:12).
- He puts them behind His back (Isaiah 38:17).
- He covers them (Psalm 32:1 and Romans 4:7).
- He blots them out (Psalm 51:1 and Isaiah 43:25).
- He bore our sins in his body on the cross (1 Peter 2:24).
- He takes them away (1 John 3:5).
- He will remember our sins no more (Jeremiah 31:34 and Hebrews 8:12).

It is safe to say that when God forgives us of sin, He gets rid of it! Praise His Holy Name! "Then he adds: 'Their sins and lawless acts I will remember no more.'" Hebrews 10:17.

July 21 – **The High Cost of Pride**

As you read through the Bible, you should notice God's reaction to pride and it's direct opposite, humility, in both believers and the ungodly. Pride is characterized by an inordinately high opinion of one's self; humility acknowledges submission and dependence on God. Both attract His attention and response. He never ignores either in anyone, no matter how righteous or evil a person may be.

King Sennacherib and his massive Assyrian army are bearing down on Judah with impending devastation. "When King

Hezekiah heard this, he tore his clothes and put on sackcloth and went into the temple of the Lord." 2 Kings 19:1. Sackcloth is course loose cloth made from goat's hair and worn as a symbol of humbling one's self before God. On the other end of the spectrum, hear what God has to say to the godless king of Assyria in Isaiah 37:23: "Who is it you have ridiculed and blasphemed? Against whom have you raised your voice and lifted your eyes in pride? Against the Holy One of Israel!" God doesn't let anything slip by Him. God's response to his pride is the death of 185,000 of his soldiers in a single night. Soon after, Sennacherib is murdered by his own sons (Isaiah 37:36-38).

God delivers King Hezekiah because he humbles himself before God. "So the Lord saved Hezekiah and the people of Jerusalem from the hand of Sennacherib king of Assyria and from the hand of all others. He took care of them on every side." 2 Chronicles 32:22. I love the part, "He took care of them on every side." That's the way God takes care of us too when we humble ourselves before Him and acknowledge Who He is and how much we need Him.

Do you remember King Nebuchadnezzar of Babylon? "But when his heart became arrogant and hardened with pride, he was deposed from his royal throne and stripped of his glory." Daniel 5:20. How about King Herod? "Immediately, because Herod did not give praise to God, an angel of the Lord struck him down, and he was eaten by worms and died." Acts 12:23.

"When pride comes, then comes disgrace, but with humility comes wisdom." Proverbs 11:2.

July 22 – **Musings from Hezekiah**

Hezekiah is recorded as one of Judah's good kings, a very interesting character in Judah's history. Here are a few reflections from his life worthy of our thoughtful consideration.

2 Kings 20 tells the story of his sickness and recovery. God decides that Hezekiah will soon die, but the king turns his face to the wall and prays earnestly. He does not want to die. Is it because he has no heir to his throne? God answers his prayer and adds fifteen years to his life during which time his son Manasseh is born, who becomes one of the more wicked kings to ever rule Judah. It reminds me of the time the children of Israel grumble against God in the desert. "In the desert they gave in to their craving; in the wilderness they put God to the test. So he gave them what they asked for, but sent a wasting disease among them." Psalm 106:14, 15. Perhaps our prayer should look more like the Lord's prayer. "your kingdom come, your will be done, on earth as it is in heaven." Matthew 6:10.

How we must guard against pride! It always looks for a way in. Because God answers Hezekiah's prayer, he becomes proud (2 Chronicles 32:25) but soon repents of the pride in his heart, and God delays His wrath.

Later, envoys from Babylon come to visit King Hezekiah, and he shows them all his treasures. Does this indicate his self-confidence? Is he trying to impress Babylon with his sense of power and wealth? At Isaiah's rebuke and word from the Lord, note these words from Hezekiah: "'The word of the Lord you have spoken is good,' Hezekiah replied. For he thought, 'There will be peace and security in my lifetime.'" Isaiah 39:8. Is that all he thinks about – his personal peace and security? What about those who will come after him? His great grandson, King Josiah, takes the opposite approach when the Prophetess Huldah speaks of the soon coming disaster. "Therefore I will gather you to your ancestors, and you will be buried in peace. Your eyes will not see all the disaster I am going to bring on this place." 2 Kings 22:20. Instead of sitting back and enjoying the rest of his life, he goes to work and does everything he can to bring the nation back to God. "Then the king called together all the elders of Judah and Jerusalem." 2 Kings 23:1.

The Apostle Paul cares deeply that people everywhere have an opportunity to know the truth of Jesus Christ and His sacrifice on the cross for the sins of the world. Jesus saved him, but he refuses to live comfortably and does everything humanly possible to spread the Good News – at the risk of great personal loss (2 Corinthians 11:16-33). "Are they servants of Christ? (I am out of my mind to talk like this.) I am more. I have worked much harder, been in prison more frequently, been flogged more severely, and been exposed to death again and again." 2 Corinthians 11:23.

July 23 – **Prepare the Way for the Way**

It was customary in the ancient Near East to send representatives ahead in preparation for a monarch's visit. Their mission was to remove any obstacles along the roadway, make causeways over valleys, and level hills.

"A voice of one calling: 'In the wilderness prepare the way for the Lord; make straight in the desert a highway for our God. Every valley shall be raised up, every mountain and hill made low; the rough ground shall become level, the rugged places a plain.'" Isaiah 40:3, 4. This passage has several applications. One is calling Israel's exiles back to their homeland, restoring their hope and future. Another applies to John the Baptist who heralds the coming of Jesus Christ. "And so John the Baptist appeared in the wilderness, preaching a baptism of repentance for the forgiveness of sins." Mark 1:4.

What is God saying to us? Remove the obstacles in your heart and life which are preventing you from knowing Christ. If you're depressed and bowed down with the guilt of sin, stand up and receive His comfort, for this is a valley which must be raised up. If you're prideful and haughty in your own righteousness, humble yourself today before God, for this is the mountain and hill that must be made low. If you're prejudiced against the Word and ways of God because it agrees not with your corrupt ideas and interests, submit to the wisdom of God, for this is the rough and rugged ground that must be made level.

John makes it clear that the way to prepare for the Lord's coming is through repentance. True repentance involves a radical break from sin. It involves a change of lords – from the lordship of Satan and self to the lordship of Jesus Christ and His Word. We must not only accept Him as Savior but as Lord over all of our life. Only then can we see clearly the way to the Lord. "Jesus answered, 'I am the way and the truth and the life. No one comes to the Father except through me.'" John 14:6.

July 24 – **No Other God**

Cyrus the Great and his massive army conquer Babylon in 539BC by simply walking into the city and taking over. In his life-time, Cyrus conquers many wealthy cities and nations and establishes the vast Persian Empire. He is not a believer in the God of Israel but is well known for his benevolence and toleration for the religions of local populations and allows captive peoples to return to their homelands and restore their places of worship. He dies in 530BC, and his tomb in Iran still exists today.

Through the Prophet Isaiah, God describes the foolishness of idol worship and then lowers the boom in Isaiah 44:28 and 45:1 and 13 when He declares His sovereignty by announcing the Jews' deliverance from Babylonian captivity by the hand of Cyrus (who wasn't even born until over 100 years later!). God raises up Cyrus for this task, and he will fulfill the work appointed for him, even though he doesn't actually know what he's doing or why. What an awesome God we serve!

"This is what the Lord says – Israel's King and Redeemer, the Lord Almighty: I am the first and I am the last; apart from me there is no God." Isaiah 44:6. "I am the Alpha and the Omega, the First and the Last, the Beginning and the End." Revelation 22:13.

July 25 – **Our Missionary God**

As a ship's crew at sea in the dark of night searches for the speck of light that is the lighthouse, so the Prophet Isaiah paints slivers of light that point us to the Lighthouse that is Jesus Christ. These dots of light soon become strong beacons incorporating much detail which only God could know about the coming Messiah, born 700 years later. Throughout his prophecies of captivity and restoration during this dark time in Israel's history, Isaiah speaks the Word of the Lord that sparks hope deep in the heart of God's people.

"...I will also make you a light for the Gentiles, that my salvation may reach to the ends of the earth." Isaiah 49:6. Since the Garden of Eden, God's missionary heart longs to be in relationship with the people He has created in His image. Read Psalm 67 and hear God's heart that all nations may know His salvation. It's up to us to tell them. May God's heart for the lost all over the world grow in us!

"When Jesus spoke again to the people, he said, 'I am the light of the world. Whoever follows me will never walk in darkness, but will have the light of life.'" John 8:12. He is the Light and Hope that shines in all the world. Get ready! There will be people from every nation and every language from every time period in heaven. "After this I looked, and there before me was a great multitude that no one could count, from every nation, tribe, people and language, standing before the throne and before the Lamb. They were wearing white robes and were holding palm branches in their hands." Revelation 7:9. What are you doing to reach those far from Christ?

July 26 – **Stubborn as a Mule**

So you think you have it all figured out. You want God to answer your prayer the way you want. You've thought about it a lot, and your way is definitely the best way. Hogwash! Who do you think you are – to tell God how to do His work? You remind me of that proverbial old stubborn mule sitting in the roadway, not budging. You don't listen to other people's advice, and you don't read your Bible to find out what God has to say about it. You're not listening! You're about to be run over by a freight truck, and you don't even know it!

"'For my thoughts are not your thoughts, neither are your ways my ways,' declares the Lord. 'As the heavens are higher than the earth so are my ways higher than your ways and my thoughts than your thoughts.'" Isaiah 55:8, 9. You have a decision to make. You can keep that stubborn as a mule/stick in the mud attitude, or you can submit your life to God and His Word. The choice is yours – be run over and lose everything or move in God's direction and live. Which will it be? God is God, and He is much smarter than you.

We must live life on God's terms to achieve any resemblance of peace and fulfillment. We start by repenting and submitting our will to God's will, and then we renew our minds by reading and meditating on His Word (Romans 12:2). To do otherwise is to invoke Romans 2:5 which reads: "But because of your stubbornness and your unrepentant heart, you are storing up wrath against yourself for the day of God's wrath, when his righteous judgment will be revealed."

July 27 – **Blessing Street**

I am directionally challenged. When I get behind the steering wheel in an unfamiliar city, I have been known to turn the wrong way on a one-way street only to be greeted by honking horns and irate drivers. I did not see that sign! Then I must take evasive action like driving up on curbs, backing up and turning around, praying loudly that no one plows into me, to correct the situation. Not fun!

Isaiah 58:3-7 teaches us the wrong way and the right way to fast. Jesus confirms this in Matthew 6:16-18. He knows the difference, because He knows the truth about us. Fasting is a good thing when done in the right way. We must follow God's blueprint to see His hand move in our lives.

There are one-way and two-way streets in God's Kingdom. There is only One Way to God the Father, and that is through His Son Jesus Christ. Blessing Street, for the most part, is a two-way street. Isaiah 58:8-14 talks about God's "ifs" and "thens." These are very important to God; each is mentioned five times in this short passage. We must travel the "if" side first before embarking on "then." "and if you spend yourselves in behalf of the hungry and satisfy the needs of the oppressed, then your light will rise in the darkness, and your night will become like the noonday." Isaiah 58:10. Then is only then if we do if first! Got it? God requires something from us first; it's a two-way street.

"If you remain in me and my words remain in you, ask whatever you wish, and it will be done for you." John 15:7.

July 28 – **God's Holy Mountain**

I've seen Mt. McKinley from 40 miles away, and it is magnificent. If I were to take a plane ride over the mountain, I would see quite a different view; there are many valleys and glaciers between those peaks. Isaiah chapter 65 reminds me of these mountain ranges. The prophet views several mountain tops of prophecy from a distance, but there are sometimes many years between the peaks. "...They will neither harm nor destroy on all my holy mountain." Isaiah 65:25.

I see one peak in 65:13, 14 pertaining to the here and now as well as to the believer's future home in heaven and the unbeliever's destiny in hell. Think of "servants" as believers and "you" as an unbeliever. "Therefore this is what the Sovereign Lord says: 'My servants will eat, but you will go hungry; my servants will drink, but you will go thirsty; my servants will rejoice, but you will be put to shame. My servants will sing out of the joy of their hearts, but you will cry out from anguish of heart and wail in brokenness of spirit.'" The only difference is that the reality of eternity is multiplied millions of times for those in heaven and hell.

Please re-read Isaiah 65:17-19. This is another peak of prophecy that speaks to me of heaven. I look at verses 20-25 as another peak in this mountain range, a depiction of the millennium. What an incredibly stunning description of mountain tops the prophet gives us!

I see Jesus all over this mountain! He is my Hope today and tomorrow. "while we wait for the blessed hope – the appearing of the glory of our great God and Savior, Jesus Christ," Titus 2:13.

July 29 – **Because of Him**

Are you praying for someone's salvation? Perhaps you've prayed for them a very long time and have seen nothing to indicate a change of heart or direction; in fact they seem farther from God than ever. Why is it that some people must hit rock bottom before looking up to God? Is it because there is nowhere else to look but up? Don't stop praying.

Manasseh does not follow in his father's footsteps. He is a very evil king and leads Judah into more evil than the nations around them whom God destroys (2 Kings 21:9). "The Lord spoke to Manasseh and his people, but they paid no attention."

2 Chronicles 33:10. God allows Manasseh to be taken prisoner to Babylon with a hook in his nose and bound with bronze shackles. "In his distress he sought the favor of the Lord his God and humbled himself greatly before the God of his ancestors. And when he prayed to him, the Lord was moved by his entreaty and listened to his plea; so he brought him back to Jerusalem and to his kingdom. Then Manasseh knew that the Lord is God." 2 Chronicles 33:12, 13. Salvation is not inherited; each one must encounter God's love and forgiveness personally.

Please understand this: It is not because of who Manasseh is or what he does that saves him; it is because of who God is and His great love, mercy, and grace. All attention and praise belong to our Lord and Savior. No one deserves or can earn salvation. Salvation comes from God alone, and He hears the cry of brokenness and prayer for mercy. With God, all things are possible.

"He has saved us and called us to a holy life – not because of anything we have done but because of his own purpose and grace. This grace was given us in Christ Jesus before the beginning of time," 2 Timothy 1:9.

Holy Father, I lift up this one again to you in prayer. Save, heal, restore. Thank You for Your mercy that is new every morning. Thank You that You are not willing any should perish, but that all should come to a saving knowledge of Jesus Christ. I pray this one will look up and find You. Amen.

July 30 – **Not So Different**

Jeremiah is known as the weeping prophet. Called to be a prophet from the womb, God lays some of the grief and anguish He feels with the sins of Israel and Judah upon Jeremiah. One can sense Jeremiah's deep sorrow as he delivers God's message to the people. God will soon send much suffering, death, and captivity to His people because of their rebellion, forsaking Him for false gods, and their unrepentant hearts. The prophecies rip Jeremiah's heart apart because of his love and compassion for his people as he pleads with them to turn back to God. No one listens (Jeremiah 5:1).

People today are not so different from Israel 2700 years ago. God hasn't changed His ways; He is always the same; He still judges sin, and He is always right. We can learn much about God and His dealings with man in the 21st century by reading the Bible, Old and New Testaments.

Hear what God says to us today from the book of Jeremiah. It sounds like He is describing us.

- "…They have turned their backs to me and not their faces; yet when they are in trouble, they say, 'Come and save us!'" (2:27).
- "Your own conduct and actions have brought this on you…" (4:18).
- "…They made their faces harder than stone and refused to repent." (5:3).
- "They have lied about the Lord; they said, 'He will do nothing! No harm will come to us; we will never see sword or famine.'" (5:12).

God states in Genesis 8:21 that every inclination of the human heart is evil from childhood. And Jesus says in Matthew 15:19, "For out of the heart come evil thoughts – murder, adultery, sexual immorality, theft, false testimony, slander." Only the shed blood of Jesus Christ can cleanse man's heart from sin.

July 31 – **Old Paths**

I have known people who left their homes and communities where they grew up only to return in later years. Sometimes we are invisibly drawn back to our roots as we long for simpler days gone by. And that's not always a bad thing.

"This is what the Lord says: 'Stand at the crossroads and look; ask for the ancient paths, ask where the good way is, and walk in it, and you will find rest for your souls. But you said, 'We will not walk in it.'" Jeremiah 6:16. Judah is in chaos because the people have strayed so far away from the path God gave them in the Law of Moses. As long as they follow the wrong path, they will never find rest. God calls them back to the former paths, but they refuse.

Has the church strayed from the path of the Spirit's power and righteousness? God gives us His path and pattern for the church in the New Testament. Do we pay more attention to man-made patterns for the church? Perhaps it's time to reevaluate and ask for the ancient and proven paths. God's full blessing is for those who are committed to live according to the pattern set forth in the New Testament. Following His path is the only way to find rest for our souls. "Take my yoke upon you and learn from me, for I am gentle and humble in heart, and you will find rest for your souls." Matthew 11:29.

AUGUST

August 1 – **One More**

Oskar Schindler was a wealthy German businessman who saved the lives of more than a thousand mostly Polish-Jewish refugees during the Holocaust by employing them in his factories. He spent his entire fortune, much of it in bribes, to save these people destined for slaughter and regretted he could not save "just one more." Why did he do it when millions were killed? Did he really make a difference? Ask those he saved from death if he made a difference.

King Josiah knows God's fierce wrath is about to be poured out upon Judah and Jerusalem. Yet he institutes major reforms hoping to turn as many of his people as possible back to the God of their fathers. Why does he do it when he knows many thousands will die and others exiled to Babylon? Because he cares – because he loves his people. "Neither before nor after Josiah was there a king like him who turned to the Lord as he did – with all his heart and with all his soul and with all his strength, in accordance with all the Law of Moses. Nevertheless, the Lord did not turn away from the heat of his fierce anger, which burned against Judah because of all that Manasseh had done to arouse his anger." 2 Kings 23:25, 26.

Let me remind you that you are precious to the Lord. You are so valuable to God that He sent His one and only Son to die for you. "But God demonstrates his own love for us in this: While we were still sinners, Christ died for us." Romans 5:8. You can't put a price tag on that!

The Bible teaches us that God's judgment will come on this world. What are we doing to reach one more for Christ? Someone told me about the Lord. Who have I told recently about the love of Jesus Christ? Am I as passionate about seeing people saved as King Josiah or Oskar Schindler?

Lord, help me to reach one more for You today.

August 2 – **Rejoice in the Lord – Always**

Soon after our daughter, Jamie, died, the Lord spoke to my heart early one morning while in prayer through the words of a little chorus I had learned years before: "Rejoice in the Lord always and again I say rejoice." I quickly came back with, "Are you kidding me, God? What do I have to rejoice about? My daughter is dead, and You're telling me to rejoice?" I was angry with God, and nothing in me wanted to rejoice at that moment. He kept telling me, "Rejoice anyway." So I looked it up in the Bible and found it in Philippians 4:4. "Rejoice in the Lord always. I will say it again: Rejoice!" It says always – not just in the good times when I feel like rejoicing – but always. Even on those days when I'm sad and angry, He says to rejoice. Now this is where living by faith comes into the picture; and that's another verse! "For we live by faith, not by sight." 2 Corinthians 5:7. So I remind myself of God's Word every day, and I rejoice in the Lord always, for He gives me strength.

Habakkuk learns to rejoice in the Lord with enemy invasion looming on the horizon. Even when there is little to eat and financial reserves are depleted (Habakkuk 3:16, 17), he rejoices. "yet I will rejoice in the Lord, I will be joyful in God my Savior. The Sovereign Lord is my strength; he makes my feet like the feet of a deer, he enables me to tread on the heights…" (3:18, 19). In Habakkuk's day and time and in our day and time, this life with God is purely a walk by faith. "See, the enemy is puffed up; his desires are not upright – but the righteous person will live by his faithfulness." Habakkuk 2:4. In this verse, faith and faithfulness are interchangeable.

God's Word is powerful in its working. We obey it, and it works in our lives. Live your life by faith in the living God and His Word, and not by your feelings or what you see around you. Therein lies our victory!

August 3 – **God Sings**

When our youngest daughter, Janet, was a small child, she was the songbird of the family. If she didn't know a song to fit the occasion, she would make up one on the spot! She made everyone smile with her songs. God created music both in nature and man. We worship and praise God with our music and song. But do you know that we are objects of God's great love and delight and that He sings over His children?

The Prophet Zephaniah in chapter three of his book describes Jerusalem's rebellion and redemption. At the same time, the prophet looks down through the centuries to a day of universal blessedness for the Israel of God. As children who have been redeemed by the blood of the Lamb, God has adopted us into His family. We are now joint heirs with Jesus Christ and redeemed Israel, both national and spiritual. "The Lord your God is with you, the Mighty Warrior who saves. He will take great delight in you; in his love he will no longer rebuke you, but will rejoice over you with singing." Zephaniah 3:17. What a beautiful picture this is of an amazing God Who delights in His children! Read this verse several more times for the full effect.

As you may know, there is music and song in heaven as well. "and sang the song of God's servant Moses and of the Lamb: 'Great and marvelous are your deeds, Lord God Almighty. Just and true are your ways, King of the nations. Who will not fear you, Lord, and bring glory to your name? For you alone are holy. All nations will come and worship before you, for your righteous acts have been revealed.'" Revelation 15:3, 4.

August 4 – **Don't Let This Happen to You**

"It's your own fault! You brought this on yourself! If you would only listen! You made your bed; now lay in it!" We've probably heard these words spoken to us, or we may have said them to someone else. We can really make a mess of our lives, and there is no one to blame but ourselves.

God is extremely long-suffering with His people. He warns Jerusalem so many times to repent and change their ways, but because of their disobedience, they leave Him no choice but to judge their sin and rebellion. He would much rather show mercy than deliver judgment. However, the people don't listen to Jeremiah or any of the prophets God sends.

The same words God speaks to Judah and Jerusalem through Jeremiah, He says to us today. He tells them to do what is just and right (Jeremiah 22:3). "Perhaps they will listen and each will turn from their evil ways. Then I will relent and not inflict on them the disaster I was planning because of the evil they have done." (26:3). "'But you did not listen to me,' declares the Lord, 'and you have aroused my anger with what your hands have made, and you have brought harm to yourselves.'" (25:7).

God loves us. He gives us multiple opportunities to get our lives right with Him. However, if we continue in our sin and rebellion toward God, there will come a day when He will judge our sin. "It is a dreadful thing to fall into the hands of the living God." Hebrews 10:31. Don't let this happen to you.

August 5 – **Always True – Nationally and Personally**

Just because someone does not believe God's Word or chooses to reject it does not nullify it or make it untrue. It will accomplish God's purpose (Isaiah 55:11). King Jehoiakim hears the Word of God given through Jeremiah; he then burns the scroll piece by piece (Jeremiah 36:23). Does he think for a moment that his actions annul what God has spoken?

Jeremiah pronounces God's approaching judgment on Judah as well as many other nations. His prophecies depict the immediate as well as the distant future. God's Word is fulfilled in Jeremiah's day; it will be true in our day as well. "See, I am beginning to bring disaster on the city that bears my Name, and will you indeed go unpunished? You will not go unpunished, for I am calling down a sword on all who live on the earth, declares the Lord Almighty." Jeremiah 25:29. God uses the surrounding wicked nations as His instruments of judgment on Israel. He then turns around and pronounces judgment on those nations for their pride and ungodliness. God always gives nations and individuals opportunities to repent and turn to Him. He is forever fair and just in everything He does.

What God says to a nation, He says to you and me personally. We in America are no better than the nations of Jeremiah's day. Satan has deceived us. We have swallowed his lie: "Surely God is not talking about me! Surely America is special to God, and His wrath will never come to our shores!" We better keep an eye on our pride, for all pride will bite the dust one day. God does not show favoritism (Acts 10:34). However, God is also able to protect His own, His Church, in the midst of disaster.

"And, if it is hard for the righteous to be saved, what will become of the ungodly and the sinners?" 1 Peter 4:18. God never leaves us without hope; read again Jeremiah 46:27, 28.

August 6 – **Young and Devoted**

Four little boys of noble birth grow up as best friends, playing in the streets of Jerusalem. They learn well the Law of Moses from their parents and teachers, and develop a strong love and respect for the One True God. All the while, they hear their elders discuss prophecies of Judah and Jerusalem soon to be invaded and people murdered or displaced. They wonder what their future will be, but they resolve to follow God no matter what happens. The day comes. Nebuchadnezzar, king of Babylon, besieges Jerusalem. As young men they are kidnapped from their homes and families and taken to Babylon. Do they see their families slaughtered? Scripture does not tell us.

Their devotion to the God of Israel is soon put to the test. In Babylon, the king assigns the four young men a daily amount of food and wine. The food and drink have evidently been consecrated by a heathen religious rite, and to eat it would, in Daniel's opinion, make them guilty of idol worship. "But Daniel resolved not to defile himself with the royal food and wine, and he asked the chief official for permission not to defile himself this way." Daniel 1:8. God gives Daniel and his friends favor with the chief official, and he allows the young men to eat vegetables and drink water. When the ten day trial run is complete, they look healthier and better nourished than anyone else. Daniel and his friends make the decision to stay true to God and do the right thing before the test.

The Apostle Paul gives a young Timothy good advice. "Don't let anyone look down on you because you are young, but set an example for the believers in speech, in conduct, in love, in faith and in purity. Until I come, devote yourself..." 1 Timothy 4:12, 13. The big question is: Can one be young and devoted at the same time? Absolutely! Make the decision today to be a life-long Christ-follower no matter what tomorrow brings. Make that a non-negotiable in your life, so that when the test comes (and it will come), the decision has already been made; you will do the right thing according to God's Word. An A+ for you!

August 7 – **Walking in the Fire with Jesus**

Shadrach, Meshach and Abednego – Daniel's friends – stay true to God even in the face of certain death. They made their decision a long time ago, and it still stands. Whatever God chooses to do with them, they will not deny Him under any circumstances. They refuse to jeopardize their eternity (Matthew 10:33). "But even if he does not, we want you to know, Your Majesty, that we will not serve your gods or worship the image of gold you have set up." Daniel 3:18. King Nebuchadnezzar is so furious that he orders the furnace heated seven times hotter than usual. Really? Does he think the young men are wearing flame-retardant robes? (They aren't invented yet, King Neb!) What does dissolve in the fire are the cords that bind them. Now they are free to walk about, and Who should meet them there, but the Incarnate Christ! The king is shocked! Notice he calls for only the three to come out of the furnace. He doesn't want to face the fourth One who "looks like a son of the gods" (v. 25). I can imagine that Shadrach, Meshach, and Abednego turn to the fourth Man and say, "Thanks for the nice walk, Lord. We'll see you later." They walk out, unscathed, not even a hair singed and no smell of fire on them. (Have you ever smelled burned hair?) "When you pass through the waters, I will be with you; and when you pass through the rivers, they will not sweep over you. When you walk through the fire, you will not be burned; the flames will not set you ablaze." Isaiah 43:2.

God delivers the three Hebrew young men from the fire and from King Nebuchadnezzar. Others God delivers directly into heaven! "the world was not worthy of them..." Hebrews 11:38. Read about these saints of God in Hebrews 11:32-40. Our responsibility is to keep the faith. God decides how He delivers and when, and His decisions are always just and true. The final outcome is a glorious eternity with God for all who keep the faith.

August 8 – **Playground Boasting**

Two six year old boys on the school playground: "I'm bigger than you are!" "Oh yea, I've got bigger muscles than you!" "Well, I can run faster than you!" "Well, I have chocolate chip cookies in my lunch!" "But I can whistle, and you can't!" I think at times God must look at us like children on the playground when we boast and brag to others about our achievements, our possessions, and our intelligence. The Bible tells us we have only one thing to really boast about – knowing Him. All other boasting is silliness. Our speech should direct attention to Jesus Christ and Him alone. Some of us really never grow up.

"This is what the Lord says: 'Let not the wise boast of their wisdom or the strong boast of their strength or the rich boast of their riches, but let the one who boasts boast about this: that I am the Lord, who exercises kindness, justice and righteousness on earth, for in these I delight,' declares the Lord." Jeremiah 9:23, 24. When we brag about God to others – what He means to us and what He has done in our lives – it makes God smile. Notice also from this passage that God is kind, just, and righteous – not only in heaven – but on earth. Yes, He is!

"For who makes you different from anyone else? What do you have that you did not receive? And if you did receive it, why do you boast as though you did not?" 1 Corinthians 4:7. "But, 'Let the one who boasts boast in the Lord.'" 2 Corinthians 10:17.

August 9 – **Don't Make This Your Theme Song**

"Gloom, despair, and agony on me; Deep, dark depression, excessive misery. If it weren't for bad luck, I'd have no luck at all. Gloom, despair, and agony on me." Do you remember this little song from the old TV program, Hee Haw, (1969-1997)? It makes us smile, but it pretty much describes some people. Perhaps you know someone who wears this song like a badge. Perhaps it is your own personal theme song.

Can we just get real for a minute? Yes, we live in a fallen world; and yes, bad things happen to good people. It rains on the righteous and the unrighteous (Matthew 5:45). But if you currently find yourself in a difficult situation and things aren't going well, could it be because of your sin? God says this in Jeremiah 13:22: "And if you ask yourself, 'Why has this happened to me?' – it is because of your many sins…" Maybe it's time to stop blaming others, take ownership of your sin, and confess it (get real and honest) before God. It does no good when you confess someone else's sin to God. God is waiting for you to acknowledge and repent (turn away from) your own sin. You need forgiveness today; you need a clean slate today.

None of us want to hear these words from God's mouth: "'You have rejected me,' declares the Lord. 'You keep on backsliding. So I will reach out and destroy you; I am tired of holding back.'" Jeremiah 15:6. Does God really get tired of holding back? I guess He does, or He would not say this.

We do know that the day of the Lord is coming soon (1 Thessalonians 5:1-3). "for you know very well that the day of the Lord will come like a thief in the night." 1 Thessalonians 5:2. Don't be caught off guard. Take care of any unfinished business with God today. You are not outside his range of love and forgiveness. Throw away that old theme song, and God will give you a new one! "He put a new song in my mouth, a hymn of praise to our God. Many will see and fear the Lord and put their trust in him." Psalm 40:3.

Lord, here I am, a broken sinner. I confess all my sins to you. Please forgive me. I need You in my life. I believe in You. Give me strength; make me a new person; and give me a new song. You are my Savior and my Lord. Thank You for forgiving me and saving me. I love You. In Jesus' Name. Amen.

August 10 – **It's Up to Us**

Jeremiah knocks on the door of Mr. Potter's house. Mrs. Potter comes to the door and opens it, only to see the prophet everyone is talking about. Nobody in Jerusalem likes what Jeremiah is saying these days – always disaster at every turn. Needless to say, the prophet has few friends. She just stares at him. "Is your husband home? God has given me instructions to observe him at his work." She thinks, "Well, you certainly could stand to change occupations!" "Come in. Mr. Potter is working in the back room," as she leads the way. They step into the workshop. "You have company. He says God told him to come here." Mr. Potter looks up briefly from his wheel, unable to shake hands because his are covered with wet clay, and motions with his eyes for Jeremiah to have a seat.

Mr. Potter works a few minutes with the wet clay on the spinning wheel but doesn't like how it looks, so he "smashes" it and starts over. His hands skillfully shape another vessel, one without flaw, one that will be useful. Perfect. He takes it off the wheel, puts it on the shelf to dry, and picks up another lump of clay.

Jeremiah hears God's message as he watches Mr. Potter. After all, God is an expert teacher, often using object lessons to help convey His point. "Then the word of the Lord came to me. He said, 'Can I not do with you, Israel, as this potter does?' declares the Lord. 'Like clay in the hand of the potter, so are you in my hand, Israel.'" Jeremiah 18:5. (Please read Jeremiah 18:1-10 again for this important truth that is as applicable to us today as it was in Jeremiah's day.) So much of our future is up to us!

"But who are you, a human being, to talk back to God? Shall what is formed say to the one who formed it, 'Why did you make me like this?' Does not the potter have the right to make out of the same lump of clay some pottery for special purposes and some for common use?" Romans 9:20, 21.

August 11 – **A Fire and Hammer**

What do a fire and a hammer have in common? God uses them to describe His Word. "'Is not my word like fire,' declares the Lord, 'and like a hammer that breaks a rock in pieces?'" Jeremiah 23:29.

We know that fire is used to purify precious metal, burning up the dross, and leaving pure gold or silver. It gets rid of scum, waste, and foreign matter which are mixed with the metal prior to refining. The more we read God's Word, the more it burns up the world, sin, filth, and impurities in our lives, and the more we shine like Christ. It's not fun going through the fire process, but the end result – the final product – resembles the pure and Holy Christ. We desire God to see His Son clearly in our hearts and lives, and the only way to achieve that is to spend time in His Word and allow Him to purify us. "for our God is a consuming fire." Hebrews 12:29.

"Anyone who falls on this stone will be broken to pieces; anyone on whom it falls will be crushed." Matthew 21:44. Think about this verse. When we come to Christ, the Rock, realizing our sin and need for a Savior, we are broken before Him. Only then can he pour in the Balm of Gilead (Jeremiah 8:22) and mend our broken and contrite hearts. "He heals the brokenhearted and binds up their wounds." Psalm 147:3. It is better for us to heed the first part of this verse, so God won't have to do the second part.

A hammer pounds until it breaks or crushes its objective. God will do this if that is what it takes to break our sin and pride before Him. Do you remember the statue in Nebuchadnezzar's dream in Daniel chapter two and the Rock cut out, but not by human hands, striking the statue and breaking it into pieces?

Humble yourself before God today. Give Him all your imperfections and brokenness and ask Him to do His work of purifying and healing in your life. He will.

August 12 – **It's a Wonderful Life**

George Bailey has a wonderful life and doesn't realize it. His life takes a turn he had not planned, and he finds himself giving up on life and giving in to despair. His guardian angel, Clarence, shows him how life in Bedford Falls would be if he had never been born – much worse. Family and friends pray for George, and he finds his purpose for living again. We watch this delightful movie, It's a Wonderful Life (1946), starring Jimmy Stewart during the Christmas holidays every year.

Babylon has captured Jerusalem, and many people are taken into exile to that heathen nation. As much as they did not want to believe Jeremiah's prophecies, they have come true. Now what? Life has not gone as they had planned for their families. God sends them His Word to build houses, plant gardens, marry and have children, and pray that God will bless the city in which they live (Jeremiah 29:4-9). God still has good plans for their lives, even though the plans they had for their lives seem to have vanished.

"'For I know the plans I have for you,' declares the Lord, 'plans to prosper you and not to harm you, plans to give you hope and a future. Then you will call on me and come and pray to me, and I will listen to you. You will seek me and find me when you seek me with all your heart.'" (Jeremiah 29:11-13).

Paul and Silas are preaching the Gospel of Jesus Christ and doing the work of the ministry; this is God's plan for their lives, and they love it. They understand the very real possibility of persecution and imprisonment, but it doesn't deter them. Then it happens; they are severely beaten and thrown into the inner prison, their feet in stocks. Life has suddenly turned an abrupt corner. What will they do now? "About midnight Paul and Silas were praying and singing hymns to God, and the other prisoners were listening to them." Acts 16:25.

When we leave our parents' home as young adults, we may have big and wonderful plans for our lives – higher education, good job, nice home, successful ministry, beautiful family. We know difficult things happen in life, but they happen to other people. Right? Suddenly, we find our lives going down a path we did not anticipate – a death of a loved one, a serious illness, loss of job, estrangement. This is not supposed to happen! God, where are you? "Never will I leave you; never will I forsake you." Hebrews 13:5.

God is not finished with us. He still has good plans for our lives. We don't have to look very far to see people who are walking through much harder times than we are. Our lives are not over – just going in another direction; and with God's help, we will make it! Remember, others are listening to you and watching your life while you walk this strange path. Will they hear your song of praise to God in the storm? Will they know beyond a shadow of a doubt that your faith is the real deal?

August 13 – **Never!**

One thing scientists know positively from space exploration is that space is so big, man will never find the end of it; because there is no end. We also know there are areas on our planet earth that man will never be able to fully explore because of the depth. These areas are beyond man's reach and capabilities.

God uses the world to illustrate a truth in Jeremiah 31:37. "This is what the Lord says: 'Only if the heavens above can be measured and the foundations of the earth below be searched out will I reject all the descendants of Israel because of all they have done,' declares the Lord." In other words, God says He will never reject all of Israel or Israel's seed (that's us) regardless of the sins we have committed in the past. This is true forgiveness and a love that is incomprehensible. God promises that Israel will endure forever. "But from everlasting to everlasting the Lord's love is with those who fear him, and his righteousness with their children's children – with those who keep his covenant and remember to obey his precepts." Psalm 103:17, 18.

"persecuted, but not abandoned; struck down, but not destroyed." 2 Corinthians 4:9. God will never reject or abandon us. His love for us is an everlasting love. Praise the Lord!

August 14 – **Babylon**

God uses Babylon to bring judgment on Israel for their many sins against Him. God never shall make a complete end of Israel, but He does make a complete end of Babylon. Jeremiah gives this word from the Lord approximately 100 years before its fulfillment: "The Lord will destroy Babylon; he will silence her noisy din… Babylon's thick wall will be leveled and her high gates set on fire…" Jeremiah 51:55, 58.

Just as God uses Cyrus the Great of the Medo-Persian Empire to help restore the Israelites back to their homeland after 70 years exile in Babylon, He uses Cyrus to help bring about the downfall of Babylon. Excavations of the ruins of ancient Babylon, located 53 miles south of Baghdad in modern Iraq, show the city encompassed about 2,100 acres. Nebuchadnezzar was its most famous king; he had a magnificent palace occupying an area of about 50 acres. The fortification protecting the city consisted of both outer and inner walls resulting in a total defense depth of 57 feet. Outside the outer wall was a moat, fed by the Euphrates River, ranging in width from 60 to 250 feet. The city was destroyed and the walls leveled. God always does what He says He will do. "Heaven and earth will pass away, but my words will never pass away." Luke 21:33.

In Revelation chapter 18, Babylon represents godless human culture. "…Fallen! Fallen is Babylon the Great!...Woe! Woe to you, great city, you mighty city of Babylon! In one hour your doom has come!" Revelation 18:2, 10. Babylon fell once, and it will fall again.

August 15 – **Where Are You?**

No matter where we may find ourselves in this life – in a pit up to our waist in mud with no place to go, or far from home and even farther from God – He never stops searching for us to give us hope and encouragement where there is none. We don't deserve the least of God's blessings, but He still reaches for us, to pull us up out of the pit like He does Jeremiah. "and they pulled him up with the ropes and lifted him out of the cistern…" Jeremiah 38:13. He still reveals Himself to us like He does to Ezekiel who is far from home. "And he said to me, 'Son of man, listen carefully and take to heart all the words I speak to you.'" Ezekiel 3:10.

God knows where we are physically and spiritually, and He loves us. God is everywhere. "Where can I go from your Spirit? Where can I flee from your presence? If I go up to the heavens, you are there; if I make my bed in the depths, you are there." Psalm 139:6, 7. (Read Psalm 139:6-12.)

If you want God to rescue you, first stop running away from Him and start running toward Him – not only in physical miles but spiritual miles as well. You can be many miles away from God, spiritually speaking, in the middle of a church service. You can be in a deep spiritual mud pit and no one else can see it, but you know where you are. Today is a good day to hear God's voice of hope and encouragement and be rescued. Listen. "So, as the Holy Spirit says: 'Today, if you hear his voice,'" Hebrews 3:7.

August 16 – **Stern Warning**

Ezekiel is living among the captives in Babylon. God makes him a watchman for Israel and charges him to warn the people of the dangers and consequences of sin. As a watchman commissioned by God, Ezekiel has a responsibility to deliver these messages. One stern warning and rebuke is found in Ezekiel 3:18-21 where he warns both the wicked and the righteous of continuing in sin. "Again, when a righteous person turns from their righteousness and does evil, and I put a stumbling block before them, they will die. Since you did not warn them, they will die for their sin. The righteous things that person did will not be remembered, and I will hold you accountable for their blood." Ezekiel 3:20. This is a hard truth to hear, but God's Word has much to say about sin – all sin.

"Because of the increase of wickedness, the love of most will grow cold, but the one who stands firm to the end will be saved." Matthew 24:12, 13. "Repent, then, and turn to God, so that your sins may be wiped out, that times of refreshing may come from the Lord." Acts 3:19.

August 17 – **In Order According to Plan**

"Now, son of man, take a sharp sword and use it as a barber's razor to shave your head and your beard…" Ezekiel 5:1. This is exactly why I don't recommend closing your eyes, opening your Bible at random, and putting your finger on a Scripture and declaring, "This is the word of the Lord for me today!" Your finger just might land on Ezekiel 5:1!

I must approach God's Word systematically, because God is a God of order and planning; nothing happens by chance in God's world. God had a plan and an order for creation and a plan for Israel. He has a plan for our salvation, a plan for marriage and family, and a plan on how to live life (called the Ten Commandments). He had a plan for the temple, and He is planning and preparing my home in heaven, perfect for me and made to order; it will be ready and waiting the day I step into heaven. He has a plan for the End Times and a plan to banish Satan and all evil from the earth forever.

It's good to follow a reading or study plan of the Bible to learn the full counsel of God. This helps prevent us from falling into error (one of Satan's many traps). It takes more discipline and perseverance to follow a daily plan and to read the Bible completely through, but these are great qualities we must develop in our lives. "But everything should be done in a fitting and orderly way." 1 Corinthians 14:40.

(Note: If a daily devotion on shaving off your hair with a sword is not what you're looking for, then please read December 13!)

August 18 – **A Heart Transplant**

Approximately 3500 heart transplants are performed worldwide annually with the vast majority of those taking place in the United States. A heart transplant is a surgical procedure performed on patients with end-stage heart failure. Post-operation survival periods average fifteen years.

God actually invented the first heart transplant. "I will give them an undivided heart and put a new spirit in them; I will remove from them their heart of stone and give them a heart of flesh." Ezekiel 11:19. It requires no donor, leaves no scar, and life expectancy is for all eternity!

The Israelites still residing in Jerusalem at the time of Ezekiel's prophecies believe God's power is limited to the land of Israel, but God says otherwise. He says He is a sanctuary for those scattered to other countries. He states He will bring them back to their homeland, and they will have new hearts within them. This new heart is completely fulfilled at Jesus' resurrection, and the Holy Spirit is poured out into those hearts on the Day of Pentecost. The new heart of flesh inside the believer is healthy, clean, pliable, and pumping royal blood. It is undivided and totally focused on Jesus Christ as Savior and Lord.

When God removes our hard stony heart and gives us a new undivided heart of flesh, we have a responsibility to take care of that new heart, to nourish and protect it. Even the hearts of Jesus' disciples grow hard following His resurrection. "Later Jesus appeared to the Eleven as they were eating; he rebuked them for their lack of faith and their stubborn refusal (hardness of heart in KJV) to believe those who had seen him after he had risen." Mark 16:14.

Jesus, I remember the day You gave me a new heart, but I have neglected You. My heart has grown hard. Restore my heart and fill it with Your Holy Spirit. Forgive me. Heal me. Thank You that Your life-giving blood is pumping through my veins once again.

August 19 – **Repentance and the Everlasting Covenant**

Repentance is a theme found throughout Scripture. God tells men everywhere and in every time period to repent. We cannot be right with God without true repentance. "Therefore say to the people of Israel, 'This is what the Sovereign Lord says: Repent! Turn from your idols and renounce all your detestable practices!'" Ezekiel 14:6. Both John the Baptist, the forerunner of Jesus Christ, and Jesus urge people to, "Repent, for the kingdom of heaven has come near" (Matthew 3:2 and 4:17).

"This is what the Sovereign Lord says: I will deal with you as you deserve, because you have despised my oath by breaking the covenant. Yet I will remember the covenant I made with you in the days of your youth, and I will establish an everlasting covenant with you." Ezekiel 16:59, 60. God promises the children of Israel a new covenant. Jesus' life, death, and resurrection fulfill the Old Covenant, the Law, and at the same time, usher in a new and better covenant – an everlasting covenant. "Do not think that I have come to abolish the Law of the Prophets; I have not come to abolish them but to fulfill them." Matthew 5:17. "In the same way, after the supper he took the cup, saying, 'This cup is the new covenant in my blood, which is poured out for you.'" Luke 22:20.

God still requires all people today to repent for the Kingdom of God is near. We enter the Kingdom of God through the Gate, Jesus Christ (John 10:9). When we do that, we enter into the Everlasting Covenant with God through the precious shed blood of His Son. Praise His Holy Name!

August 20 – **Sour Grapes**

"The parents eat sour grapes, and the children's teeth are set on edge" (Ezekiel 18:2). God rejects this proverb as untrue. Ezekiel's contemporaries allege that they are being punished for the sins of the previous generation – probably in reference to Exodus 20:5 – which teaches that children are affected by the sins of their parents. However, they fail to realize their own sins exceed those of their fathers. Ezekiel uses the illustration of three generations: a righteous man who continues in his righteousness (18:5-9), his son who behaves wickedly (10-13), and his grandson who renounces the evil of his father (14-17). This chapter teaches the fundamental truth that each of us is accountable to God for our own life.

"The one who sins is the one who will die. The child will not share the guilt of the parent, nor will the parent share the guilt of the child. The righteousness of the righteous will be credited to them, and the wickedness of the wicked will be charged against them." Ezekiel 18:20. Paul emphasizes this same truth in Romans 2:6-8: "God 'will repay each person according to what they have done.' To those who by persistence in doing good seek glory, honor and immortality, he will give eternal life. But for those who are self-seeking and who reject the truth and follow evil, there will be wrath and anger."

God promises salvation to anyone who will repent, turn away from their sins, and turn to God. No one is forced to follow the sins of their family. God desires everyone to come to Him. "Do I take any pleasure in the death of the wicked? declares the Sovereign Lord. Rather, am I not pleased when they turn from their ways and live? For I take no pleasure in the death of anyone, declares the Sovereign Lord. Repent and live!" Ezekiel 18:23, 32. "who wants all people to be saved and to come to a knowledge of the truth." 1 Timothy 2:4.

Likewise, a righteous person can choose to be unfaithful, rebel against God, and go back into a life of sin. Such people will die, just like the one who has always lived in sin (18:24). Paul tells believers in Romans 8:13, "For if you live according to the flesh, you will die..."

Whoever eats sour grapes, their teeth will be set on edge.

August 21 – **Reminders and Hope**

"...my laws, by which the person who obeys them will live..." Ezekiel 20:11, 13, 21. God reminds the children of Israel three times in this one chapter of the better way, which they rejected. May it also serve as a reminder to us today. Let's listen and obey the Divine Teacher, the written Word of God. "Your word is a lamp for my feet, a light on my path." Psalm 119:105.

At times it is difficult to read through certain portions of Scripture because of so much suffering caused by sin. However, God never leaves us without shining His light on the hope that we find in His Son, Jesus Christ. God tells His people through Ezekiel that despite all their idolatry, the Davidic line will continue. However, there will be no king or throne for many years in Israel. It will be reinstated only when the Messianic King comes to establish His rule. "...The crown will not be restored until he to whom it rightfully belongs shall come; to him I will give it." Ezekiel 21:27.

The first time, Jesus rode into Jerusalem on the colt of a donkey (Matthew 21:1-11); he was crucified. The next time, He will ride in on a white horse (Revelation 19:11-16). "His eyes are like blazing fire, and on his head are many crowns. He has a name written on him that no one knows but he himself." Revelation 19:12. He is King of kings and Lord of lords!

August 22 – **Gap Crossing**

There is a simple stick-man illustration (the height of my artistic ability!) of the cross of Christ creating a bridge from sinful man to God. I have drawn this picture when talking to someone about salvation, explaining there is no other way to God the Father except through the cross of His Son Jesus Christ. There is a great expanse between man and God that only the cross can bridge. Man may try other ways to God but everything else falls short and plunges man to certain eternal death. We must all go by way of the cross and faith in Jesus Christ to eternal life in Him. He is the Way to forgiveness, peace, and true joy.

God reveals to the Prophet Ezekiel that there is so much corruption among the leaders and people of Judah that He cannot find a single man who is able to lead the nation back to Him and avert His judgment. How tragic! Therefore, God's wrath and judgment will be poured out on His people in full. "I looked for someone among them who would build up the wall and stand before me in the gap on behalf of the land so I would not have to destroy it, but I found no one." Ezekiel 22:30.

God is beyond grieved for His chosen people because of their sin and rebellion. He compares the pain He feels to that of a loving husband whose wife continues a life of adultery and prostitution in spite of His love for her and constant efforts to win her back. I believe what God says to Israel and Judah, He says to America today. After all, He is the same God, and He never changes. "Therefore this is what the Sovereign Lord says: Since you have forgotten me and turned your back on me, you must bear the consequences of your lewdness and prostitution." Ezekiel 23:35.

"for they have committed adultery and blood is on their hands. They committed adultery with their idols; they even sacrificed their children, whom they bore to me, as food for them." Ezekiel 23:37. Could this verse also speak to our world today of the millions of babies we have murdered through abortion on the altars of greed and self-centeredness? It is something to think about and definitely something to pray about.

God is looking for people to stand in the gap for America today. Will He find anyone in our churches and government who will intercede for our nation? Is there anyone who can lead the way in true repentance and humble prayer for revival? Is America on the path to God's wrath and judgment?

God, in His great mercy and love, found a way to bridge the gap so that you and I can know Him and have eternal life. "Very truly I tell you, whoever hears my word and believes him who sent me has eternal life and will not be judged but has crossed over from death to life." John 5:24. Have you "crossed" over?

August 23 – **Choose**

In case you haven't noticed, the Prophets Jeremiah and Ezekiel are contemporaries; Jeremiah still lives in Jerusalem while Ezekiel lives some 600 miles away among the exiles in Babylon. Each one is delivering God's message to the people where they live. Many of their prophecies include the surrounding nations. No individual or nation escapes the watchful eye of God. He deals with each one according to their deeds. "I will punish you as your deeds deserve, declares the Lord…" Jeremiah 21:14. This word from God is still true today for individuals and nations alike.

"Furthermore, tell the people, 'This is what the Lord says: See, I am setting before you the way of life and the way of death.'" Jeremiah 21:8. God is a God of justice, and at the same time, a God of compassion and mercy. Again, He gives the people in Jerusalem a choice and a chance to live. Whoever stays in the city will die; but whoever goes out and surrenders will live; they will escape with their lives (21:9). God always would rather extend mercy; but if it is refused, He judges. When we refuse God's mercy and grace, we give Him no other choice.

"…choose for yourselves this day whom you will serve…" Joshua 24:15. We choose life when we go out from where we are and surrender to God. We leave our old way of life and surrender control of our life and our future to God. It's the only way; we must obey Him in order to live. "Therefore, 'Come out from them and be separate, says the Lord. Touch no unclean thing, and I will receive you.'" 2 Corinthians 6:17. This is really when life begins!

August 24 – **Cross My Heart!**

"Cross my heart, hope to die!" I remember saying that as a child. It meant I was telling the truth and nothing but the truth. You could count on it! And if I added, "I promise," – well, it was a done deal! The fact is kids have been quoting that since 1908 when it was first recorded.

God's Word is filled with promises – of judgment and blessing – of consequences and restoration. To date, some of His promises have already been completely fulfilled, others partially, and others await the Last Days. Rest assured; everything God says He will do – He will do – in His own time and His own way – which is the best time and the best way.

"This is what the Lord says: As I have brought all this great calamity on this people, so I will give them all the prosperity I have promised them…I will heal my people and will let them enjoy abundant peace and security. I will bring Judah and Israel back from captivity and will rebuild them as they were before." Jeremiah 32:42; 33:6, 7.

Reread Jeremiah 33:15, 16. These Scriptures have been fulfilled, partially fulfilled, and will be completely fulfilled at Jesus' second coming. "I am the Lord, the God of all mankind. Is anything too hard for me?" Jeremiah 32:27.

Everyone except God is capable of lying. "God is not human, that he should lie, not a human being, that he should change his mind. Does he speak and then not act? Does he promise and not fulfill?" Numbers 23:19. "…it is impossible for God to lie…" Hebrews 6:18. He is faithful to His promises and commitments.

All things are in God's hands. We can trust Him and His Word completely. "Heaven must receive him until the time comes for God to restore everything, as he promised long ago through his holy prophets." Acts 3:21.

August 25 – **Tyre**

The history of the ancient city of Tyre is quite interesting. Before we get into our brief history lesson for the day, here are the Scriptures I want you to think on. "I will bring you to a horrible end and you will be no more. You will be sought, but you will never again be found, declares the Sovereign Lord." Ezekiel 26:21. "But do not forget this one thing, dear friends: With the Lord a day is like a thousand years, and a thousand years are like a day. The Lord is not slow in keeping his promise, as some understand slowness…" 2 Peter 3:8, 9.

The fall of Jerusalem (586 BC) happens in the same year as Ezekiel's prophecy concerning Tyre (Ezekiel 26:1-28:19). Keep in mind that the construction of ancient cities is even more amazing when we remember they were built with sheer manpower and beasts of burden; there was no heavy machinery.

Tyre was occupied by the middle of the third millennium BC, and by the 14th century BC was already a city on an island. Located on the shore of the Mediterranean Sea, it consisted of two parts – a rocky coast defense of great strength on the mainland, and a city on a small but well-protected island, about one half mile from the shore.

The Prophets Ezekiel, Isaiah, Jeremiah, Amos, and Zechariah all talk about Tyre. King David formed an alliance with Tyre for trading purposes. King Ahab's wife, Jezebel, was from there.

Following Nebuchadnezzar's destruction of Jerusalem, he turned his attention to Tyre, laying siege against it for thirteen years (585-572 BC). He captured the mainland, but without a navy, could not defeat the island fortress. Tyre eventually came under Persian domination. Alexander the Great invaded the

Persian Empire in 332 BC. He literally pulled down the buildings on the mainland and used its stones, timber, and debris (Ezekiel 26:4, 12) to build a causeway, 200-300 yards wide and one half mile long to the island city. His victory over Tyre came following a seventeen month siege. (That causeway is an isthmus today.)

Under Greek rule, Tyre once again became an important trade city. It became a Roman province in 64 BC. People traveled from Tyre to hear Jesus (Mark 3:8), and Jesus visited Tyre (Matthew 15:21 and Mark 7:24). Following Stephen's, death, a church was formed there. The Apostle Paul spent seven days there (Acts 21:3-7).

Located in modern Lebanon, Tyre is a predominantly Shi'a Muslim city with a small but noticeable Christian community. However, the city of Tyre is home for more than 60,000 Palestinian refugees who are mainly Sunni Muslim.

August 26 – **Helpers**

We know from reading through the Bible that the Bible is not written in chronological order. And we know from reading through the Book of Jeremiah that this book is definitely not written in the order of the events as they happen. Jeremiah's faithful scribe, Baruch, is credited with putting Jeremiah's book in final form shortly after Jeremiah's death in Egypt (585-580 BC), where he is taken against his will after the final destruction of Jerusalem.

Jeremiah is known as the weeping prophet because of his expressed sadness and heartache at the devastation of the city and people he loves. His tender spirit intensifies his suffering even more. He is lonely and rejected, forbidden by God to marry and have children. Jeremiah preaches to deaf ears for forty years and reaps only hate from his fellow countrymen, yet he is one of the boldest and bravest prophets in the Bible.

Do you remember the promise God makes to Baruch that he will escape the destruction with his life (Jeremiah 45:1-5)? God also makes a promise to Ebed-Melek, the Ethiopian eunuch, who saves Jeremiah's life from the pit (Jeremiah 38:7-13). "But I will rescue you on that day, declares the Lord; you will not be given into the hands of those you fear. I will save you; you will not fall by the sword but will escape with your life, because you trust in me, declares the Lord." Jeremiah 39:17, 18.

Not everyone is called to be a prophet, pastor, or teacher. But God does call people to help support those who are; and He notices and rewards those who do so faithfully. Aaron and Hur stand beside Moses and help him hold up his arms so the children of Israel can defeat the Amalekites (Exodus 17:12). Many women travel with Jesus and His disciples ministering to them, so they can better do what God called them to do. "After this, Jesus traveled about from one town and village to another, proclaiming the good news of the kingdom of God. The Twelve were with him, and also some women...These women were helping to support them out of their own means." Luke 8:1-3. Are you aware that "helping" is one of the gifts God gives to His Church (1 Corinthians 12:28)? Are you called to be a helper?

August 27 – **Tomorrow**

Jamie was in first grade in 1982 when the Annie movie came out. Jamie and Janet both loved Annie – the little orphan girl, although living a difficult life, could always find something to celebrate. She was an eternal optimist and believed tomorrow would be a better day. Our girls sang her song for the longest time, and Jamie loved wearing her red Annie dress with the white collar.

Lamentations, written by the Prophet Jeremiah, is exactly that – expressions of grief and sorrow. But in the middle of those five chapters is chapter three and some very encouraging words. Jeremiah remembers (3:21) and looks for the good in the middle of the bad. When we open our eyes in the middle of our storms and struggles, we will see hope and the goodness of God as well. So go back and read again Lamentations 3:21-40. "Because of the Lord's great love we are not consumed, for his compassions never fail. They are new every morning; great is your faithfulness." (vs. 22, 23). Jesus has compassion on people everywhere He goes. "When he saw the crowds, he had compassion on them, because they were harassed and helpless, like sheep without a shepherd." Matthew 9:36.

God gives us a new day every 24 hours; it's a chance to start over! His compassions and faithfulness are new every morning; His supplies are never exhausted! Praise God for that! So whatever you're going through at this moment, things will get better with God. He inserts His love, compassions, faithfulness, and hope right in the middle of it all. Look for Him! Today is yesterday's tomorrow!

August 28 – **Will the Violence Ever End?**

As I read through the Bible, I ask, "Will the killing, hatred, and violence ever end?" I ask myself that same question as I watch the evening news or read the headline stories on the internet. I could allow myself to get fearful, anxious, overcome with worry and dread, or I can look up and know that my redemption is drawing near (Luke 21:28). I won't find the answer to my question in today's news reports, but I do find it in God's Word. Each day brings me one day closer to seeing Jesus!

"The day of the Lord is near for all nations. As you have done, it will be done to you; your deeds will return upon your own head." Obadiah 1:15. What is in store for the United States of America in God's plan? Will He remember the good this nation has done for over 200 years in sending out missionaries around the world to proclaim His Good News? Will He remember our friendship to Israel and our aid to nations struggling with the ravages of natural disasters and wars over the years? Yes, there is so much wrong and evil in America today, but there also lives within its shores a people (His true Church) who love God and serve Him with all their hearts and lives. One thing we know for sure: God is a God of justice and mercy, and He always does the right thing. Our lives are in His hands. Our responsibility is to stay faithful to Him and help others know Him in any way we can.

Will we ever experience peace in our world? Only when the Prince of Peace comes and establishes His Kingdom in the earth! "And this gospel of the kingdom will be preached in the whole world as a testimony to all nations, and then the end will come." Matthew 24:14.

Thankfully, each of us can know His peace when He lives within our hearts as Savior and Lord. Such a sweet foretaste of heaven to come! We can also experience community with other believers in His Church, the Bride of Christ. We must find our place within a local Bible-believing, Holy Spirit-filled church, serve God by serving others, learn and grow in Christ daily, and point others to Jesus. We don't have to be filled with fear and trepidation; we can have His peace as we walk this earth, and then spend an eternity in peace and glory with Him in heaven. Hope can only be found in Jesus Christ. So, the answer to my question is YES!

August 29 – **Don't Just Talk the Talk, but...**

The remnant left in Jerusalem following its destruction by King Nebuchadnezzar and his Babylonian army come to the Prophet Jeremiah. "Then they said to Jeremiah, 'May the Lord be a true and faithful witness against us if we do not act in accordance with everything the Lord your God sends you to tell us. Whether it is favorable or unfavorable, we will obey the Lord our God, to whom we are sending you, so that it will go well with us, for we will obey the Lord our God.'" Jeremiah 42:5, 6. The people can really talk the talk, but will they walk the walk now? Ten days later, God speaks to Jeremiah. The people do not agree with God's message. "…You are lying! The Lord our God has not sent you to say, 'You must not go to Egypt to settle there.'" Jeremiah 43:2. So everyone travels to Egypt, disobeying God again; and they force Jeremiah to go with them. Soon they will endure another Babylonian invasion, this time in Egypt. Most will die in Egypt; only a few fugitives will return to Judah (Jeremiah 44:14).

Meanwhile, back in Babylon, the Prophet Ezekiel has a hard time with the Jewish exiles. God says this to him: "My people come to you, as they usually do, and sit before you to hear your words, but they do not put them into practice. Their mouths speak of love, but their hearts are greedy for unjust gain." Ezekiel 33:31.

Are we all talk and no walk? Do we walk what we talk? God is pleased when no discrepancy exists between my heart and my talk and my walk; and He knows when there is a disconnect. We must talk and walk to honor God; both are important to Him. "Do not let any unwholesome talk come out of your mouths…" Ephesians 4:29. "And this is love: that we walk in obedience to his commands…" 2 John 1:6.

August 30 – **Know That I Am the Lord**

Do you hear the theme running through the Book of Ezekiel? "Then you/they will know that I am the Lord." Ezekiel 35:9, 15; 36:11, 38. We read those exact words 26 times in Ezekiel. God wants us to know Him, really know Him, and His great love for us. God has been very tough on Israel, because He loves His kids!

Now He's coming down hard on the shepherds (church leaders) over His flock (Ezekiel 34:1-10), because they are not doing what is right in God's eyes. God would rather us know Him through His loving kindness instead of His judgment, but He gives us what our actions deserve.

God makes it clear to Israel that He will again bless Israel and restore the remnant scattered among the nations to their homeland, and He will do it for the sake of His Holy Name (Ezekiel 26:22, 23). He will once again bless His chosen people. But more than anything else, He wants them to know Him. Such blessings await them – showers of blessing (34:26) – such as favor, cleansing, a new heart and a new spirit, and fruitfulness everywhere!

"If you really know me, you will know my Father as well. From now on, you do know him and have seen him." John 14:7. Jesus Christ wants you to know Him today; in knowing Him, you will know the Father. Take time and get to know the One Who loves you so much that He gave His life for you. Know Him better and love Him more each day. He loves you more than you can possibly imagine.

August 31 – **God's Breath**

I have been to Xian, China and have seen the famous Terracotta Warriors, a remarkable sight. They were discovered by local farmers digging a water well in 1974. China's first emperor, Qin Shi Huang, in the third century BC, created this army of 8,000 life-size warriors, each one different from the other, 130 chariots, 529 horses, 150 cavalry horses, and many kinds of weapons. His plan was for this army to protect him in the afterlife. They were all buried with him in his mountain tomb in 210-209 BC.

God gives Ezekiel a vision of a valley full of dry bones. "He asked me, 'Son of man, can these bones live?' I said, 'Sovereign Lord, you alone know.'" Ezekiel 37:3. God causes the bones to come together; tendons and flesh appear and skin covers them; but they are lifeless without breath. "So I prophesied as he commanded me, and breath entered them; they came to life and stood up on their feet – a vast army." (v. 10). God goes on to say that these bones are the people of Israel. "I will put my Spirit in you and you will live, and I will settle you in your own land. Then you will know that I the Lord have spoken, and I have done it, declares the Lord." (v. 14).

The valley of dry bones is a picture of the nation of Israel living again, so that Israel and the nations of the earth will know that He is the Lord. (In reality, everything God does is so that people and nations will know He is the One True God!) It is also a picture of each of us who are dead in our sins before we meet Jesus Christ. But He comes in and gives us new life. "And with that he breathed on them and said, 'Receive the Holy Spirit.'" John 20:22. I thank God that He breathed on me one day and gave me new life, filling me with His Holy Spirit!

The Terracotta Warriors have never lived and never will live. I'm afraid they weren't much help to Qin Shi Huang in his afterlife!

SEPTEMBER

September 1 – **Current or Convenient**

Have you seen the commercial of the man who finds a note that reads: Tonight you will have your heart attack? Sorry, but life doesn't happen that way. None of us knows what each day will bring. We don't know when our heart will beat for the last time. God calls the man a fool in Luke 12:20 who is making all these big plans for his life without regard for his soul. This doesn't mean we should live in fear; it means we can have peace that comes with knowing Jesus Christ as our Savior and Lord; and should we die or should He return for His Church today, we are ready to meet Him! Our sins are washed away! That's security and confidence and peace, precious commodities in today's world.

We hear God saying it again in Ezekiel 33:1-20; it is one of His repeated calls to man – Keep it current! "Since they heard the sound of the trumpet but did not heed the warning, their blood will be on their own head. If they had heeded the warning, they would have saved themselves. Say to them, 'As surely as I live, declares the Sovereign Lord, I take no pleasure in the death of the wicked, but rather that they turn from their ways and live. Turn! Turn from your evil ways! Why will you die, people of Israel?'" Ezekiel 33:5, 11. God wants more than anything to extend His mercy and saving grace; but we must turn away from sin and turn to Him, and receive this gift from His hand.

Paul is brought before Felix, governor of Caesarea, and given the opportunity to state his case (Acts 24:1-27). Felix is well acquainted with the Way. Also his wife, Drusilla, who is Jewish, has probably talked to Felix concerning the God of her ancestors. "As Paul talked about righteousness, self-control and the judgment to come, Felix was afraid and said, 'That's enough for now! You may leave. When I find it convenient, I will send for you.'" (Acts24:25). Scripture does not record if Felix ever found that "convenient" time.

Do you have sin in your life today? Don't put it off any longer. Repent; get your life right with God. Keep your relationship with God current. Right now is a convenient time.

September 2 – **Good Journalism**

I remember an English class in my high school (many years ago!) that stressed the importance of answering these questions when writing an article: Who? Where? What? When? Why? How? Let's apply these questions to an easily over-looked passage of Scripture in today's text. "They were helped in fighting them, and God delivered the Hagrites and all their allies into their hands, because they cried out to him during the battle. He answered their prayers, because they trusted in him." 1 Chronicles 5:20. What are the facts?

- Who? Verse 18 tells us that "they" are the Reubenites, the Gadites and the half-tribe of Manasseh. "He" is obviously God.
- Where? They are on the battlefield.
- What? "...because they cried out to him..."
- When? "...during the battle..."
- What? "...He answered their prayers..."
- Why? "...because they trusted in him."

- How? "…and God handed the Hagrites and all their allies into their hands…" No other details are given or needed. God just does the work; that's all we need to know.

Is there any significance in this passage for us today? Always. The facts are we must know who we are in Christ Jesus, Who is God, and who is our enemy. In this life, there is always a battlefield. When we cry out to God for help in the midst of battle, He hears and answers our prayers, because we trust in Him. How will He do it? However He sees fit; that's His decision. "Some trust in chariots and some in horses, but we trust in the name of the Lord our God." Psalm 20:7. "May the God of hope fill you with all joy and peace as you trust in him, so that you may overflow with hope by the power of the Holy Spirit." Romans 15:13. Find the Who, What, When, What, and How in that verse!

September 3 – **Two Kings**

King Nebuchadnezzar is notably the greatest king who ever rules the ancient kingdom of Babylon. This heathen king reigns for 43 years (604-562 BC), and he worships false gods, particularly Bel-Marduk whose temple he builds and adorns. Daniel chapter four describes the dream King Nebuchadnezzar has and the interpretation by Daniel. The dream comes true, and the king is insane for seven years (582-575 BC) and is kicked out of his kingdom to live with the beasts of the field – all because of his pride (vs. 28-32). God teaches King Neb a valuable lesson. "At the end of that time, I, Nebuchadnezzar, raised my eyes toward heaven, and my sanity was restored…Now I, Nebuchadnezzar, praise and exalt and glorify the King of heaven, because everything he does is right and all his ways are just. And those who walk in pride he is able to humble." (vs. 34, 37). Notice that this evil king, whom God has used as an instrument of His wrath and judgment upon Judah and surrounding nations, looks up to the God of heaven, and God restores him to his throne.

"Pride goes before destruction, a haughty spirit before a fall." Proverbs 16:18. This proves true in Nebuchadnezzar's life, and it is true for all of us. What God says for one, He says for all. "But he gives us more grace. That is why Scripture says: 'God opposes the proud but shows favor to the humble.'" James 4:6. How much better it is – and safer – to walk humbly with God as He requires (Micah 6:8)!

Here's another thought to mull over. We know King Nebuchadnezzar acknowledges God, and King Solomon forsakes God – both of them later in life. Who do you think we will see in heaven? I guess we will have to wait to find out for sure. I've heard it said that God's Kingdom is somewhat of an "upside down" kingdom. "So the last will be first, and the first will be last." Matthew 20:16. No doubt there will be surprises in heaven. God makes these calls, because only He really knows the state of a man's soul when he dies; He is the righteous judge. I think we can all agree with King Neb when he says about God, "everything he does is right and all his ways are just."

September 4 – **Zadok**

God gives Ezekiel another vision (chapters 40-43) in which He describes the future temple in detail (God is a God of the details!). Whether the temple is symbolic or literal, God emphasizes His presence and glory will be restored to His people forever.

"...These are the sons of Zadok, who are the only Levites who may draw near to the Lord to minister before him." Ezekiel 40:46. "But the Levitical priests, who are descendants of Zadok and who guarded my sanctuary when the Israelites went astray from me, are to come near to minister before me..." Ezekiel 44:15. Zadok's name means "just and righteous," and he lives up to his name. Zadok, the priest, first joins up with King David early in his reign in Hebron. Like Benaiah, David's bodyguard who becomes his Commander in Chief, and the Prophet Nathan, Zadok is unwavering in his loyalty to King David. Through the years, when other Levites abandon God's ways, Zadok and his family remain faithful. As an older man, he anoints Solomon as King and is the first High Priest in Solomon's temple.

Zadok and his descendants are granted the privilege of ministering before the Lord in the future temple. This honor bestowed on Zadok reveals to us that our faithfulness to God during our earthly lives determines our place in God's eternal Kingdom. God's Word teaches a future judgment of believers when we will give an account, and rewards will be given (2 Corinthians 5:10 and Ephesians 6:8).

"God is not unjust; he will not forget your work and the love you have shown him as you have helped his people and continue to help them." Hebrews 6:10.

September 5 – **Spiritual Receptivity**

Here's what I know about antennas: 1) Ants have them; 2) My Favorite Martian (1963-1966) had them; and 3) The TV antenna on top of my house when I was a kid had to be pointed in the right direction for our family to get good reception, so we could watch My Favorite Martian.

"The Lord said to me, 'Son of man, look carefully, listen closely and give attention to everything I tell you..." Ezekiel 44:5. In other words, God tells Ezekiel to adjust his antenna and be spiritually receptive. Why? So he doesn't miss anything God wants to teach him, and so that he can instruct others. "They are to teach my people the difference between the holy and the common and show them how to distinguish between the unclean and the clean." (v. 23).

How is your spiritual receptivity? Are you learning more about God, His ways, and His will for your life every day? He wants to teach you, but you must be receptive to Him. Are you looking carefully into His Word, listening closely to the Holy Spirit, and giving Him your attention daily?

"Now the Berean Jews were of more noble character than those in Thessalonica, for they received the message with great eagerness and examined the Scriptures every day to see if what Paul said was true." Acts 17:11. May we be like the Bereans and be eager to learn and search God's Word for ourselves! Our Jesus journey begins when we, like Martha, invite Him into our heart's home. "As Jesus and his disciples were on their way, he came to a village where a woman named Martha opened her home to him." Luke 10:38.

September 6 – **River of Life**

What an incredible vision of the river of life Ezekiel receives! You must read Ezekiel 47:1-12 again! Now turn to Revelation 22:1, 2 and read John's description of his vision. Approximately 650 years separate the two visions. Everyone who goes to heaven will see and enjoy this beautiful river.

Let's look more closely at Ezekiel's vision. The angel taking Ezekiel on this grand tour actually leads him into the water. This is a big river! Ezekiel walks through ankle-deep water for 1700 feet. He keeps walking another 1700 feet in knee-deep water. He stays in there and keeps walking (I wonder if Ezekiel can swim!) another 1700 feet up to his waist. He moves a little closer to the angel for the next 1700 feet because now the water is deep enough in which to swim! "He asked me, 'Son of man, do you see this?' Then he led me back to the bank of the river." Ezekiel 47:6. Back on shore, Ezekiel looks around and sees the luscious fruit trees. He observes that this river enters the Dead Sea, and the sea comes to life with large numbers of fish of every kind, and he sees fishermen fishing. (Do you think we will be able to fish in heaven? I love it!) "...so where the river flows everything will live." (v. 9).

Jesus talks about rivers of living water in John 7:37-39. "...Let anyone who is thirsty come to me and drink. Whoever believes in me, as Scripture has said, rivers of living water will flow from within them. By this he meant the Spirit, whom those who believed in him were later to receive." Jesus may be referring to Isaiah 58:11 and Joel 2:28.

So where this Holy Spirit river of living waters flows, everything lives! How much of Jesus and His Holy Spirit do you want? Just enough to get your big toe wet? You must not be very thirsty. I want more than my big toe to experience life! I want to swim in His river of life! Dive in! His living water is just right!

September 7 – **The King and I**

Daniel doesn't know the name of the One he sees in his vision, but you and I know Him as Jesus Christ. "He was given authority, glory and sovereign power; all nations and peoples of every language worshiped him. His dominion is an everlasting dominion that will not pass away, and his kingdom is one that will never be destroyed." Daniel 7:14.

The Apostle Paul knows His Name and knows Him personally. "Therefore God exalted him to the highest place and gave him the name that is above every name, that at the name of Jesus every knee should bow, in heaven and on earth and under the earth, and every tongue acknowledge that Jesus Christ is Lord, to the glory of God the Father." Philippians 2:9-11.

You and I and every person who has ever been conceived will bow before Jesus Christ, the Son of the Living God – King of kings and Lord of lords. God does not give us a choice in the matter. We do get to choose, however, when we do so – today or in eternity. Why not both? Of my own free will, I choose Christ as my King and submit my life to Him. I humbly bow before Him daily – physically and with my heart. He alone is worthy of my devotion and worship. He shares His position and glory with no other. Those who never bow before Him on earth will acknowledge Him in eternity on their way to hell. He is forever King over my life, and I am not.

September 8 – **Sufficient Evidence**

Enough evidence has been presented to find the defendant guilty; the jury is convinced and presents their verdict. "Guilty as charged!" And the judge slams the gavel down! (I love Matlock!)

Daniel serves God faithfully throughout his long life while exiled in Babylon. He is also a faithful and diligent worker in the king's court; his life is above reproach. Because of jealousy, his co-workers attempt to find grounds for charges against him in his conduct of government affairs. "...They could find no corruption in him, because he was trustworthy and neither corrupt nor negligent. Finally, these men said, 'We will never find any basis for charges against this man Daniel unless it has something to do with the law of his God.'" Daniel 6:4, 5. Side Note: Wouldn't it be nice if this could be said about some of our government officials?

Daniel's colleagues persuade the king to sign into law, "that anyone who prays to any god or human being during the next thirty days, except to you, Your Majesty, shall be thrown into the lions' den." (v. 7). Daniel hears about the decree, but he continues to do what he does every day. "...Three times a day he got down on his knees and prayed, giving thanks to his God, just as he had done before." (v. 10). Got Him! The spies report to the king, and Daniel ends up in the lions' den. Long story short: God sends His angel to "lullaby" to sleep the lions, and Daniel is safe. The angel is nowhere around, however, when Daniel's accusers are thrown to the lions. Well, you know the outcome – not a pretty sight.

Peter and John find themselves in trouble with the Sanhedrin (the supreme Jewish court of justice of the day). "Then they called them in again and commanded them not to speak or teach at all in the name of Jesus. But Peter and John replied, 'Which is right in God's eyes: to listen to you, or to him? You be the judges! As for us, we cannot help speaking about what we have seen and heard.'" Acts 4:18-20.

The evidence is stacked against Daniel, Peter and John. They are all guilty of loving God, serving Him, obeying Him, and staying faithful to Him no matter the cost. What about you? Is there sufficient evidence to convict you of being a Christian?

September 9 – **Are You Experiencing Opposition?**

The exiles, after seventy years in Babylon, have returned to Jerusalem at King Cyrus' command (and God's plan) and are busy rebuilding the temple. The enemies of Judah and Benjamin, however, endeavor to oppose the work of God through discouragement, fear, and frustration (three of the most effective weapons in Satan's arsenal). "Then the peoples around them set out to discourage the people of Judah and make them afraid to go on building. They bribed officials to work against them and frustrate their plans…" Ezra 4:4, 5.

Jesus says, "…I will build my church, and the gates of Hades will not overcome it." Matthew 16:18. If you are a born again believer in Jesus Christ, you are a member of His Church. As members, He calls us to come alongside Him and build His Church in all nations (Matthew 28:19). Just as Satan opposed the building of the temple, he opposes the expansion of the Church of Jesus Christ around the world today.

Hear what Jesus says about the prince of demons in Mark 3:26: "And if Satan opposes himself and is divided, he cannot stand; his end has come." To oppose something is to be against it, to disapprove, to stop it. One sure way we know we're doing the will of God is by the opposition against us. Satan doesn't oppose himself; if he does, he destroys his own work. He opposes God and God's children and the growth of God's Kingdom on earth. If you aren't experiencing any opposition as you "do the work of the ministry," it's probably time to take inventory.

Know what God has called you to do, and do it with all your might. Expect opposition. Expect discouragement, fear, and frustration (to name a few). But also remember that greater is He Who is within you than he who is in the world (1 John 4:4). God's work will go forward with or without you. We are not doing God a favor by serving Him. He gives us the honor and privilege to work in His Church; He is blessing us. Doing God's work will never be easy; there will always be opposition. It's one way we know we're on the right track. "Therefore encourage one another and build each other up, just as in fact you are doing." 1 Thessalonians 5:11.

September 10 – **Are You Shiny?**

I have a few pieces of silver in my kitchen. Over time, my little coffeepot and creamer will tarnish and become dull. I must apply a little elbow grease (to me) and silver polish (to them) and work hard to regain that "see my face in the reflection" shine. I also have to take the time to do it. They won't shine themselves!

"Those who are wise will shine like the brightness of the heavens, and those who lead many to righteousness, like the stars for ever and ever." Daniel 12:3. (I wonder if Daniel speaks from personal experience. Has he lead people to God in Babylon?) Think about it. Daniel knows the words of Solomon in Proverbs

11:30: "...and the one who is wise saves lives." Daniel separates these two thoughts and then brings them back together again. The wise and those who lead many to righteousness shine brightly – forever. Is it their crowns or a radiant glow surrounding them – or both? So, if you're wise, you will lead many to Jesus Christ; and if you are a soul-winner, you are wise. You'll be so bright and shiny, that people will have to squint to see you!

How are you doing in the "evangelism/witnessing" department? It all begins with Jesus. "'Come, follow me,' Jesus said, 'and I will send you out to fish for people.'" Matthew 4:19. I must be an active follower of Jesus Christ. Others should see and hear Him in me. It will take my time and effort to win the lost. It will take prayer and being sensitive and obedient to the Holy Spirit. But when God uses me to help someone know Him as their personal Savior and Lord, God says I'm wise – and shiny – forever.

September 11 – **The Apple of His Eye**

"...for whoever touches you touches the apple of his eye." Zechariah 2:8. This is a common expression to us, first found in five different Scriptures in the Bible. In four of those five places, it can literally be translated as "little man of the eye." This is in reference to the tiny reflection of yourself that you can see in other people's pupils. If someone were to touch the apple of your eye, it would be very painful, and so it is protected by the eyelid. The Biblical imagery is that we are the apple of God's eye, and He protects us with His eyelids. The phrase refers to something or someone that one cherishes above all others, someone of great worth. We are precious to the Lord!

King David prays for protection from his enemies in Psalm 17:8: "Keep me as the apple of your eye; hide me in the shadow of your wings." This is how God sees His chosen ones; and this is how we should see God and His Word as He says in Proverbs 7:2:

"Keep my commands and you will live; guard my teachings as the apple of your eye." Do we do that? Does the Lord know how much we love Him and His precious Word? Do we protect and nourish our relationship with Him and time spent in His Word?

"Greater love has no one than this: to lay down one's life for one's friends." John 15:13. That's how much God loves us. Here's one final reflection for married couples: Do you cherish and protect your love for each other? "Husbands, love your wives, just as Christ loved the church and gave himself up for her." Ephesians 5:25. Be the apple in each other's eyes.

September 12 – **The New is Here!**

The children of Israel have lived far from God for so many years and have suffered greatly for their apostasy and rebellion. Yet, when they finally obey God and return to Him and their homeland and begin to rebuild their lives that the enemy has ripped apart, they begin to experience the blessings of the Lord. "Just as you, Judah and Israel, have been a curse among the nations, so I will save you, and you will be a blessing. Do not be afraid, but let your hands be strong." Zechariah 8:13. God says He will save them; and let me remind you it is not because of their righteousness, but because of God's great mercy and love for His people. God will not only bless His people, but He will make them a blessing to other nations. He goes on to encourage them to not be afraid but to be strong and do the work He has given them to do.

God says this to Israel, but He says it to you today as well. Put your name in that verse. "Just as you, ____________, have been..."

All is not lost! It is not hopeless! When you return to Him, He will receive you. He will take the curse off your life, save you, and make you a blessing. How wonderful is that! So don't be afraid, but be strong in the Lord. "Therefore, if anyone is in Christ, the new creation has come: The old has gone, the new is here! All this is from God..." 2 Corinthians 5:17, 18. He always gives back to us so much more than we deserve. Praise His Holy Name!

September 13 – **That Precious Fountain**

"There is a fountain filled with blood, Drawn from Immanuel's veins; And sinners, plunged beneath that flood, Lose all their guilty stains." (William Cowper, 1731-1800). This old hymn of the church speaks of a fountain; so does the Prophet Zechariah.

Zechariah says some very interesting things in his book. A few of his prophecies are very precise and point directly to Jesus Christ (550 years before the fact):

- The king riding into Jerusalem on a donkey (Zechariah 9:9)
- The thirty pieces of silver paid to Judas Iscariot for betraying Jesus (Zechariah 11:13)
- The piercing of Jesus on the cross (Zechariah 12:10)

"On that day a fountain will be opened to the house of David and the inhabitants of Jerusalem to cleanse them from sin and impurity." Zechariah 13:1. That day is the day Jesus dies on the cross. That fountain is His blood which has the power to cleanse all sin and impurity in everyone, from royalty to common folk. "But if we walk in the light, as he is in the light, we have fellowship with one another, and the blood of Jesus, His Son, purifies us from all sin." 1 John 1:7.

"Instead, one of the soldiers pierced Jesus' side with a spear, bringing a sudden flow of blood and water." John 19:34. Blood is needed for atonement (reconciliation of man with God), as the countless sacrifices of the Old Testament indicate. The Spirit is required for sanctification (to free from sin; set apart), as the many washings of the law show. Both issue from the same fountain.

When Jesus Christ died, he opened that fountain and made it available to all mankind – you and I included. Have you stepped into that precious and holy fountain?

September 14 – **History Makers**

God controls history as is evident in the Book of Esther, even though "God" is never mentioned. Esther is a young Jewish girl raised by her cousin, Mordecai, after her parents die. Their families were among those taken captive to Babylon during the reign of Nebuchadnezzar. Many thousands of Jewish people still live in exile at this time. King Xerxes rules Persia (modern Iran). Queen Vashti upsets the King, and at the advice of his experts, he deposes her from her royal position. After a few years, he begins to miss Vashti, so his personal attendants propose a plan to find a new queen. They know if Vashti regains her position, she will recommend their deaths.

Many beautiful virgins are gathered from around the kingdom and brought in before the king so he can select his new queen. Esther wins! Mordecai lives near the palace and keeps close tabs on everything concerning Esther. He instructs her to never reveal her Jewish heritage.

It just so happens (actually God directs this incident as well) that Mordecai overhears a plot to assassinate the king (Esther 2:21-23). He reports it to Esther who takes care of the situation.

Meanwhile, Haman, King Xerxes' right hand man, begins to have issues with personal pride. The king has commanded everyone to kneel down and pay Haman honor whenever he walks by, and everyone does, except Mordecai. This infuriates Haman! So he devises a plan to exterminate, not only Mordecai, but every Jew in the king's jurisdiction.

Mordecai and Esther are just ordinary people whom God uses to accomplish a big task. "For if you remain silent at this time, relief and deliverance for the Jews will arise from another place, but you and your father's family will perish. And who knows but that you have come to your royal position for such a time as this?" Esther 4:14.

God orchestrates when and where and to whom we are born in this world, because He also controls our history. We're ordinary people, but He has something for us to do that matters. If we don't do what He wants us to do, He will find someone else to carry out His plans. Jesus takes a little boy (we don't even know his name) and uses his lunch that his mother packed for him to feed a great crowd of people. "Here is a boy with five small barley loaves and two small fish, but how far will they go among so many?" John 6:9. He is in the right place at the right time and is willing to give it all to Jesus. If he had chosen to run away and keep his lunch to himself, Jesus would have found another way to feed the people. Is God arranging events in your life to make history?

September 15 – **Backfire!**

When you hear the word backfire, you may think of a car that backfires. I think of a gun that may fire in the opposite direction due to an obstruction in the barrel, which could be deadly. When something backfires on you, the effect is opposite to the one intended. Haman experiences backfire.

"Haman boasted to them about his vast wealth, his many sons, and all the ways the king had honored him and how he had elevated him above the other nobles and officials." Esther 5:11. Haman is deceived by his own pride and self-worth, and it becomes his downfall.

The king can't sleep one night, so he orders someone to read him a bedtime story (actually the book contains the record of his reign), and he realizes that nothing was ever done for Mordecai for saving the king's life. The next morning, Haman appears with the intention to ask for Mordecai's execution. Instead... "'Go at once,' the king commanded Haman. 'Get the robe and the horse, and do just as you have suggested for Mordecai the Jew, who sits at the king's gate. Do not neglect anything you have recommended.'" Esther 6:10. Backfire! (I wish I could have been a fly on the wall just to see Haman's expression!)

Haman begins to realize the truth of his situation. His family and friends begin to see the truth. Others realize the truth (7:9). "For whatever is hidden is meant to be disclosed, and whatever is concealed is meant to be brought out into the open." Mark 4:22.

"But when the plot came to the king's attention, he issued written orders that the evil scheme Haman had devised against the Jews should come back onto his own head, and that he and his sons should be impaled on poles." Esther 9:25. Backfire again!

Pride never ends well. It always backfires on the one who has it. "The Lord detests all the proud of heart. Be sure of this: They will not go unpunished." Proverbs 16:5.

September 16 – **True Devotion**

Ezra, the priest, leads the second expedition of Jews back from Babylonian exile into Palestine. "For Ezra had devoted himself to the study and observance of the Law of the Lord, and to teaching its decrees and laws in Israel." Ezra 7:10. This one statement about Ezra tells us much about this godly man. I believe God wants many Ezras today. Are you called to be an Ezra?

Ezra's life is one of devotion to God, but he doesn't stop there. He is devoted to studying God's Word. Not only that; he does what it says. "Do not merely listen to the word, and so deceive yourselves. Do what it says." James 1:22. Also, he teaches others to do the same. Are you getting the picture of what Ezra's devotion looks like? Devotion = Study, Observe (put into practice) and Teach.

To study God's Word takes time. You gotta love it! If your love for God's Word is lacking, pray about it. Carve out time in your day to read, study, pray, and meditate on God's Word, and then protect that time and don't allow the enemy to steal it from you. Read John 5:39.

Observe it. Live it. Make it your identity. Read Psalm 119:34.

Once you're devoted, and you're a student of God's Word, and you're a doer of God's Word – then what? You can't keep it all to yourself. Teach it to others. Talk about what God is teaching you to someone else; it may be just what they need to hear. If God has called you to teach, then find your place in His Church and teach others. The Church needs you.

Is God calling you to be an Ezra? Start today. I believe this verse can apply here: "I am saying this for your own good, not to restrict you, but that you may live in a right way in undivided devotion to the Lord." 1 Corinthians 7:35.

September 17 – **Confession and Intercession**

"I didn't do it! She did!" Children are quick to put the blame where it belongs, and sometimes where it doesn't. It's easy to carry this same tendency into adulthood.

Ezra and Nehemiah are different. They confess sin that doesn't belong to them personally. "I am too ashamed and disgraced, my God, to lift up my face to you, because our sins are higher than our heads and our guilt has reached to the heavens." Ezra 9:6. "We have acted very wickedly toward you. We have not obeyed the commands, decrees and laws you gave your servant Moses." Nehemiah 1:7. Daniel does the same thing (Daniel 9:5). It's called intercession. You can probably think of others who have taken on the sin, guilt, and shame of others as if it was their own – Jesus

Christ being our supreme example. He suffered and died for the penalty of our sins; He had no sins. "Therefore he is able to save completely those who come to God through him, because he always lives to intercede for them." Hebrews 7:25.

Before Christ, Satan tries repeatedly over the years to contaminate and eradicate the Holy Seed from which Jesus would be born (Ezra 9:2). He attempts to destroy God's plan for man's redemption but is always unsuccessful, because God's plan and Word will forever prove true. Today, Satan continues his never-ending assault upon the nation of Israel and the Church of Jesus Christ. Again, he will not succeed, and he knows it; nevertheless, Satan continues to attack God's people in an attempt to hurt God. (And you thought Satan was after you because of who you are. In reality, he attacks you because of Who you belong to. His goal is to hurt God, so he goes after God's children.)

We need more Ezras, Nehemiahs, and Daniels in the world today. Will you be an intercessor like Ezra and "mourn over the unfaithfulness…until the fierce anger of our God in this matter is turned away from us"? Ezra 10:6, 14. Notice that Ezra has those who oppose him from inside the ranks (Ezra 10:15), and Nehemiah has opposition from outside Israel (Nehemiah 2:19). Expect it. Whenever you obey God and follow His will, opposition will come out of the woodwork.

Intercession is vitally important today. Will you intercede for our nation? Will you pray for the lost? Notice that Ezra and Nehemiah put feet to their prayers as well. They got busy doing God's work. Do we have that same love and concern for God and people?

September 18 – **Diligent in Business**

Let's look at a couple of diligent individuals today. What does diligence mean to you? Is it a work ethic? Is it the virtue of hard work? God calls some people to work in full time ministry; others He calls to fields in the secular workplace. Both areas are significant to God, and how we accomplish the work He gives us is of utmost importance to Him.

Nehemiah is a cupbearer to a heathen king (I would compare that to the secular workplace!); then God calls him into ministry. God gives him the job to return to Jerusalem and oversee the rebuilding of the wall around the city. It's a big responsibility, but God is with him. Nehemiah learns to keep his (God's) priorities in order, for there are challenges, distractions, and opponents galore. "so I sent messengers to them with this reply: 'I am carrying on a great project and cannot go down. Why should the work stop while I leave it and go down to you?'" Nehemiah 6:3. He must keep his focus in order to complete the project God has given him.

Tabitha is a Christ follower who serves God diligently while working in the clothing industry. "In Joppa there was a disciple named Tabitha (in Greek her name is Dorcas); she was always doing good and helping the poor. Peter went with them, and when he arrived he was taken upstairs to the room. All the widows stood around him, crying and showing him the robes and other clothing that Dorcas had made while she was still with them." Acts 9:36, 39.

Both Nehemiah and Tabitha are diligent in fulfilling God's call on their lives. God honors them and is pleased with their work. He blesses the work of their hands. Where are you today? What project are you accomplishing for God? Maintain your priorities and commitments against all odds and finish what you've started. "We want each of you to show this same diligence to the very end, so that what you hope for may be fully realized. We do not want you to become lazy, but to imitate those who through faith and patience inherit what has been promised." Hebrews 6:11, 12.

September 19 – **Too Blessed**

Do you know how many Holy Bibles you have in your home right now? Neither did I until I counted – just now. I counted those on shelves, in drawers, and in closets. I'm shocked. I have 36 Bibles in my home at this moment. That's not counting commentaries, children's Bible story books, study books from Bible college days (yes, I still have every single one), devotionals, Christian books, and Bibles on electronic devices. I'm blessed beyond measure, but I'm also saddened at the same time; because I know that most people in the world today don't even own one complete Bible in their own language.

One day, Ezra, the priest and teacher, begins to read aloud the Book of the Law of Moses (Ezra 8:1-12) to thousands of people as they gather in the square. Can you imagine? There is no microphone, no words on a screen, no scrolls in their hands – only a few Levites scattered throughout the crowd to help the people understand what they just heard. The people begin to weep when they hear and understand God's Word. "Nehemiah said, 'Go and enjoy choice food and sweet drinks, and send some to those who have nothing prepared. This day is holy to our Lord. Do not grieve, for the joy of the Lord is your strength." Nehemiah 8:10.

Everyone deserves a chance to hear the Words of Life. "Again Jesus began to teach by the lake. The crowd that gathered around him was so large that he got into a boat and sat in it out on the lake, while all the people were along the shore at the water's edge. He taught them many things…" Mark 4:1, 2.

Missionaries as well as nationals risk their lives every day around the world smuggling Bibles to those who have none. I know some personally; my daughter was one of those. Is it fair that I have 36 Bibles and that I can sit down and read one at any time without fear of persecution? No, it's not. I'm very blessed and at the same time humbled. I'm not doing enough to help get God's Word into the hands of people who are spiritually starving to death. Again, hear the words of Nehemiah (paraphrased): "Go and enjoy your spiritual food, and send some to those who have nothing. This day is holy to our Lord. Do not grieve, for the joy of the Lord is your strength."

September 20 – **STOP! Remember. Obey.**

Turn over that leaf! Isn't it about time? The Israelites finally do. What can we learn from them? First of all they stop and listen to God's Word. Second, they remember (Nehemiah 9); and third, they agree to obey (Nehemiah 10).

Let's assume we have stopped and heard. Now it's time to remember. Remember what? The Israelites remember their history as a nation and where God brought them from – slavery. They remember God's provision. They recall the bread from heaven (manna) and water from the rock (foretastes of the Messiah). They remember their wickedness and sin and God's goodness to them time and time again. "…But you are a forgiving God, gracious and compassionate, slow to anger and abounding in love…" Nehemiah 9:17. God gives them the Promise Land (a glimpse of heaven). "…they took possession of houses filled with all kinds of good things…" Nehemiah 9:25. And they remember history repeating itself numerous times with their backsliding, crying out to God, and God giving mercy.

The third step is their pledge to obey the commandments of God. They will keep the Sabbath holy, and they will give their tithes and offerings. "…We will not neglect the house of our God." Nehemiah 10:39.

"God exalted him to his own right hand as Prince and Savior that he might bring Israel to repentance and forgive their sins." Acts 5:31. "For great is your love, higher than the heavens; your faithfulness reaches to the skies." Psalm 108:4. Turn over the new leaf today, follow God, obey Him, and stay faithful to His house.

September 21 – **Full of Life**

Do you consider today's reading boring? I find it teaming with life! The people are occupying Jerusalem and surrounding villages. Everyone is important; look at all those names! And everyone has something to do. Here are just a few of the positions and responsibilities listed: priests in charge of the house of God and associates who carry on work for the temple, Levites in charge of the outside work of the house of God, those who lead in thanksgiving and prayer, gatekeepers who keep watch at the gates and others who guard the storerooms at the gates, temple servants, musicians responsible for the service of the house of God, king's agent in charge of all affairs relating to the people, those responsible for the rooms and treasuries in the house of God, those in charge of the furnishings and articles used in the temple services, and those who take care of mixing the spices and baking the offering bread. Work responsibilities are shared around the clock. Every person and every responsibility is important for the smooth operation of the temple. Life is busy and fulfilling.

God still considers His people and His work vital in the church today. God knows your name, and He knows your place in His church. Do you know your place in God's work today? You need to find out what He wants you to do, because your role is crucial to the function of the local church. "Just as a body, though one, has many parts, but all its many parts form one body, so it is with Christ." 1 Corinthians 12:12. (Read all of 1 Corinthians 12.)

"However, do not rejoice that the spirits submit to you, but rejoice that your names are written in heaven." Luke 10:20. If Jesus Christ is your Savior and Lord, your name is in His book. I believe that just as God had a plan and order in the ancient temple in Jerusalem, and He has designed organization in His Church today, there will be meticulous order to life in heaven. When you step into heaven, you won't be left on your own to find your way around. You will be greeted by someone who knows your name and will show you to your home prepared by Jesus Himself. Your guide will introduce you to friends and loved ones, new and old alike, and show you around. Life with Jesus is busy and fulfilling on earth and in heaven. And life in heaven will be a billion times better than we ever imagined!

September 22 – **God Remembers**

God never has to tie a string on His finger to remember anything! (Hebrews 6:10). Nehemiah asks God several times to remember everything he is doing for the house of God. "Remember me for this, my God, and do not blot out what I have so faithfully done for the house of my God and its services." Nehemiah 13:14. Nehemiah's first trip to Jerusalem lasts twelve years. All during that time he provides for his own needs; he refuses to overburden the people as the former governors had done or take advantage of the system. "…But out of reverence for God I did not act like that. Instead, I devoted myself to the work on this wall…" Nehemiah 5:15, 16.

The accolades in this life fade quickly. Seriously, which would you rather have? Recognition and compensation on earth (so temporary) or appreciation and rewards in heaven (never ending)? What you do for God may go unnoticed on earth (and that's okay), but God always notices. "And if anyone gives even a cup of cold water to one of these little ones who is my disciple, truly I tell you, that person will certainly not lose their reward." Matthew 10:42. God even remembers your acts of love and kindness which you may have long forgotten.

God also wants us to remember Him all the days of our lives. That's why He instituted Communion in the church, so we will never forget what Jesus Christ did for us in His death on the cross (1 Corinthians 11:24, 25).

Why do you do what you do for God? "...They do it to get a crown that will not last, but we do it to get a crown that will last forever." 1 Corinthians 9:25.

September 23 – **On Change, Marriage and Faithfulness**

You've heard it said that the only one who likes change is a baby with a wet diaper. I don't particularly enjoy change; that's one reason I always loved going to my grandparents' home. Nothing ever changed in that house! I can still see their home clearly in my mind's eye – the chest of drawers with her perfumes on top, the coffee grinder mounted on the wall in the kitchen that gave a handful of change whenever a grandchild turned the handle, the bathtub with feet, and the door at the top of the stairs that you had to lift up like a window – it was wonderful! My grandparents have been with the Lord many years now, and their house is no longer the same. There is only One Who has never changed since the beginning of time and Who will never change – God.

"I the Lord do not change..." Malachi 3:6. Since He never changes, His design and plan for marriage has never changed. The first book in the Bible gives good marriage advice in Genesis 2:24: leave, cleave, and then become one flesh (in that order). The last book in the Old Testament also talks about marriage (Malachi 2:13-17). "Has not the one God made you? You belong to him in body and spirit. And what does the one God seek? Godly offspring. So be on your guard, and do not be unfaithful to the wife of your youth." (v. 15).

God calls each of us to faithfulness to Him and to our spouse. Think about it: If you are faithful to God, you will be faithful in marriage; if you're unfaithful in your marriage, you are unfaithful to God. If you are currently unfaithful in either relationship, God has something to say to you. "'...Return to me, and I will return to you,' says the Lord Almighty…" Malachi 3:7. He says it again in Joel 2:12, 13.

Malachi and Joel are preparing us to enter the world of the New Testament and the New Covenant through Jesus Christ. First we return and repent. God then restores us (Joel 2:18-27). And then comes the Lord's promise to pour out His Spirit on all people (Joel 2:28).

"And everyone who calls on the name of the Lord will be saved…" Joel 2:32. "for, 'Everyone who calls on the name of the Lord will be saved.'" Romans 10:13. I'm so thankful God never changes.

September 24 – **The Living Word**

The Living Word of God is none other than Jesus Christ, God's Son, the Savior of the world. "The Word became flesh and made his dwelling among us. We have seen his glory, the glory of the one and only Son, who came from the Father, full of grace and truth." John 1:14. As a whole, the nation of Israel does not receive Jesus as their Messiah the first time He comes to earth (v. 11); but a few do believe and they become children born of God (vs. 12-13).

Before his death, Moses recites all the words God has given him for the children of Israel. "They are not just idle words for you – they are your life…" Deuteronomy 32:47. "He was in the assembly in the wilderness, with the angel who spoke to him on Mount Sinai, and with our ancestors; and he received living words to pass on to us." Acts 7:38. God's Word is alive in spoken, written, and living form. Jesus Christ is the Living Word of God.

The angel says to Mary, "'For no word from God will ever fail.' 'I am the Lord's servant,' Mary answered. 'May your word to me be fulfilled.' Then the angel left her." Luke 1:37, 38. Jesus Christ physically grows in Mary. At some point in Mary's life, even she must receive Him as her Lord and Savior, and she becomes God's child. Jesus Christ is alive and well and growing in me. Is the Living Word of God growing in you?

September 25 – **The Heavenly Host**

It starts out like any other night. It's dark and quiet on the hillside; the moon and stars are out; the sheep are asleep. The shepherds settle in for a peaceful night of rest. Then it happens, and there will never be another night like this one! "An angel of the Lord appeared to them, and the glory of the Lord shone around them, and they were terrified." Luke 2:9. The sleepy shepherds are now wide awake and hearing the good news of the birth of the Messiah. How fitting that the birth of the Good Shepherd (John 10:11) is announced to these lowly shepherds first. This good news will change their lives forever.

All of a sudden, their night has turned to day. "Suddenly a great company of the heavenly host appeared with the angel, praising God and saying, 'Glory to God in the highest heaven, and on earth peace to those on whom his favor rests.'" Luke 2:13, 14. It's not so dark and quiet any more. God's Son is born! Every square inch of heaven is exploding with praise at that moment! And these shepherds bask in the overflow from heaven's portals! "Praise him, all his angels; praise him, all his heavenly hosts." Psalm 148:2.

It starts as an ordinary night but ends with hearts and lives forever changed. Jesus Christ is born! And He changes everything.

September 26 – **Renounce/Repent**

One lie can't stand alone but requires another to prop it up, then another, then another, and so on. Honesty is the best policy, especially when it comes to trying to conceal our sins. "Whoever conceals their sins does not prosper, but the one who confesses and renounces them finds mercy." Proverbs 28:13. Nobody wins when we try to hide, ignore, minimize, justify, bury, pretend, or forget our sin. It's still there and we know it; God sees it, and it will be exposed one day. The only way to eradicate it is to confess and renounce it. To renounce means to give up, to disown. The truth is we all need God's mercy to make it through this life and into heaven, and this is a requirement.

"In those days John the Baptist came, preaching in the wilderness of Judea and saying, 'Repent, for the kingdom of heaven has come near.'" Matthew 3:1, 2. To repent means to turn around, turn from evil ways and turn to Christ. Repentance is a decision we make, made possible by God's grace. It is a radical break from sin and nothing less. This saving faith is not mere trust. We receive Jesus Christ as our Savior and make Him Lord over our life. As our Lord, we give Him complete control over our life. God's forgiveness and mercy are available for all who come to God in sincere repentance.

Don't live with the lie any longer. Humble yourself before God. He loves you and is rich in mercy, grace, and forgiveness.

September 27 – **No Plan B**

If Plan A doesn't work for me, I usually have a Plan B in my back pocket. Let's say my family is planning a Saturday afternoon at the park. In case of rain, we will go instead to the movie at the mall. It's no big deal in this case.

I believe God has a Plan A for each life. Satan's plan is to destroy God's plan, so he puts temptations, snares, and stumbling blocks in our path. When sin enters the picture of our life and throws everything off course, God may resort to Plan B. It's a little more serious than a rainy Saturday afternoon. Fortunately for us, God provides forgiveness and restoration through His Son Jesus Christ, and everything can work out okay. It may not be His original plan for our life, but He redeems us and the situation and brings good out of it (Romans 8:28).

"Then Jesus was led by the Spirit into the wilderness to be tempted by the devil." Matthew 4:1. In Jesus' case, there is no Plan B. Satan knows if he can make Jesus succumb to temptation, God's plan for the redemption of all mankind would be ruined; we would forever be separated from God. "The animals you choose must be year-old males without defect, and you may take them from the sheep or the goats." Exodus 12:5. Jesus Christ is the spotless Lamb of God, the Passover Lamb; there is no other way. Jesus uses the all powerful Written Word of God to defeat Satan's temptations, and so can we. It's another very good reason to know your Bible. Jesus wins, so we win! He is forever Plan A for our lives! Praise His Holy Name!

September 28 – **Look Up**

Nicodemus wakes up Jesus to tell Him something He already knows (John 3:2). Jesus seizes the opportunity to explain to Nic about rebirth. "Flesh gives birth to flesh, but the Spirit gives birth to spirit." John 3:6. It's a little confusing to him, but apparently Nic "gets it," because we see him later defending Jesus (John 7:50) and also helping prepare Jesus' body for burial (John 19:39). Jesus helps "Israel's teacher" (John 3:10) understand by referring to a story of which Nic is familiar. "Just as Moses lifted up the snake in the wilderness, so the Son of Man must be lifted up, that everyone who believes may have eternal life in him." John 3:14, 15.

You can read the story in Numbers 21:4-9. The children of Israel are complaining again in the wilderness, so the Lord sends snakes among them; many people are bitten and die. The people confess their sin and ask Moses to pray for them. "So Moses made a bronze snake and put it up on a pole. Then when anyone was bitten by a snake and looked at the bronze snake, they lived." Numbers 4:9. This is another event in Israel's history which anticipates the sacrificial death of Jesus Christ, who is lifted up on the cross in order to bring life to all who look to Him.

There are people all around us today who have been bitten by the devil and are in varying stages of dying. Are we helping people to look up at the cross of Jesus and live? We know some will refuse to look, and they will die; but all who do look to Jesus in faith believing in Him will live. Looking to Jesus Christ is the only Way for people to experience spiritual birth before they close their eyes in death.

O Lord, I want to help others look up to You so they can be saved from death. I pray for opportunities, the help of Your Holy Spirit, and boldness.

September 29 – **David and Jesus**

David and Jesus share many similarities in Scripture. After all, David is a man after God's own heart (1 Samuel 13:14). We learn that mornings are special to David. "In the morning, Lord, you hear my voice; in the morning I lay my requests before you and wait expectantly." Psalm 5:3. "But I will sing of your strength, in the morning I will sing of your love; for you are my fortress, my refuge in times of trouble." Psalm 59:16. "Very early in the morning, while it was still dark, Jesus got up, left the house and went off to a solitary place, where he prayed." Mark 1:35.

David and Jesus love and take care of their mothers! "From there David went to Mizpah in Moab and said to the king of Moab, 'Would you let my father and mother come and stay with you until I learn what God will do for me?'" 1 Samuel 22:3. "When Jesus saw his mother there, and the disciple whom he loved standing nearby, he said to her, 'Woman, here is your son,' and to the disciple, 'Here is your mother.' From that time on, this disciple took her into his home." John 19:26, 27.

However, there is a striking contrast between the two. Notice how David feels about his enemies. "For the sins of their mouths, for the words of their lips, let them be caught in their pride. For the curses and lies they utter, consume them in wrath, consume them till they are no more. Then it will be known to the ends of the earth that God rules over Jacob." Psalm 59:12, 13. Even on his death bed, David seeks revenge by charging Solomon to deal with Joab and Shimei who wronged him. "But now, do not consider him innocent. You are a man of wisdom; you will know what to do to him. Bring his gray head down to the grave in blood." 1 Kings 2:9. Do you remember the words of Jesus as he dies on the cross? "Jesus said, 'Father, forgive them, for they do not know what they are doing.' And they divided up his clothes by casting lots." Luke 23:34. May God help us to be more like Jesus in our most difficult moments.

September 30 – **The Seen and Unseen**

I love the true story of the paralytic and his four best friends who go to a lot of trouble to get their sick friend in front of Jesus. Not easily discouraged by the thick crowd, they get very creative in what to do to achieve their goal. The homeowner may not think so, but what they do works! "...When Jesus saw their faith, he said to the man, 'Take heart, son; your sins are forgiven.'" Matthew 9:2. At that moment, the man becomes aware of a cleansing inside his heart and a joy filling his soul. Jesus takes care of the most important business first – forgiveness. All five have faith that the man will be healed; but notice, Jesus speaks only to the paralytic that his sins are forgiven. Jesus sees an additional faith in the sick man – faith for salvation.

"'But I want you to know that the Son of Man has authority on earth to forgive sins.' So he said to the paralyzed man, 'Get up, take your mat and go home.'" Matthew 9:6. The visible miracle of getting up and walking is the miracle that is seen; the larger miracle of forgiveness and salvation is unseen and undetected by all except the man to whom it happens. The visible miracle is temporary; the internal miracle is eternal. This in no way minimizes the miracle of healing. Our Savior suffers greatly to provide healing for us by subjecting Himself to the torturer's whip, for it is by his wounds we are healed (1 Peter 2:24). Nevertheless, the greater miracle is that of salvation through faith in Jesus Christ, when our spirit is born again, cleansed and forgiven, and our names are written in the Lamb's Book of Life.

The former paralytic is healed inside and out! "Praise the Lord, my soul, and forget not all his benefits – who forgives all your sins and heals all your diseases," Psalm 103:2, 3.

OCTOBER

October 1 – **Stop Sinning!**

The pool at Bethesda is a familiar place to the Jews in Jerusalem. The surface area of the enclosed water is over 3.10 square miles (a little larger than what we think of when we hear the word pool!). Jesus finds the man who has been an invalid for 38 years and asks him if he wants to be well (John 5:6). He knows the man has had this condition for so long that he has almost lost the desire to become whole again. Jesus' question is designed to arouse him from his apathy and awaken a sense of expectation and hope. Jesus heals him and tells him to pick up his mat and walk. Of course it is the Sabbath when Jesus does this miracle. (Do the Jewish leaders always follow Jesus around on the Sabbaths?)

The cripple knows His power but not His name. "Later Jesus found him at the temple and said to him, 'See, you are well again. Stop sinning or something worse may happen to you.'" John 5:14. Jesus wants the man to understand the moral significance of his healing. He knows his bigger problem is sin. Jesus is concerned for his soul as well as his body.

True believers in Jesus Christ commit their lives to Him, and although not perfect, through the power of the Holy Spirit, sin no longer has dominion over them (1 John 3:6-10). Jesus has high expectations of those who are born-again. He will give us strength to live our lives for Him as we daily trust Him. "Wash and make yourselves clean. Take your evil deeds out of my sight; stop doing wrong." Isaiah 1:16.

October 2 – **Love My What?**

Jesus says a lot of things that the Jewish people hear for the very first time – like the following: "But to you who are listening I say: Love your enemies, do good to those who hate you," Luke 6:27. One Jewish man looks at another and says, "Did I really hear Him say what I thought I heard Him say? Did He just tell us to love our enemies? Is He serious?" The nation of Israel has had more than their fair share of enemies for hundreds of years. They're used to hearing things like this from King David: "In your unfailing love, silence my enemies; destroy all my foes, for I am your servant." Psalm 143:12. Jesus not only tells them to embrace a whole new way of thinking, but an entirely new way of responding and acting toward their enemies. They must not only love them but do good to them, bless them, pray for them, turn the other cheek to them, give them their shirt and anything else they have without expecting anything in return (Luke 6:27-36). Are they listening?

Am I listening? Jesus says the same thing to me today. I can forgive someone who has wronged me. God's Word tells me I have no choice but to forgive if I want to be forgiven, and I most definitely want to be forgiven (Matthew 6:15). Just as I choose to forgive, I must also choose to love, because it is what God requires of me. I have discovered that whatever God asks of me, He will supply the grace and strength I need to accomplish it. I must have His help to love as He loves.

This has been my prayer: Lord, You tell me to love this person, but I'm having a really hard time doing that. Please forgive me. Use Your two-edged sword to cut deep into my heart and remove anything that should not be there. O Lord, that hurts, but take it out. Plant Your seeds of love, water them with Your Holy Spirit, and let love grow in my heart. Give me Your grace and strength to do good to those who hurt me. Thank You. In the precious Name of Jesus I pray. Amen.

October 3 – **Priority One**

"If you scratch my back, I will scratch yours. If I do this for You, God, then You will do this for me. Okay? Let's make a deal, God!" Well, it may work sometime, but that's not the gist of Matthew 6:33. "But seek first his kingdom and his righteousness, and all these things will be given to you as well." It's talking about more than just food and clothes. It means more than a fast way to get what I want; it's not a "get-rich-quick" scheme. It even goes much deeper than my worry.

"But Jehoshaphat also said to the king of Israel, 'First seek the counsel of the Lord.'" 1 Kings 22:5. That's good advice. Why is it that God is not usually the first one we turn to when we need help? We often enjoy doing things ourselves; we take pride in being independent. However, it is so much better for all concerned to be totally dependent upon God. Seeking God first is a habit we must develop; this tendency does not come naturally to us. Begin by seeking Him first in your day – early in the morning – time spent with Him in prayer and reading His Word. Put Him first in your finances – tithes and offerings. Make God and living by His Word your top priority. When we practice this every day, it will become a forever lifestyle.

God has promised to meet our needs, not make us rich. We think material blessings; God thinks spiritual blessings. When we are teachable before God, we will receive more from Him than we bargained for. (Sometimes we think we're teachable when we're really not.) He will reveal to us areas in our life where godliness is severely lacking; we will receive that from Him if we're teachable.

Seek first His kingdom and His righteousness; that's our number one job; that's our first priority. God will take care of every need and every worry. Our thoughts can get splintered out in a hundred different directions, when all God tells us to do is focus on one thing – Him. Make Him Priority One today.

October 4 – **Tangled**

"A woman in that town who lived a sinful life learned that Jesus was eating at the Pharisee's house, so she came there with an alabaster jar of perfume. As she stood behind him at his feet weeping, she began to wet his feet with her tears. Then she wiped them with her hair, kissed them and poured perfume on them." Luke 7:37, 38. She is a woman with a past, a tangled life of sin, and she knows it. Is there anyone anywhere who can help her? Then she hears stories about this Jesus Who heals people with His touch. He drives out demons and sets people free. It has even been reported that He forgives sin! She must find Him! He is her only hope!

One day, she hears that Jesus is visiting in the home of a Pharisee; she knows the place. She takes with her the costliest possession she owns and bravely makes her way to the house. Will He even notice her? Will He even care? She sees Him, and her tears begin to fall. She has nothing to lose but her sin. She humbles herself at His feet, washes them with her tears, loosens her hair and wipes His feet with her hair, kisses His feet, and pours perfume on them. It doesn't matter what others say or think, only what the Savior thinks. As she washes His feet, He washes her sins away. Only the two of them know the miracle taking place at that moment. Forgiveness, true love, new life, and joy begin to flow into her heart from the Savior.

Almost a thousand years before, Absalom, King David's son, tried to steal the throne. He was a handsome man with no blemish in him, known for his beautiful thick hair (2 Samuel 14:25, 26). Prideful and arrogant, he built a monument in his own honor (2 Samuel 18:18). "Now Absalom happened to meet David's men. He was riding his mule, and as the mule went under the thick branches of a large oak, Absalom's hair got caught in the tree. He was left hanging in midair, while the mule he was riding kept on going." 2 Samuel 18:9. His hair got tangled in the tree! Was Absalom trying to work out the tangles to keep from having to chop off his hair when Joab found him and murdered him?

The very thing we take pride in could become our downfall. Your outward appearance may wow others, but God is not impressed. He's more interested in the content of your heart. Use what God has given you for His glory.

October 5 – **Fertile Ground**

Do you remember the condition of your heart the first time you heard the Gospel? Was it the tender heart of a child, or was it hard, shallow, or thorny? Because a child's heart is usually soft and receptive, it's vital that we reach children with the Good News of Jesus Christ and give them an opportunity to receive Jesus as Savior. Next comes the work of discipleship, teaching them to be followers of Jesus Christ. As we grow older, the challenge becomes greater to plant the seeds of God's Word, because over time our hearts can become cold and calloused.

"Listen! A farmer went out to sow his seed." Mark 4:3. He sows seed (the Word) in four different places: 1) the well-traveled path that is caked from use; 2) the rocky ground with very little soil and moisture; 3) the ground covered with thorns; and 4) the good soil. These are four different people with four very dissimilar hearts. The seed can only grow and produce a crop if it's planted in the good soil, the heart that's been plowed, prepared, and opened. Here's a thought: Is Jesus telling us that, on average, one in four people come to Him who hear the Word? Jesus tells us in Matthew 7:13-14 that few find that narrow gate, and many more walk the broad road to destruction. We want to believe more people go to heaven every day than go to hell, but is that really the case?

"Sow righteousness for yourselves, reap the fruit of unfailing love, and break up your unplowed ground; for it is time to seek the Lord until he comes and showers his righteousness on you." Hosea 10:12. Maybe your heart is hard from being walked on so much; perhaps you have more rocks than good soil and moisture to sustain life; possibly life is choking His life out of you. Stop! You can humble yourself before God right now and ask Him to break up the unplowed ground in your life. Understand the process may be uncomfortable. Plowing is hard work and the instrument sharp. Our hearts and lives are turned upside down and inside out. In the end, healthy soil is ready to receive the healthy seed of God's Word and His showers of blessing that produce eternal life. The enemy can't steal that away!

If you are a farmer, don't stop slinging seed! You can't see the heart that is hungry and waiting to receive it. God brings the results. Our job is to plant and water; God makes it grow. You will never see all the results of your farming today, but one day in heaven you will.

October 6 – **Rare Treasure**

Who hasn't wanted to find buried treasure? It's one of those things kids and adults alike dream about! As kids growing up in the small East Texas town of Colmesneil, my friends and I had to entertain ourselves. One of the things we did was to create, bury, and discover our own treasure chest! Like I said, not a whole lot to do in Colmesneil! Now with grandchildren, I have several times hidden little containers of change, candy, and small toys, drawn treasure maps, and let the grands discover their own buried treasure. I still enjoy an afternoon once in a while with my metal detector. So far, all I've "discovered" are lots of pop-tops from aluminum cans and a little loose change (not even enough to buy a coke) – but I have fun!

"The kingdom of heaven is like treasure hidden in a field. When a man found it, he hid it again, and then in his joy went and sold all he had and bought that field." Matthew 13:44. This man realizes that all his combined worldly goods can't begin to compare to this treasure. Nothing is more beautiful or valuable. He must do whatever is necessary to claim this treasure. This rare treasure, of course, is Jesus Christ; and the joy accompanying this acquisition will never end. "and if you look for it as for silver and search for it as for hidden treasure," Proverbs 2:4. "It" is wisdom or Jesus Christ in the Book of Proverbs.

Do you know that Jesus has a treasure as well? "For the Lord has chosen Jacob to be his own, Israel to be his treasured possession." Psalm 135:4. If you are a born-again believer in Jesus Christ, you are part of that promised seed; you are one of His jewels. And Jesus is always searching to add more jewels to His cache to go in His crown (Zechariah 9:16). The most important thing here is not who finds whom; but that you find each other. Don't step into eternity and realize you allowed the most Wonderful Treasure in all of heaven and earth to slip through your fingers.

October 7 – **Welcome!**

I have a mat outside my front door with the word "Welcome" on it. I want people to feel they are welcome when they step into our home. Jesus knocks on our heart's door (Rev. 3:20), but if we don't open the door and invite Him in and make Him feel welcome, He will turn away. Jesus is a gentleman; He will never force Himself on us.

Jesus heals a demon-possessed man in the region of the Gerasenes (Mark 5:1-20). The population on this side of the lake is probably mixed or mainly Gentile, for Jews would not be raising pigs because they consider them unclean animals. The man knows when Jesus delivers him from the demons because of the visible demonstration: They come out of him and go into the swine that in turn plunge down the cliff into the water and drown. Yes, someone lost their property that day, but someone else is set free by the power of God which is far more significant. The townspeople are notified and quickly come see what all the ruckus is about. They find Jesus and the former town demoniac (who is now at rest, dressed, and in his right mind) having a decent conversation.

"Then the people began to plead with Jesus to leave their region." Mark 5:17. Are they scared of the supernatural? Are they afraid if Jesus stays longer that other things in their lives may have to go as well? He will never stay where He is not wanted. This is sad, because there is no record of Jesus ever returning to the region of the Gerasenes.

"But my people would not listen to me; Israel would not submit to me. So I gave them over to their stubborn hearts to follow their own devices." Psalm 81:11, 12. How it must hurt the heart of God for people to reject Him, because He knows we need Him. Welcome Him in today. He has good things to give you.

October 8 – **The Harvest**

The need for workers in God's kingdom on earth has always been great (Matthew 9:35-38). "Then he said to his disciples, 'The harvest is plentiful but the workers are few. Ask the Lord of the harvest, therefore, to send out workers into his harvest field.'" Matthew 9:37, 38. The need here is for prayer. Each of us must pray for more workers; it won't happen until we pray. These Scriptures imply that many can be saved if only someone will present the Gospel to them. Are you praying?

"Then I heard the voice of the Lord saying, 'Whom shall I send? And who will go for us?' And I said, 'Here am I. Send me!'" Isaiah 6:8. Only after Isaiah is cleansed (v. 7) will God send him. Are we afraid to pray for God to send forth more laborers like Jesus asks us to pray for fear that He may want to send us? God tells each of us to "Go" in the Great Commission (Matthew 28:19). May God's heart for the lost grow so mightily in us that we will eagerly say, "Here am I. Send me!"

Today is the day to work in His harvest fields. Eternity will hold no harvest fields. It is too late for those in hell, and there are no lost people in heaven! So pray and go! What are you waiting for?

October 9 – **Flare Prayers**

There are times in our lives when all we have time for is a short prayer. We've all shot those flare prayers up to heaven just before a test, a public speaking engagement, a near-miss accident, a sticky confrontation, or any of a hundred other close calls. Peter finds himself sinking fast with no time for a long eloquent prayer. "But when he saw the wind, he was afraid and, beginning to sink, cried out, 'Lord, save me!'" Matthew 14:30. Just in the nick of time! Nehemiah goes before the king (445 BC) with a question that could cost him his life. "The king said to me, 'What is it you want?' Then I prayed to the God of heaven, and I answered the king..." Nehemiah 2:4, 5. No time for a long prayer in that moment either. Both experience God's help and intervention. Jesus wants us to pray, and He wants us to get to the point. "And when you pray, do not keep on babbling like pagans, for they think they will be heard because of their many words." Matthew 6:7.

Don't misunderstand. All of us should spend more One-on-one time with the Lord in prayer, meditation, worship, reading the Bible, and listening to Him. Our prayer life should not only consist of crisis prayers. If that is the only time we seriously pray, some readjusting is in order. But thank God He always hears us whenever we pray! God's mercy is greater than we can possibly imagine; I believe many step into heaven because of "deathbed" prayers. The thief on the cross is one example. But how close is too close for comfort? "save others by snatching them from the fire…" Jude 1:23. The truth is no one knows when they close their eyes at night if that is the last time. Spend relaxed time in prayer today, talk to Jesus, listen to Him, and make everything right with Him. You may not have time to make another emergency prayer.

October 10 – **Heart Deep**

"Go to your room and think about what you've done. And while you're there, find twenty Scriptures in your Bible that talk about lying, and write them all out on paper, and then we'll talk about it." My twelve year old daughter was not happy. She was caught in a lie and now must pay the consequences. It would have been so much easier on both of us if the punishment was a simple grounding from friends, phone, and TV for a week. To have a difficult discussion takes time and effort. To make her look inward at her heart was painful for both of us.

The people following Jesus want an easy "step 1-2-3" formula. "Then they asked him, 'What must we do to do the works God requires?' Jesus answered, 'The work of God is this: to believe in the one he has sent.'" John 6:28, 29. There goes Jesus getting deep again! They just want to "do" something; they don't want to think about it. Jesus takes them back to the beginning; they must believe in Him. The condition of man's heart and spirit are of utmost importance to Jesus. "The Spirit gives life; the flesh counts for nothing. The words I have spoken to you – they are full of the Spirit and life." John 6:63.

This tent of flesh that houses my spirit will return to dirt one day. The spirit within me is the real me; that's the part of me that will live forever somewhere. And it all starts with believing in Jesus Christ. "'You are my witnesses,' declares the Lord, 'and my servant whom I have chosen, so that you may know and believe me and understand that I am he. Before me no god was formed, nor will there be one after me. I, even I, am the Lord, and apart from me there is no savior.'" Isaiah 43:10, 11.

October 11 – **A Test of Faith**

"Are you calling me a dog?" I wonder how many of us would have said that to Jesus. Jesus and His disciples are in Gentile territory; they have entered a home, perhaps for a much needed rest, but it is not to be. A Canaanite woman hears that Jesus is in town and rushes to the home, crying and pleading with Him to heal her daughter who is suffering terribly from demon possession. He seems to ignore her. Finally He tells her that He is sent only to the lost sheep of Israel. That doesn't stop her.

"The woman came and knelt before him. 'Lord, help me!' she said. He replied, 'It is not right to take the children's bread and toss it to the dogs.' 'Yes it is, Lord,' she said. 'Even the dogs eat the crumbs that fall from their master's table.' Then Jesus said to her, 'Woman, you have great faith! Your request is granted.' And her daughter was healed at that moment." Matthew 15:25-28.

Why does Jesus speak to her in this way? His attitude is intended to test her faith. She is probably a believer in Jesus Christ (perhaps the first heathen convert) and understands the Gospel must be taken to the Jews first. She also knows that Gentiles receive blessings indirectly when He blesses Israel. She knows Jesus is referring to the Jews as children and Gentiles as dogs, but the term He uses here refers to a household companion, not an outside scavenger.

The woman has faith in Jesus, even faith that He can heal her daughter from a distance. She perseveres. She trusts Him even when He does not seem to answer or care. Possibly she knows the story of Elijah and the poor widow when he demands her last morsel of bread (1 Kings 17:13). That woman's faith was tested; she passed the test, and God met her need. Maybe she is acquainted with God's Word in Proverbs 15:1: "A gentle answer turns away wrath, but a harsh word stirs up anger." She cannot get defensive, but must remain humble, believing, and trusting. She passes the test!

October 12 – **Spiritual Eyes**

We are so quick to judge people and situations merely by outward appearance and their effect on us. That's the carnal mind at work! How unlike Christ can we be? Physical vision is very limited. If you see the world and your circumstances only through eyes of flesh, you are definitely missing the bigger picture.

Jesus is explaining to His disciples how He must suffer and die and on the third day be raised to life. Peter, thinking carnally and missing the big picture entirely, rebukes Jesus. Jesus must suddenly have a flashback to His time in the wilderness when Satan tries to tempt Him to avoid the cross. "Jesus turned and said to Peter, 'Get behind me, Satan! You are a stumbling block to me; you do not have in mind the concerns of God, but merely human concerns.'" Matthew 16:23. Peter is well-meaning but completely unspiritual at the moment. It can happen to any of us – the old foot in mouth dilemma – and we easily become a tool of Satan.

Jesus still loves Peter, but He is teaching him a powerful lesson: You have spiritual eyes! Use them!

Our spiritual eyes open as we spend more time with the Savior. Our spiritual eyes open when He supernaturally opens them. We draw false conclusions based on what we see with our natural eyes and what we hear with our natural ears. Jesus opens blind eyes and deaf ears every day; He can open mine. May we see others with His eyes of compassion and love. He will pull back the covers and help us see people and situations as He sees them.

"And Elisha prayed, 'Open his eyes, Lord, so that he may see.' Then the Lord opened the servant's eyes, and he looked and saw the hills full of horses and chariots of fire all around Elisha." 2 Kings 6:17.

October 13 – **Unlimited Possibilities**

Matthew is a tax-collector by profession when Jesus calls him into the ministry. He finds the hilarious story of how Jesus pays his taxes so interesting that he includes it in his book, and he is the only writer who does. "But so that we may not cause offense, go to the lake and throw out your line. Take the first fish you catch; open its mouth and you will find a four-drachma coin. Take it and give it to them for my tax and yours." Matthew 17:27.

Meanwhile, back in the lake, God prepares a fish, but not just any fish. Just a few months before, God created hundreds of fish eggs in the bottom of that lake, and one egg in particular. This would be a special fish. He watched it hatch, swim away, and grow. And what about the coin? Perhaps it is part of a treasure in a sunken ship, resting undisturbed at the bottom of the sea for many years. Or maybe a little boy drops the coin his grandfather gave him while walking along the seashore, and the tide carries it out to sea. God knows where the coin came from and where it is now. At just the right time, the fish sees a coin, thinking it is something delicious, and scoops it up. It's not just any coin either; it is a four-drachma coin. Gulp! It's a little difficult to swallow and lodges in his throat. About that time, the fish swims directly to Peter's line, which he just cast into the lake. The rest is history. You see, God had this all figured out before there was ever a need.

Do you remember the story of King Ahab and how he dies? "But someone drew his bow at random and hit the king of Israel between the sections of his armor. The king told his chariot driver, 'Wheel around and get me out of the fighting. I've been wounded.'" 1 Kings 22:34.

The truth is, nothing is ever random or coincidence with God. He knows how to perform His Word. The odds are in our favor when God directs our lives. Nothing is impossible with Him. He has ways and resources that have never entered our imagination.

October 14 – **Don't Walk Away**

"Who can say, 'I have kept my heart pure; I am clean and without sin'"? Proverbs 20:9. I can't. I am a sinner saved by the grace of God alone. Let's look at the story in John chapter eight when the woman caught in adultery is brought to Jesus. Her accusers try to trap Him in His words. He confuses them by hesitating, bending down and writing on the ground with his finger. "When they kept on questioning him, he straightened up and said to them, 'Let any one of you who is without sin be the first to throw a stone at her.'" John 8:7. You know the rest of the story. Conviction descends upon the crowd. Soon everyone turns and walks away except the woman and Jesus. The 'high and mighties' take their sin and guilt and walk away from the only One Who can make all things new.

Jesus, in no way, looks casually at adultery or any sin. He is leading the woman to repentance and forgiveness with His kindness. It's up to her. He doesn't condemn her but offers her salvation and a way out of her sin. "Go now and leave your life of sin." (v. 11). Jesus says the same to us today.

Lord Jesus, I believe in You. I know I am a sinner in need of a Savior. I believe you died for me on the cross and paid the price for my sin. Please forgive me; wash me. I give you my life. Thank you for saving me. I will live for you. Amen.

October 15 – **Go and Do Likewise**

I've heard it said that when you're all wrapped up in yourself, you make a very small package! Some people are content to live in a mini-world that includes only themselves and who and what belong to them. Jesus is definitely not that way since He left His beautiful heavenly home and came to our earth. He teaches us in the story of the Good Samaritan that we should be good neighbors and step out of our world to help others. Dr. Luke shares Jesus' story in Luke 10:30-37. Luke is a Gentile convert writing to Gentiles, and he is the only non-Jewish author of a book in the Bible.

Jesus tells this story to an audience who can partially relate. They know the road from Jerusalem to Jericho is dangerous, descending more than 3,000 feet in less than fifteen miles through gorges that are infested with robbers. They may know people who have been victims along this same road. The man in Jesus' story is robbed, stripped, beat, and left for dead. Two "religious" people pass by and can't help but notice the man, but they don't stop. They are too busy and important. They are on a tight schedule. If they stopped to help, they might get dirty; it would certainly eat up their valuable time, and may even cost them money. It's just too much trouble. Besides, there may be more robbers lurking behind those rocks; they better keep moving.

Jesus knows of the open hostility between Jews and Samaritans, for Jews consider Samaritans as half breeds, both physically and spiritually. "But a Samaritan, as he traveled, came where the man was; and when he saw him, he took pity on him." Luke 10:33. The Samaritan doesn't see him as a hated Jew; he sees him as someone needing help. He pours his own oil and wine on the man's wounds and then bandages them. He takes time to help him, ignoring possible danger to himself. He puts him on his own donkey and takes him to an inn and cares for him. He gets a little blood and dirt on himself, and he uses his own money (two days wages) to pay the innkeeper. He also follows up on the man later and pays any extra expense. "'Which of these three do you think was a neighbor to the man who fell into the hands of robbers?' The expert in the law replied, 'The one who had mercy on him.' Jesus told him, 'Go and do likewise.'" Luke 10:36, 37.

God wants you to grow up spiritually. He wants to expand your vision beyond yourself, but it takes you stepping out of your all exclusive world first. Do something you've never done before! Help someone in need. It will take your courage, time, money, and possibly get a little dirt under your fingernails. But it will open up a whole new world of adventure and blessing!

"The foreigner residing among you must be treated as your native-born. Love them as yourself, for you were foreigners in Egypt. I am the Lord your God." Leviticus 19:34. The call to love God is a call to love others. Is your love for God evident in your love for others?

October 16 – **Stuck in Neutral**

A car in neutral is going nowhere fast. It's the same for a life. Jesus says in Luke 11:23, "Whoever is not with me is against me, and whoever does not gather with me scatters." There are no gray areas in the spiritual realm. Neutrality is not possible in relation to spiritual things. There is no straddling the fence with Jesus. To walk with Jesus requires two feet; you can't have one foot in the devil's world and one foot in God's Kingdom. You're either all in or you're out. God spits anything lukewarm out of His mouth (Rev. 3:16). He doesn't tolerate "wishy-washiness." No "maybe" is allowed. You can't serve two masters, and you can't serve both God and money (Luke 16:13). "You cannot drink the cup of the Lord and the cup of demons too; you cannot have a part in both the Lord's table and the table of demons." 1 Corinthians 10:21. And may I add that Satan has a huge table spread in front of your computer called internet pornography? People who feast there are eating death.

"Elijah went before the people and said, 'How long will you waver between two opinions? If the Lord is God, follow him; but if Baal is God, follow him.' But the people said nothing." 1 Kings 18:21. God is not pleased with neutrality, compromise, indecision, partial obedience, or half-heartedness. The Lord requires undivided service. Every person is fighting either on the side of Christ or on the side of Satan; it is impossible to be neutral in the conflict.

If you don't know with certainty where you are in relationship with Jesus Christ, you need to settle that now. Do you really want to be straddling the fence should you step into eternity today? That's a gamble none of us should want to take. Turn away from sin and turn to God with all of your heart. "But if from there you seek the Lord your God, you will find him if you seek him with all your heart and with all your soul." Deuteronomy 4:29.

October 17 – **Life's Lessons**

Life's lessons, well learned, make us who we are. Look with me into the life of Obed-Edom. "The divisions of the gatekeepers…

Obed-Edom also had sons…(For God had blessed Obed-Edom.) 1 Chronicles 26:1, 4, 5.

We first learn of Obed-Edom in the story of David's attempt to bring the ark of God to the City of David some thirty years prior. David neglects to follow God's strict guidelines in transporting the ark, thus incurring God's wrath and the death of Uzzah. "David was afraid of God that day and asked, 'How can I ever bring the ark of God to me?' He did not take the ark to be with him in the City of David. Instead, he took it aside to the house of Obed-Edom the Gittite. The ark of God remained with the family of Obed-Edom in his house for three months, and the Lord blessed his household and everything he had." 1 Chronicles 13:12-14.

Obed-Edom learned two valuable lessons during that time which become part of his DNA. The first lesson is to respect and obey God's Word or suffer the consequences. He remembers what happened to Uzzah, so he becomes a gatekeeper. One of the chief duties of a gatekeeper or doorkeeper is to guard the door of the temple to prevent anyone from coming carelessly to the ark. "Do your best to present yourself to God as one approved, a worker who does not need to be ashamed and who correctly handles the word of truth." 2 Timothy 2:15.

The second lesson he learns is that blessings are found in God's Presence, and that is where he wants to be. "Better is one day in your courts than a thousand elsewhere; I would rather be a doorkeeper in the house of my God than dwell in the tents of the wicked." Psalm 84:10.

Are you learning life's lessons well, and are you using them to bless others? "…From everyone who has been given much, much will be demanded; and from the one who has been entrusted with much, much more will be asked." Luke 12:48.

October 18 – **From Hopelessness to Joy**

"For his anger lasts only a moment, but his favor lasts a lifetime; weeping may stay for the night, but rejoicing comes in the morning. You turned my wailing into dancing; you removed my sackcloth and clothed me with joy, that my heart may sing your praises and not be silent. Lord my God, I will praise you forever." Psalm 30:5, 11, 12.

The enemy of our soul, the devil, is a liar and the father of lies (John 8:44). He is a master at taking God's powerful Word and twisting it, attempting to reduce it to meaningless rubble, undermining its eternal truth, and creating doubt. He did it to Eve. "Now the serpent was more crafty than any of the wild animals the Lord God had made. He said to the woman, 'Did God really say, 'You must not eat from any tree in the garden"?" Genesis 3:1.

The devil wants us to believe we're stuck and nothing will ever change. Lie! He tells us God will always be angry with us; we will always be sad; the grief will never end; there is no hope. All lies! While in this state of mind when one feels completely hopeless, convinced the pain will never end, that we try to numb the pain with drugs, alcohol, porn, or any of a host of demonic substitutes; we may even consider suicide. Satan just smiles; this is exactly what he wants. But Jesus says, "The thief comes only to steal and kill and destroy; I have come that they may have life, and have it to the full." John 10:10. God says sadness is temporary; His favor lasts a lifetime; joy will come soon; we will dance and sing again. You choose who to believe. Turn your eyes on Jesus; look into His face.

Extend love, hope, and encouragement to someone today. It could be their turning point. "Though you have not seen him, you love him; and even though you do not see him now, you believe in him and are filled with an inexpressible and glorious joy, for you are receiving the end result of your faith, the salvation of your souls." 1 Peter 1:8, 9.

October 19 – **Selective Hearing**

I've accused my husband of having selective hearing; he hears what he wants to hear! I do that myself occasionally – just hear the part I agree with and forget the rest. Selective hearing is not our friend when it comes to the words of Jesus. We truly need to hear Him, even when His words bite.

"Salt is good, but if it loses its saltiness, how can it be made salty again? It is fit neither for the soil nor for the manure pile; it is thrown out. Whoever has ears to hear, let them hear." Luke 14:34, 35. Let's study these Scriptures a few minutes, then you hear God and draw your own conclusions.

Most of the salt used in Israel in Jesus' day came from the Dead Sea. It was full of impurities which caused it to lose some of its flavor. It was used in sacrifices to the Lord, so people connected salt to covenant making. To "eat salt with" a person symbolized hospitality. When covenants were made, they were usually confirmed with sacrificial meals, at which salt was always present. "Season all your grain offerings with salt. Do not leave the salt of the covenant of your God out of your grain offerings; add salt to all your offerings." Leviticus 2:13.

Salt is a necessary part of the daily diet. Even today, salt is used for flavoring and preserving, with its power to strengthen food and keep it from decay. We instantly know when our favorite food lacks salt or has too much.

Jesus tells us we are the salt of the earth and the light of the world (Matthew 5:13, 14). In a round-about way, here are a few questions for you concerning Luke 14:34, 35. Is Jesus referring to our salvation or our witness? Our witness is connected to our credibility. Is it possible to lose our witness and keep our salvation?

Can we lose our salvation and lose it all? There are no loopholes in God's Word. Is it possible to make it into heaven by the skin of our teeth? Think about it: Do teeth really have skin?

October 20 – **What's It Gonna Take?**

"What do you say?" "I really want chocolate ice cream!" exclaims my four year old grandson as his friend's mother hands him a vanilla ice cream cone. "No," I reply, slightly embarrassed. "You say 'Thank you.'" We try hard to teach our small children and grandchildren to say please and thank you. As adults, we're not always as appreciative as we should be either. We really want chocolate ice cream! It's the same with believing God. What's it gonna take for us to truly believe Him?

"Therefore many of the Jews who had come to visit Mary, and had seen what Jesus did, believed in him. But some of them went to the Pharisees and told them what Jesus had done." John 11:45, 46. Many Jews are at Mary and Martha's house comforting them in their time of loss. Now Jesus comes and raises Lazarus from the dead. Some of the Jews believe Him at this point; others run to go tattletale. Do you remember the parable Jesus tells of the other Lazarus, the beggar at the rich man's gate (Luke 16:19-31)? They both die; the rich man goes to hell, and Lazarus goes to heaven. The rich man asks Father Abraham, whom he sees in heaven with Lazarus, to please send Lazarus to his five brothers and warn them about hell. "He said to him, 'If they do not listen to Moses and the Prophets, they will not be convinced even if someone rises from the dead.'" Luke 16:31.

Jesus heals ten lepers in Luke 17:11-19. Only one returns to say thank you. "Jesus asked, 'Were not all ten cleansed? Where are the other nine?" Luke 17:17. Are they in such a hurry that they forget to say thank you? What's it gonna take for some people to say thank you to the Lord?

There are unbelieving and ungrateful people around us every day – even in our churches. Jesus tells us in John 20:29 that blessed are those who have not seen and yet believe. "Now, our God, we give you thanks, and praise your glorious name." 1 Chronicles 29:13.

Lord Jesus, I believe in You. I believe Your Word, the Holy Bible that I hold in my hands. Thank You for dying in my place; thank you for saving my soul. You are so good to me, and You do all things well. I love You, Lord.

October 21 – **No One**

It sounds like David is congratulating himself in 2 Samuel 22:21-25. "The Lord has dealt with me according to my righteousness; according to the cleanness of my hands he has rewarded me." 2 Samuel 22:21. Then we read these words of David four times in Psalms 14 and 53: There is no one who does good. "Everyone has turned away, they have become corrupt; there is no one who does good, not even one." Psalm 53:3. He must include himself in this statement. David realizes his righteousness is as filthy rags in the presence of the Living God (Isaiah 64:6).

Just when I think I'm so good – I do all the right things; I do such a great job, and I'm busily patting myself on the back – then I better repent of pride and acknowledge the fact that the only good thing in me is Jesus Christ and Him crucified. "'Why do you call me good?' Jesus answered. 'No one is good – except God alone.'" Mark 10:18. "May I never boast except in the cross of our Lord Jesus Christ, through which the world has been crucified to me, and I to the world." Galatians 6:14.

October 22 – **My Ransom**

I remember watching television shows as a child in which someone was kidnapped and held for ransom. The kidnappers would demand money in exchange for the release of the captive. Usually, in the end, the ransom price was paid and the person set free. (It was a much simpler world back then.)

At one time, I was held captive to sin. I didn't like where I was. It was a sad place, and even as a child, I hurt inside. I knew I was a sinner and wanted to be free. Then my grandfather introduced me to Jesus. I knelt on the hardwood floor beside my bed that night and asked Jesus to forgive me and come into my heart. When I climbed into bed, something was different inside. I was forgiven and free. It was real then, and He is still real inside of me today.

Psalm 46:8 reads "the ransom for a life is costly, no payment is ever enough." There is nothing in this world that can equal the value of the human soul. Therefore, God sent His only Son into the world to be my Redeemer. He paid my ransom price with His own blood. "But God will redeem me from the realm of the dead; he will surely take me to himself." Psalm 46:15.

"...just as the Son of Man did not come to be served, but to serve, and to give his life as a ransom for many." Matthew 20:28. I'm so thankful Jesus Christ willingly paid the price for my freedom. Have you accepted the price He paid for your soul? Ask Him today to be your ransom.

October 23 – **His Triumphal Entry**

All four Gospels record Jesus' Triumphal Entry into Jerusalem. "When Jesus entered Jerusalem, the whole city was stirred and asked, 'Who is this?' The crowds answered, 'This is Jesus, the prophet from Nazareth in Galilee.'" Matthew 21:11. "So the

Pharisees said to one another, 'See, this is getting us nowhere. Look how the whole world has gone after him!'" John 12:19.

The Triumphal Entry – a beautiful few hours for Jesus. How deserving He is of all our praise and worship! In no way do I want to diminish His glory that day, but the thought occurs to me that there are actually four triumphal entries for Jesus, this being the first one.

The second triumphal entry happens several weeks later, after His crucifixion and resurrection, at His ascension (Luke 24:51) into heaven, as all the heavenly host welcome Him back home, victorious and glorified! What a celebration that must have been!

The third triumphal entry will be when He returns to earth again, this time as King of kings and Lord of lords, The Rider on the white horse – in the not too distant future (Revelation 19:11-16)! "For the earth will be filled with the knowledge of the glory of the Lord as the waters cover the sea." Habakkuk 2:14. Look! This is Jesus! The whole world has gone after him!

I like to think of the fourth triumphal entry as a personal one – the day He came into my heart. O happy day! The day my Savior took my sins away! There was celebration that day in heaven as well (Luke 15:10)!

Has He made His triumphal entry into your heart? I am reminded of the words of an old hymn of the church, Come Into My Heart, O Lord Jesus (1924) by Harry Dudley Clark:

Come into my heart, Lord Jesus. Come in today, come in to stay.

October 24 – **Figlicious!**

When I think of a fig tree, I always remember the fig trees behind my grandparents' home in the country. As a child I popped many sweet ripe figs into my mouth right off the tree. Figlicious!

You'll find figs and fig trees mentioned in the Bible many times. "Early in the morning, as Jesus was on his way back to the city, he was hungry. Seeing a fig tree by the road, he went up to it but found nothing on it except leaves. Then he said to it, 'May you never bear fruit again!' Immediately the tree withered." Matthew 21:18, 19. Don't be critical of our Lord's action here; He wants to teach us a few things we need to know. Allow me to share several lessons I see.

This is Christ's only miracle of judgment on an inanimate object to teach a moral lesson. We understand the fig tree to be a symbol for the Jewish nation which abounds in religious profession (leaves) but is barren of righteousness (fruit). Its cursing is prophetic of the fate of the Jewish leaders who are about to reject their Messiah. Jesus is desperately looking for fruit in the nation of Israel as a whole and finds none.

Jesus looks for fruit in the lives of His followers. He desires us to bear fruit; He is doing everything He can to help us bear fruit (Luke 13:6-9). It is only as we are planted by His Living Water that we will thrive. "They will be like a tree planted by the water that sends out its roots by the stream. It does not fear when heat comes; its leaves are always green. It has no worries in a year of drought and never fails to bear fruit." Jeremiah 17:8. "They will still bear fruit in old age, they will stay fresh and green," Psalm 92:14. However, Jesus does not mince words in Matthew 7:19: "Every tree that does not bear good fruit is cut down and thrown into the fire." We may be full of green lush leaves, but are we a hypocrite tree? Be sure He will push back our branches and search diligently for fruit. And we all know how Jesus feels about hypocrites (Matthew 24:51). Are you figlicious?

Jesus teaches us about faith and prayer in His encounter with the barren fig tree (Mark 11:22-25). Our effectiveness in prayer depends upon our relationship with God and others. Our faith must rest in God alone. Also, we cannot hold unforgiveness in our hearts for it will affect our attitude when we pray and the effectiveness of our prayers.

Everything recorded in God's Word is for our learning and growing. What have you learned today, and how will it change you?

October 25 – **Is He King or Not?**

The narratives in Judges reveal how depraved and immoral some in Israel have become after turning away from God, which is the usual outcome when God and His Word are forsaken. Israel fails to keep their heritage of true religious faith and assimilates too much of the surrounding cultures. This cruelty and paganism generates God's tragic judgment on the nation. "In those days Israel had no king…" Judges 19:1. The nation is devoid of spiritual and national leadership. Many thousands die needlessly in civil war. The tribe of Benjamin is almost obliterated except for 600 men. How very sad.

God established human government thus endorsing it. "Let everyone be subject to the governing authorities, for there is no authority except that which God has established. The authorities that exist have been established by God." Romans 13:1. "Then Jesus said to them, 'Give back to Caesar what is Caesar's and to God what is God's.' And they were amazed at him." Mark 12:17. We learn from Scripture, as well as everyday life around us, that chaos and death breed in the absence of God's presence, so also in the heart of man where God is not welcome. God, not only desires to be our national King, but He also wants to be King in our hearts where He reigns supreme. "which God will bring about in his own time – God, the blessed and only Ruler, the King of kings and Lord of lords," 1 Timothy 6:15.

October 26 – **A Cover Up**

If you've ever read The Adventures of Tom Sawyer (1876) by Mark Twain, you may remember Tom having to whitewash a fence as punishment. Perhaps you've heard the expression, "Too poor to paint and too proud to whitewash!" Whitewash is a cheap white paint or coating of chalked lime used to quickly give a uniform clean appearance. It does serve a purpose, but mostly it is used in an attempt to hide something unpleasant or untrue – a cover up. It gives a false impression of what is underneath the surface. Whitewash is also a metaphor meaning to gloss over or cover up vices, crimes, or scandals.

Jesus doesn't "whitewash" anything when he addresses the teachers of the law and Pharisees in Matthew 23:13-36. "Woe to you, teachers of the law and Pharisees, you hypocrites! You are like whitewashed tombs, which look beautiful on the outside but on the inside are full of the bones of the dead and everything unclean. In the same way, on the outside you appear to people as righteous but on the inside you are full of hypocrisy and wickedness." Matthew 23:27, 28. Things are not always what they appear.

In Ezekiel's day, there are many false prophets leading people astray with their false words and lying visions. God compares them to flimsy walls covered in whitewash. It all looks and sounds good, but underneath are rotten dilapidated walls. These false prophets deceive many with their words, but they're all lies. The thin layers of whitewash cover up lies and death. "So I will pour out my wrath against the wall and against those who covered it with whitewash. I will say to you, 'The wall is gone and so are those who whitewashed it,'" Ezekiel 13:15.

God is a God of truth, and no lie will stand in His Presence. All whitewash will come off and every lie exposed. We might fool people with our experienced and expert whitewashing technique, but God is never mocked and He is never deceived. And God doesn't whitewash the liar's fate but groups all liars with a who's who list of sinners. "But the cowardly, the unbelieving, the vile, the murderers, the sexually immoral, those who practice magic arts, the idolaters and all liars – they will be consigned to the fiery lake of burning sulfur. This is the second death." Revelation 21:8.

Today would be a good day to come clean with God, remove the whitewash, and ask Him for forgiveness and a new beginning.

October 27 – **Stand Firm**

Studying end times is interesting to me. We may disagree on some of the finer points, and I admit I certainly don't have all the answers. But two things I know for sure – without a doubt – that Jesus is coming back to earth soon, and I must stand firm to the end. In our Bible reading today, we are told repeatedly to "watch out," "be on your guard," and "stand firm" – all for a very good reason.

Throughout Scripture, we read the words "stand firm." God's Word is eternal and stands firm in the heavens (Psalm 119:89). His love stands firm forever (Psalm 89:2). Isaiah warns us if we don't stand firm in our faith, we will not stand at all (7:9). "When the storm has swept by, the wicked are gone, but the righteous stand firm forever." Proverbs 10:25.

"At that time many will turn away from the faith and will betray and hate each other," Matthew 24:10. "At that time" is today! "Many will turn away from the faith" implies that the "many" once had saving faith but chose to turn away. No wonder Jesus tells us to stand firm! "Everyone will hate you because of me, but the one who stands firm to the end will be saved." Mark 13:13. "Stand firm, and you will win life." Luke 21:19. That is reason enough to spend time with Jesus every day, stay close to Him, obey Him, live for Him, and tell others about Him. Who knows? Jesus may come back for His Church today (Mark 13:32)!

October 28 – **Too Little, Too Late**

Too little, too late. It's a common cliché and will describe many people the moment after Jesus returns for His Bride. "I opened for my beloved, but my beloved had left; he was gone. My heart sank at his departure. I looked for him but did not find him. I called him but he did not answer." Song of Songs 5:6. The bridegroom comes for His bride, but she misses him. In Jesus' parable of the ten virgins, five are wise and ready; five are foolish and miss the Bridegroom altogether. "But he replied, 'Truly I tell you, I don't know you.' Therefore keep watch, because you do not know the day or the hour." Matthew 25:12, 13. Too little, too late, too bad. How sad!

Most theologians believe we are living in the last days of the church, the Bride of Christ. That means, at some point, there will be a last day. Typical human nature is to think I have plenty of time; I can do that tomorrow. Recognize this for what it is: a lie from the enemy. Don't put it off another day! Get your house in order! Do today what you know God is telling you to do. Don't be a part of the too little, too late crowd. Instead, be ready and expectant to meet Jesus at any moment! "Led in with joy and gladness, they enter the palace of the king." Psalm 45:15.

October 29 – **Our Example**

We teach our children as well as others by our words and our example. Even when we're not aware of it, we are teaching by example – sometimes good and sometimes not so good. We have learned and are still learning from the examples of others – carefully eating the fish and spitting out the bones. Joshua learns from the example of Moses, Elisha from Elijah, and Timothy from Paul.

Jesus washes the feet of His disciples. "When he had finished washing their feet, he put on his clothes and returned to his place. 'Do you understand what I have done for you?' he asked them...I have set you an example that you should do as I have done for you." John 13:12, 15. Does Jesus expect His disciples to go out and wash everyone's feet? No, it means much more than that. What has Jesus done for them? A few examples are His love, mercy, compassion, forgiveness, fellowship and relationship, teaching, humbly serving others, rebuking when necessary, giving to others, meeting the needs of others, putting others first. And He's not through being their example. He will give His life for them. They learn well from His example, because all but John die a martyr (excluding Judas Iscariot, of course), and John devotes his long life to serving the Lord and dying in exile.

Paul emphasizes in First Corinthians chapter ten that everything that happened to the children of Israel in the wilderness serves as examples to us today. "Now these things occurred as examples to keep us from setting our hearts on evil things as they did. These things happened to them as examples and were written down as warnings for us, on whom the culmination of the ages has come." 1 Corinthians 10:6, 11.

Are we a good example to others of what a true follower of Christ looks like? Will we follow His example even in death? "Now that you know these things, you will be blessed if you do them." John 13:17.

October 30 – **A Glimpse**

The queen of Sheba travels a long distance to visit King Solomon. She has heard many stories about the king and his wisdom, vast riches, and glorious temple, but she wants to see for herself. "When the queen of Sheba saw the wisdom of Solomon, as well as the palace he had built, the food on his table, the seating of his officials, the attending servants in their robes, the cupbearers in their robes and the burnt offerings he made at the temple of the Lord, she was overwhelmed." 2 Chronicles 9:3, 4. "But I did not believe these things until I came and saw with my own eyes. Indeed, not even half was told me; in wisdom and wealth you have far exceeded the report I heard." 1 Kings 10:7. Do you think the queen of Sheba gets a tiny glimpse of heaven?

One day I will go to heaven. This will be part of my story: "I traveled a long distance today but arrived instantly. I have heard and read stories all my life about the King of Kings and his glorious home. I have believed for many years but longed to experience it all for myself. In my first moment in heaven, I see the King, the beautiful city, the delicious food, so many happy people and magnificent angels! I am completely overwhelmed and thankful! Not even the half was told me! The beauty and riches far exceed the report I heard! No earthly words will ever be able to describe this glorious place! Being with Jesus is absolutely the best part, but after that, the realization that this is eternal! The Queen of Sheba had to return home, but not me! I will live here forever in peace and joy with Jesus Christ, my Wonderful Savior, and my precious loved ones! I praise my Lord for all He has done for me!"

"Do not let your hearts be troubled. You believe in God; believe also in me...I am going there to prepare a place for you." John 14:1, 2. "and into an inheritance that can never perish, spoil or fade. This inheritance is kept in heaven for you," 1 Peter 1:4.

October 31 – **A Safe Place**

Toddlers are quick! I, on the other hand, felt as if I was traveling in slow motion as I ran across the dining room floor to catch my two year old before she plopped down on shards of the cut glass bowl she had just pulled off the hutch while on her tippy toes. And I thought my home was child-proof! After all the child-proof locks, electric outlet covers, household cleaners put up high, and plastic bowls put down low, she still found that cut glass bowl within her reach. What's a parent to do? Our best. As parents we attempt to keep our children safe, especially in our own home. That is our responsibility.

"When you build a new house, make a parapet around your roof so that you may not bring the guilt of bloodshed on your house if someone falls from the roof." Deuteronomy 22:8. Houses in the ancient Near East had flat roofs with outside staircases, and rooftops were places of relaxation with family and friends. God instructs the Israelites to build a low wall or barrier around their roof tops to make their homes a safe place, otherwise a fall could be deadly.

Does God also expect us to provide spiritual safety for our children, family, and friends? Of course, He does. It is our responsibility to provide safe and clear boundaries for our children. "While I was with them, I protected them and kept them safe by that name you gave me..." John 17:12. We take the time needed to patiently teach them the ways of God and the rules of the home, lead by example, and only discipline when blatant disregard is evident. "Follow my example, as I follow the example of Christ." 1 Corinthians 11:1. We want our children to be physically and spiritually healthy, because we love them.

There comes a time, however, when our children grow into adulthood and must assume responsibility for their own lives. What if they decide to climb over that protective barrier that has been in place all those years? That is their decision, and they will be the ones to suffer the consequences. Our job of raising children is over, but we continue to pray and trust God always. He is faithful, and His Word is true.

"For you know that we dealt with each of you as a father deals with his own children, encouraging, comforting and urging you to live lives worthy of God, who calls you into his kingdom and glory." 1 Thessalonians 2:11, 12.

NOVEMBER

November 1 – **Overwhelming Love**

If you have experienced the loss of a loved one through death, you know how exhausting grief and sorrow can be. Jesus Christ – 100% God and 100% man – understands how we feel. He is not a god far away and unattached from his creation; He became part of His creation. On the night of His betrayal, God's Son displays His humanity, and at the same time, submits to His Father's perfect will for His life. "Then he said to them, 'My soul is overwhelmed with sorrow to the point of death. Stay here and keep watch with me.' Going a little farther, he fell with his face to the ground and prayed, 'My Father, if it is possible, may this cup be taken from me. Yet not as I will, but as you will.'" Matthew 26:38, 39. Why does He suffer and die? Because His overwhelming love for you and me overwhelms His overwhelming sorrow.

"When he rose from prayer and went back to the disciples, he found them asleep, exhausted from sorrow. 'Why are you sleeping?' he asked them. 'Get up and pray so that you will not fall into temptation.'" Luke 22:45, 46. I've been there – exhausted from sorrow – it's not a fun place to be, but it happens to all of us at some time in our lives. Jesus gives us the solution: Get up and pray. Wake up and pray; get out of bed and pray. Are you overwhelmed with sorrow? Get up and pray. It is as we pray and read His Word and draw close to Jesus that we find encouragement, peace, comfort, and the strength to move forward in life. Jesus tells us in Luke 22:53 that this is the hour when darkness reigns. It's just an hour. His light will soon dispel that darkness and joy will come; and the best part is, it will last for all eternity; never forget that.

Remember, Jesus understands, and more than that, He has the power to do something about our sorrow. As the cliché goes: He has been there and done that. "Surely he took up our pain and bore our suffering, yet we considered him punished by God, stricken by him, and afflicted." Isaiah 53:4.

November 2 – **Like a June Bug...**

Some things are just better up close and personal! Like a hug, or eating a piece of chocolate candy rather than staring at it behind the counter, or a walk in a rose garden instead of holding a picture of one. We will never enjoy any of these experiences from a distance. Have you heard these expressions? I will stick to you like glue! I'm stuck to you like a June bug on a screen door! We're so close, we're joined at the hip! What about the jingle – "I am stuck on Band-Aid brand cuz Band-Aid stuck on me." "...but there is a friend who sticks closer than a brother." Proverbs 18:24.

"Peter followed him at a distance, right into the courtyard of the high priest. There he sat with the guards and warmed himself at the fire." Mark 14:54. It is dangerous to follow Jesus from a distance. Soon Peter finds himself in the enemy's camp, around the enemy's campfire, jawing with the enemy. He is following Jesus – but not closely. He does something he said he would never do (Mark 14:31) – deny the Lord.

The realization of his sin hit Peter like a ton of bricks. "And he went outside and wept bitterly." Luke 22:62. It was quite a different outcome with Judas Iscariot. "When Judas, who had betrayed him, saw that Jesus was condemned, he was seized with remorse...Then he went away and hanged himself." Matthew

27:3, 5. Peter messed up, admits it, is truly repentant and then is truly forgiven. God turns boisterous, outspoken, uncouth, rowdy Peter into a mighty apostle.

Let's back it up. 4) Don't sin against God and do something you say you will never do. 3) Don't warm your hands around the enemy's campfire. 2) Don't go into the enemy's camp. 1) Don't follow Jesus from a distance. The moral of the story: Walk so close to Jesus that you feel His breath and you hear His heartbeat. With Jesus, you can never be too close for comfort. It's a comfortable, beautiful, and safe place to be – under His umbrella of protection and blessing. Stick closer to Jesus than that June bug on a screen door! "My feet have closely followed his steps; I have kept to his way without turning aside." Job 23:11.

November 3 – **A Dead End**

I recall hearing a statement made by an evangelist many years ago about Pilate, judge and governor during Jesus' trial. From a legend recorded in church history, it is believed that Pilate lives the rest of his life following Jesus' crucifixion repeatedly washing his hands in an attempt to wash away his guilt. Hand-washing will never be able to accomplish what only God can do. Wearied from misfortunes, he eventually commits suicide (approximately AD 37).

All four Gospels record the trial of Jesus before Pilate. "Are you the king of the Jews?" asked Pilate. "You have said so," Jesus replied. "From then on, Pilate tried to set Jesus free, but the Jewish leaders kept shouting, 'If you let this man go, you are no friend of Caesar. Anyone who claims to be a king opposes Caesar.'" John 19:12. He ignores his wife's message; he ignores his gut feeling that Jesus is innocent. His own security and comfort are at stake; he fears the emperor's frown and the loss of place and power. Pilate allows his weakness and fear of a disturbance to override his sense of justice. "Wanting to satisfy the crowd, Pilate released Barabbas to them. He had Jesus flogged, and handed him over to be crucified." Mark 15:15.

"When Pilate saw that he was getting nowhere, but that instead an uproar was starting, he took water and washed his hands in front of the crowd. 'I am innocent of this man's blood,' he said. 'It is your responsibility!'" Matthew 27:24. So ends Pilate's share in the greatest crime ever committed.

"Do not follow the crowd in doing wrong. When you give testimony in a lawsuit, do not pervert justice by siding with the crowd," Exodus 23:2. Pilate chooses expediency above principle. Multitudes do the same thing every day. What will you do? Do the right thing according to God's Word, no matter the volume of the crowd, because a crowd apart from Jesus Christ is a dead end.

November 4 – **Jesus, Remember Me**

Death is very close – at the door – for all three: Jesus and the two criminals. "In the same way the rebels who were crucified with him also heaped insults on him." Matthew 27:44. Talk about adding insult to injury; Satan is making sure of that! But something is about to change in the heavenly realm. Both rebels are on their way to hell. Rebel #1 continues on that same trek – no change there – his choice. But the other stops, thinks about it, turns around (or does an about-face in marching lingo), and goes the other direction, meeting Jesus eyeball to eyeball.

What happens in those few hours on the cross for Rebel #2? Is a mother praying somewhere for her son's salvation? Did someone say a prayer for Rebel #2 a long time ago, and at that moment, God pulls it out of the archives in heaven and says, "It's time for this one"? The heart of Rebel #2 begins to soften and change as the reality of a lifetime of sin hits his heart head-on. He responds with repentance, and Jesus saves him then and there on his death bed (so to speak). "Then he said, 'Jesus, remember me when you come into your kingdom.' Jesus answered him, 'Truly I tell you, today you will be with me in paradise.'" Luke 23:42, 43. What beautiful music to a dying man's ears! What an awesome demonstration of God's mercy and love!

"Do not remember the sins of my youth and my rebellious ways; according to your love remember me, for you, Lord, are good." Psalm 25:7. If there is doubt in your mind of your eternal destiny, don't wait another minute. Certainly don't wait until your last hours of life. You and I don't have a clue when our heart will beat for the last time. "Then I called on the name of the Lord: 'Lord, save me!'" Psalm 116:4.

November 5 – **What Are You Preparing For?**

God spoke these words to my heart on January 1, 2012. I've lived these words many years, but He had me write them down: "Prepare today for what God wants me to do tomorrow; do today what I prepared for yesterday." In Luke 23:56, we read of women preparing. "Then they went home and prepared spices and perfumes. But they rested on the Sabbath in obedience to the commandment." Then in Luke 24:1, we see the women do that for which they are prepared. "On the first day of the week, very early in the morning, the women took the spices they had prepared and went to the tomb."

"Joshua told the people, 'Consecrate yourselves, for tomorrow the Lord will do amazing things among you.'" Joshua 3:5. God desires His people to always be prepared to serve Him, move forward, fight and win battles in His name as Joshua does, and love and worship Him as the women do on that first Easter morning. It's a lifestyle of always preparing for what God wants us to do next, and at the same time, doing today that which we are already prepared to do for Him.

We could choose to live only for ourselves like the rich man who continued to build bigger barns; but then our results would be the same. "But God said to him, 'You fool! This very night your life will be demanded from you. Then who will get what you have prepared for yourself?'" Luke 12:20. May we live every day preparing for *and* accomplishing that which God has planned for us. Our work for the Lord on this earth will not be completed until God calls us home. Get ready! God wants to do amazing things!

November 6 – **Don't Let That Stop You!**

"I would read the Bible more, but I just don't understand it." Really? And you're going to let that stop you from reading your Bible? I don't understand everything that goes into a live play or performance, but I still enjoy it. I don't understand much at all about my computer or phone, but I still benefit from using them. The more I use these new fangled electronic devices, the more familiar I become with them. I was twelve years old when I read the Bible completely through the first time. Needless to say, I understood only a small portion of what I read, but the hunger for God's Word began to grow in me, and the discipline of daily time in the Word is a definite plus. I was eighteen the second time I read it through and have read it through many times since. Each time I see new and fresh things I haven't seen before. The more I read it, the more I love it, and the more I realize I still have so much to learn! I don't understand it all, but I stand on it all!

Jesus walks alongside the two men as they walk to Emmaus, but they don't recognize him. They are discussing the current event of the day – Jesus Christ, crucified, and now some say, resurrected. "And beginning with Moses and all the Prophets, he explained to them what was said in all the Scriptures concerning himself." Luke 24:27. He opens their eyes, and then disappears. "They ask each other, 'Were not our hearts burning within us while he talked with us on the road and opened the Scriptures to us?'" (v. 32).

"Yea, but Jesus is not here to walk beside me and teach me these things." Yea, but the Holy Spirit is. He will sit with you as you read and teach you the things you need to know. Ask, seek, and knock, and He will open your mind to understand. Listen to Him, just like the two men on the road to Emmaus. Give the Word your undivided attention. You will see Jesus; your heart will burn within you; and you will want to tell others what He says. "Then he opened their minds so they could understand the Scriptures." Luke 24:45. The Holy Spirit will do the same for you. "It is to be with him, and he is to read it all the days of his life so that he may learn to revere the Lord his God and follow carefully all the words of this law and these decrees." Deuteronomy 17:19.

A baby doesn't start out eating t-bone steak, and neither will you. The Holy Spirit will teach you and give you what you need as you grow in Christ. Just don't quit. If we stop growing and learning, we start dying. It's our choice.

November 7 – **What Does This Mean?**

It is the Day of Pentecost, and strange sounds are falling into the streets from the upper room. A crowd gathers. They hear the sound of a violent wind; they see a glow of light in the windows; and they hear many different languages spoken at the same time. "Amazed and perplexed, they asked one another, 'What does this mean?'" Acts 2:12.

Luke explains in his letter to Theophilus that this is none other but the gift the Father promised (Acts 1:4). God gives good gifts to His children (including you and me). A gift is something we receive when it is given to us. How rude of us to say to God we don't want His gift. He knows we need His gift just like the 120 people gathered together in the upper room.

Jesus tells them prior to His ascension that they will receive power when the Holy Spirit comes on them, power to be His witnesses all over the world (Acts 1:8). They are all believers and followers of Christ, but they need more. The "more" is the gift of the Holy Spirit.

The people on the street ask Peter and the other apostles, "What shall we do?" "Peter replied, 'Repent and be baptized, every one of you, in the name of Jesus Christ for the forgiveness of your sins. And you will receive the gift of the Holy Spirit.'" Acts 2:38. The prophet Joel predicted this day many years before (Joel 2:28-32 and Acts 2:17-21). This outpouring of the Holy Spirit is still happening in these "last of the last" days on people of all ages, male and female! Children of the Living God need this baptism in the Holy Spirit now more than ever. The coming of the Lord is near! We must be about the Father's business of telling others, and the Holy Spirit gives us the power to be His bold and courageous witnesses. We don't hear the violent wind or see the tongues of fire as they did in the initial outpouring of His Spirit, but we can still speak in other tongues as the Spirit enables us (Acts 2:4). Speaking in tongues is the evidence; it's how we know we are baptized in His Holy Spirit.

"till the Spirit is poured on us from on high, and the desert becomes a fertile field, and the fertile field seems like a forest." Isaiah 32:15. God desires for us to be a healthy fruitful forest, not a dry desert, or even a fertile field. Peter warns and pleads with the people (Acts 2:40). Today, be filled with His Holy Spirit. We need His power for living.

Thank You, Holy Father, for Your gift of the Holy Spirit. Baptize me with Your Spirit. I receive Your gift. I praise You for Your gift today.

November 8 – **You Can't Give What You Don't Have**

One day two Christians are on their way to a prayer meeting at their church. It is a special-called prayer meeting (why else would it be at 3:00 in the afternoon?). Since they live near the church, they decide to enjoy the afternoon and walk to church together. Along the way, they encounter a middle-aged gentleman, sitting in a wheelchair, holding a sign in one hand which reads, "Please help me," and a can with loose change in the other hand. One of the Christians says to the man, "Look at us! Silver and gold I do not have, but I can take you to go get a hamburger at McDonald's." Moral: You can't give what you don't have.

Now read the better and slightly similar story in Acts 3:1-10 again. Here are some things to think about. I wonder if the lame man's path had ever crossed the path of Jesus. The man is in the temple courts; are there people right under our noses who need our help? I can definitely relate to Peter when he says, "Silver and gold I do not have." But do I possess what Peter and John possess – boldness, power, and authority in Jesus' Name? When he's healed, the man goes into the temple, walking and jumping, and praising God.

There's a church just about on every corner in the small city in which I live. There are many people who are close to a church but who never step into a church. We need more of Jesus in the marketplace, more prayer for the lost and hurting; we should give Jesus more opportunities to do His work in our places of business. Only then will we see more of our friends, neighbors, and co-workers do as the healed man – join us in church. Why? Because they have already experienced the power and love of God in their lives, and they want to know more about this Jesus! Jesus in us in the marketplace can grow our churches! Because we have freely received, we should freely give (Matthew 10:8). Pray for opportunities to share the love of Jesus with others.

The fact remains: You can't give what you don't have. But what do you have? Compassion, a smile, a meal, a prayer, a visit to the hospital or convalescent center, a ride, an act of kindness (Acts 4:9), the ability to repair something broken, faith for a miracle? Ask God to fill you with His Holy Spirit (Acts 4:8) so that you can be "Jesus with skin-on" to somebody today.

"Each of you must bring a gift in proportion to the way the Lord your God has blessed you." Deuteronomy 16:17. I love this verse in the KJV as well. "Every man shall give as he is able, according to the blessing of the Lord thy God which he hath given thee." Ask God to bless you more so that you can bless others more – then do it. This is what makes life an adventure!

November 9 – **Full**

"I'm so full! If I eat another bite, I'll explode!" "I'm fuller than a tick on a hound dog!" (More proof I am from East Texas!)

When life squeezes you, whatever you're full of will come out. "If clouds are full of water, they pour rain on the earth..." Ecclesiastes 11:3. "They pour out arrogant words; all the evildoers are full of boasting." Psalm 94:4. "You will have plenty to eat, until you are full, and you will praise the name of the Lord your God, who has worked wonders for you; never again will my people be shamed." Joel 2:26.

Scripture teaches us that Stephen is full of God. "They chose Stephen, a man full of faith and of the Holy Spirit...a man full of God's grace and power..." Acts 6:5, 8. Life soon puts the squeeze on Stephen when he is brought before the Sanhedrin on false charges of blasphemy. What comes out? "But they could not stand up against the wisdom the Spirit gave him as he spoke." Acts 6:10. "All who were sitting in the Sanhedrin looked intently at Stephen, and they saw that his face was like the face of an angel." (v. 15).

Stephen is so completely full of faith, the Holy Spirit, God's grace and power, that it comes out in his speech and on his countenance.

Stephen takes advantage of the opportunity to speak for God, so he gives the Jewish leaders a history lesson starting with Abraham, with which they are very familiar, before he lowers the boom in Acts 7:51-53, "You stiff-necked people!..." He gets in their faces with the truth, and it cuts deep, but it's the truth nonetheless. Stephen looks up to heaven; Jesus pulls back the clouds so Stephen can see Him standing at the right hand of the Father, nodding His approval. Even in his dying breath, the heart of Jesus surfaces. "...Lord, do not hold this sin against them..." Acts 7:60. Do you remember Jesus' dying words on the cross? "...Father, forgive them, for they do not know what they are doing..." Luke 23:34.

When life squeezes the breath out of you, what comes out? Jesus will fill us with His Holy Spirit, as much as we want. Many times in Scripture, oil is symbolic of the Holy Spirit. The story of Elisha helping a poor widow is recorded in 2 Kings 4:1-7. "She left him and shut the door behind her and her sons. They brought the jars to her and she kept pouring. When all the jars were full, she said to her son, 'Bring me another one.' But he replied, 'There is not a jar left.' Then the oil stopped flowing." 2 Kings 4:5, 6. He will fill us to the brim as much as we can hold to meet every need.

November 10 – **Receive the Holy Spirit**

This is my testimony. I was 14 when I received the baptism in the Holy Spirit with the evidence of speaking in other tongues (just a little bit). I was with many other teenagers at Sabine Tabernacle in Beaumont, Texas for a summer revival. It was great! But then I went back home and teenage life resumed as normal (if there is such a thing when you're a teenager). I didn't think much more about it. On my first Mother's Day (as a new mom),

Gene and I went to the church we were attending at the time in Huntsville, Texas. Brother Barnes preached on the Holy Spirit. I got so hungry for more of God. That evening at home while sitting in bed, praying and reading my Bible, Jamie asleep in her crib and Gene at work, I cried out to God to fill me with His Holy Spirit. He did, and I began to speak in other tongues. Praying and praising in the Spirit is a vital part of my everyday life.

This is Gene's testimony. God baptized him in the Holy Spirit at home on an Easter Sunday afternoon a few years later. He was so desperate for more of God in his life, and God answered that cry of his heart.

This is Jamie's testimony. She accepted Jesus as her Savior at the age of four and baptized in water at the age of six. When she was eight years old, an old time Pentecostal Evangelist, Don Brankel, conducted a revival at our current church in Lufkin, Texas. Jamie went to the altar to receive the baptism in the Holy Spirit on a Valentine's evening. God answered that little girl's prayer, filled her with the Holy Spirit with the evidence of speaking in tongues, and she couldn't stop! We were the last to leave the church, because she wanted to stay at the altar! We could hear her speaking in tongues in the back seat of the car on the way home, as she brushed her teeth before bed, and in her bed while trying to go to sleep!

This is Janet's testimony. She accepted Jesus as her Savior at the age of six and was baptized in water shortly thereafter. She was filled and refilled with the Holy Spirit with the evidence of speaking in tongues many times in children's church, at kids' camps, and youth camps.

It is quite clear to me that salvation and baptism in the Holy Spirit are two separate experiences (Acts 8:14-17). Yes, the Holy Spirit draws you to Jesus before salvation, and you are born again by His Spirit and on your way to heaven. But you can have more of Him in your life today. Hunger and thirst for more of Jesus, and you will be filled (Matthew 5:6). "When they arrived, they prayed for the new believers there that they might receive the Holy Spirit, because the Holy Spirit had not yet come on any of them; they had simply been baptized in the name of the Lord Jesus." Acts 8:15, 16. How do they know that the Holy Spirit had not yet come on any of them? Because it is an understood realization by this time that speaking in tongues is the evidence of being filled with the Holy Spirit. Peter and John know these believers receive the Holy Spirit after they place their hands on them because they hear them speak in other tongues. It works the same way today.

"...You anoint my head with oil; my cup overflows." Psalm 23:5. "I will no longer hide my face from them, for I will pour out my Spirit on the people of Israel, declares the Sovereign Lord." Ezekiel 39:29.

November 11 – **The Good News**

Have you ever watched birds feed their hungry babies? On our back porch, there is a corner of space where little red-breasted house wrens love to build their nest each spring. I derive so much pleasure in watching the mother bird sit on her eggs; and when the babies are hatched, mommy and daddy bird stay busy feeding their hungry wide-open mouth offspring!

Cornelius and his family and friends remind me of those baby birds so eager and hungry to hear everything Peter has to say (Acts 10:34-48). When Peter arrives, he shares the Good News of Jesus Christ with this house full of Gentile believers in God. They are so hungry for the truth, and they are not disappointed. "All the prophets testify about him that everyone who believes in him receives forgiveness of sins through his name." Acts 10:43. At that moment, they believe; and at that moment they are saved.

"While Peter was still speaking these words, the Holy Spirit came on all who heard the message." Acts 10:44. Wow! That didn't take long! "For they heard them speaking in tongues and praising God…" (v. 46). I have witnessed a few people in my life saved one minute and baptized in the Holy Spirit the next. However, we seem to think today there should be more time between the two experiences – not necessarily. Even if it's years after salvation that a person is filled with the Holy Spirit, better then than never!

The simple message of the Good News of Jesus Christ has the same life-transforming power today as it did then. There is no other name under heaven whereby man can be saved (Acts 4:12). When the speaker is anointed and full of the power of the Holy Spirit, and when the hearers are hungrily anticipating a touch from God, the stage is set for miracles from heaven! However, anyone can be saved at anytime and anywhere; they need only to believe. And anyone can be filled with the Holy Spirit at anytime and anywhere; they need only to be saved and believe.

"…So then, even to Gentiles God has granted repentance that leads to life." Acts 11:18. Praise God! "I, the Lord, have called you in righteousness; I will take hold of your hand. I will keep you and will make you to be a covenant for the people and a light for the Gentiles," Isaiah 42:6. God has promised to pour out His Spirit on all people (Joel 2:28). Praise the Lord!

November 12 – **A Peaceful Night's Sleep**

Insomnia is not Peter's problem this night. Many people don't sleep well because of significant life stress or anxiety – but not Peter. He sleeps like a rock. (After all, his name does mean Rock!) How does he do it? He is sound asleep on the hard prison floor, chained between two soldiers (Acts 12:6-19). Herod plans to kill Peter like he did James. Actually, a guard could come get him at any time and take off his head, but he's not worried. Perhaps he remembers the words of Jesus recorded in Matthew 6:27. "Can any one of you by worrying add a single hour to your life?" So why worry? Might as well sleep!

Peter is in such a deep sleep that not even the angel's bright light stirs him. The angel must kick him in the side and then tell him "Quick, get up!" Peter is still more asleep than awake. The angel spells it out for him. "Put on your clothes and sandals... Wrap your cloak around you and follow me." Peter thinks he is dreaming, so he's not in any hurry. After walking past sleeping guards, gates that open on their own, and a leisurely walk down the street, the angel disappears – then Peter wakes up! He realizes this is no dream and walks to Mary's house, the mother of John Mark, where friends are having an all night prayer meeting for him. Long story short, God answers their prayers and they are all astonished!

Remember Jacob's campout at Bethel? "When he reached a certain place, he stopped for the night because the sun had set. Taking one of the stones there, he put it under his head and lay down to sleep." Genesis 28:11. And we think we need our Serta and feather pillow to sleep well!

Both Jacob and Peter could have stayed awake all night and worried. They both had more than enough to stress over, but what would it have accomplished? Nothing, except to add fatigue and exhaustion to their long list of problems. We don't have to lose sleep over the worries and concerns of life. Trust God to take care of you. Rest in Him. "He will not let your foot slip – he who watches over you will not slumber;" Psalm 121:3. "When you lie down, you will not be afraid; when you lie down, your sleep will be sweet." Proverbs 3:24.

November 13 – **God Never Wastes an Experience**

Here's a Scripture that describes the Apostle Paul, pre-conversion. "Their feet rush into sin; they are swift to shed innocent blood. They pursue evil schemes; acts of violence mark their ways." Isaiah 59:7. Saul's fame as a persecutor of the church is notorious. It is believed Saul was born a couple years after Jesus. He is the son of strict Jewish parents, educated well in the Law of Moses, a Pharisee of Pharisees. "For you have heard of my previous way of life in Judaism, how intensely I persecuted the church of God and tried to destroy it. I was advancing in Judaism beyond many of my own age among my people and was extremely zealous for the traditions of my fathers." Galatians 1:13, 14. Paul knows the Holy Scriptures backwards and forwards, all to prove you can know God's Word well and still be full of the devil! The devil knows God's Word too as evidenced in the Garden of Eden with Adam and Eve (Genesis 3:1) and in the temptation of Christ in the wilderness (Matthew 4:1-11).

Then one day Saul encounters Jesus Christ, and everything changes. Everything. His life is literally turned upside down for the glory of God! God transforms this reprobate into a powerful man of God, and only His power can accomplish such a task. Shortly thereafter, Saul goes to Arabia and Damascus for three years where Jesus Christ reveals to Him what He needs to know – the Truth. Jesus takes Saul's strong and commanding prior knowledge of the Law of Moses and Scripture and builds on it. He takes all of Saul's pre-conversion experiences and uses them to make him the great Apostle Paul. Paul's life and life experiences are redeemed by the blood of Jesus Christ!

God never wastes an experience – good or bad – when we commit our lives to Him. He can use anything and everything for His glory, when we give it all to Him – our failures, mistakes, ignorance, loss, pain, heartache, successes, accomplishments, joys, past, present, and future. He is a Master at creating beauty from ashes (Isaiah 61:3). But it won't happen until we have our own personal encounter with Jesus Christ and submit our lives to Him.

God has the power to redeem our lives completely. He redeems our pain and gives us joy. He redeems every piece of our ugly baggage when we give it to Him. Why does He do this? Why does He even care? Because of His matchless love for us, and so we can help someone else (2 Corinthians 1:4).

"Here is a trustworthy saying that deserves full acceptance: Christ Jesus came into the world to save sinners – of whom I am the worst." 1 Timothy 1:15.

November 14 – **Die Daily**

When was the last time you crucified your flesh? Crucifixion is painful, and we tend to steer clear of anything that causes us discomfort. How can we slide into heaven with the least amount of pain as possible? That's what we want to know! The truth is something must die so that something better can live (John 12:24). Is your spiritual walk lacking? Do you feel as if you're at a standstill with Christ? Then what needs to die in your life, so that fresh new life can enter? More than likely, you already know the answer to that question. "Those who belong to Christ Jesus have crucified the flesh with its passions and desires." Galatians 5:24.

Paul loves to get in our business! He tells us in Galatians 5:19-21 the obvious acts of the flesh. Following this long list of sins (Let's just call it what it is!), which we all have personally experienced one or more of these at some time in our lives, he says "...and the like. I warn you, as I did before, that those who live like this will not inherit the kingdom of God." (v. 21). "and the like" includes a lot more sins not included here! But notice this: "Those who *live* like this" means those who make these sins "and the like" a way of life, not the occasional blunder of jealousy or envy. It includes those sins we commit, repent of, but later go back and do again. That's called bondage. These cycles must be crucified, put to death once and for all, so that new life can come forth. Jesus makes this possible. It's by His strength, not our own.

"Now see to it that you drink no wine or other fermented drink and that you do not eat anything unclean." Judges 13:4. The angel of the Lord appears to Manoah's wife (Samson's parents) and tells her in order for something holy to be born, she must put to death the unclean.

You must die to self so that God can birth something better in your life. Crucify that thing that is holding you back, that stands between you and God! "I have been crucified with Christ and I no longer live, but Christ lives in me. The life I now live in the body, I live by faith in the Son of God, who loved me and gave himself for me." Galatians 2:20.

"Have I now become your enemy by telling you the truth?" Galatians 4:16.

November 15 – **What a Night!**

It is doubtful you have ever had a night like Paul and Silas does in Acts 16:16-40. Please read the story there first. Here are some of the high points I see. Paul and Silas are thrown into prison, because Paul gets irritated with a female slave fortune-teller who keeps following them around. "She followed Paul and the rest of us, shouting, 'These men are servants of the Most High God, who are telling you the way to be saved.' She kept this up for many days. Finally Paul became so annoyed that he turned around and said to the spirit, 'In the name of Jesus Christ I command you to come out of her!' At that moment the spirit left her." Acts 16:17, 18. Her employers are not pleased that their money-maker has been silenced. Dragged into the marketplace, Paul and Silas are stripped and beaten with rods, and thrown into the inner cell of the prison with their feet fastened in stocks.

Since sleep is hard to come by that night, Paul and Silas decide to have church – worshiping, praying, and singing. The prisoners are awake, listening; the jailer is asleep. There's a violent earthquake, the prison shakes, doors fly open, chains fall off – now the jailer is awake! He thinks all the prisoners have escaped, so he will save his boss the trouble and go ahead and kill himself! "But Paul shouted, 'Don't harm yourself! We are all here!'" (v. 28). The jailer must have heard that fortune-teller before God set her free. "He then brought them out and asked, 'Sirs, what must I do to be saved?'" (v. 31). The jailer takes Paul and Silas to his house, wakes everybody up, so his family can hear these men. He washes their wounds. He and his entire family believe and are baptized, and the jailer gives Paul and Silas a meal. What a night! When daylight finally dawns, they are "escorted" out of prison and go to Lydia's house and encourage the brothers and sisters there. Paul and Silas are the ones who have been beaten and thrown into prison, and they encourage others!

The next time sleep escapes you, perhaps God wants you to spend time in worship and prayer. When God keeps reminding you of someone, He wants you to pray for them. Get out of bed and find a place to worship. You may have to bring it down a notch if the rest of your family is sound asleep. True worship is powerful at any time day or night. It shakes things up! Doors open! Chains fall off! Captives are set free! People get saved! And people are encouraged in the Lord!

"Ascribe to the Lord the glory due his name; worship the Lord in the splendor of his holiness." Psalm 29:2. "Worship the Lord with gladness; come before him with joyful songs." Psalm 100:2.

November 16 – **It's Called Encouragement**

While Saul sits under the tamarisk tree (1 Samuel 22:6) having a pity party (I can almost see his bottom lip protruding and quivering!), which results in the irrational and illogical deaths of 85 priests plus an entire town of men, women, children and infants, Jonathan seeks out David his friend. While Saul digs his own grave, Jonathan denies himself for the greater good of Israel and God's unmistakable will. "And Saul's son Jonathan went to David at Horesh and helped him find strength in God. 'Don't be afraid,' he said. 'My father Saul will not lay a hand on you. You will be king over Israel, and I will be second to you. Even my father Saul knows this.'" 1 Samuel 23:16, 17.

Now Jonathan can probably use some encouragement at this point. After all, he's watching his enraged father go berserk and cause misery and devastation at every turn. Even Jonathan's own life has been in jeopardy at the hand of his father. Nevertheless, his eyes are not turned inward. He goes to his friend to, "help him find strength in God."

Do I stand around waiting for someone to encourage me? Perhaps I waste too much time waiting for my path to cross the path of someone else before I offer an encouraging word. Today, there are people all around me who are in desperate need of encouragement. I will put forth effort and go to someone today to, "help him find strength in God." "Therefore encourage one another and build each other up, just as in fact you are doing." 1 Thessalonians 5:11.

November 17 – **Stand Firm and Hold Fast**

Paul warns the believers in Thessalonica (and us) to hold tightly to the teaching we receive in God's Word. In order to hold something tightly, we must first know what it is we are holding. This is another good reason to be an avid student of God's Word. It is imperative that we know what and in Whom we believe (John 4:42).

"So then, brothers and sisters, stand firm and hold fast to the teachings we passed on to you, whether by word of mouth or by letter." 2 Thessalonians 2:15. "In the name of the Lord Jesus

Christ, we command you, brothers and sisters, to keep away from every believer who is idle and disruptive and does not live according to the teaching you received from us." 2 Thessalonians 3:6. Whether in the world or in the church, we must constantly be careful that we remain true to the teaching of the Word, for it is easy to be deceived. Allow the truth of the Bible to be your filter by which you view everything. God's Word is our sure foundation and the final authority. Paul advocates helping those in real need, but able-bodied people who refuse to work steadily for a living should not be supported by the church. This is where discernment comes in and good stewardship of God's resources.

Moses answered the people, 'Do not be afraid. Stand firm and you will see the deliverance the Lord will bring you today. The Egyptians you see today you will never see again.'" Exodus 14:13. "You will be hated by everyone because of me, but the one who stands firm to the end will be saved." Matthew 10:22. "But you are to hold fast to the Lord your God, as you have until now." Joshua 23:8.

November 18 – **A Tiny Glimpse of Heaven**

"…a land flowing with milk and honey…a land with large, flourishing cities you did not build, houses filled with all kinds of good things you did not provide, wells you did not dig, and vineyards and olive groves you did not plant…a land with brooks, and deep springs gushing out into the valleys and hills; a land with wheat and barley, vines and fig trees, pomegranates, olive oil and honey; a land where bread will not be scarce and you will lack nothing…" Deuteronomy 6:3, 10-11; 8:7-9. God describes the beautiful land He is leading the children of Israel into to inherit, a land He has prepared just for them. I can't help but think this is a minuscule glimpse into heaven.

"But he brought us out from there to bring us in and give us the land he promised on oath to our ancestors." Deuteronomy 6:23. God brings us out of a life of sin and bondage to bring us into His Kingdom and ultimately to bring us into heaven, our promised land. When we connect our lives to God through faith in His Son Jesus Christ, He brings us out to bring us in. Do we deserve or earn His gift of salvation and heaven? No. "But it was because the Lord loved you..." (7:8). God always blesses us so much more than we deserve or can give Him.

As children of the Most High God, we have a lot to look forward to! Heaven is a beautiful, real, exciting, and busy place. Our imagination and vocabulary can't begin to comprehend or describe heaven. Think of your happiest moment on earth; multiply that experience a billion times; and then maybe, just maybe, you can begin to understand the eternal glory that awaits you – heaven. "However, as it is written: 'What no eye has seen, what no ear has heard, and what no human mind has conceived' – the things God has prepared for those who love him." 1 Corinthians 2:9. "My Father's house has many rooms; if that were not so, would I have told you that I am going there to prepare a place for you?" John 14:2.

November 19 – **Clearly God**

"Lord, the Lord Almighty, may those who hope in you not be disgraced because of me; God of Israel, may those who seek you not be put to shame because of me." Psalm 69:6. David is still fighting his personal and national battles. He tries to reason with God; he cries out to God to save him, so that others who hope in Him won't become discouraged and lose hope. David understands people are watching his life. He has sought to live an upright life, and he foresees other godly men who may become disheartened if his urgent need receives no response from God. He also knows there are many people around him who are seeking to know the One True God. What better way for God to show Himself strong than to rescue David from all his enemies?

I believe David also understands his own weaknesses and proclivity to sin. He is very aware people are examining his life and in no way wants to bring reproach upon God or cause someone to stumble. He desires to please God and for others to see Almighty God at work in his life. The Apostle Paul writes these words, "Therefore I urge you to imitate me." 1 Corinthians 4:16. I believe David would concur.

"Therefore I urge you to imitate me." In all honesty, can I make that statement to someone? Do others see Jesus Christ alive and well in me? Is my life above reproach? As Christians, we know others scrutinize our lives. We're not perfect; but are we reflecting Jesus Christ and His grace clearly to the world around us? Do they see Rock-solid faith in us even when we journey through the valley of the shadow of death? How do we handle life's successes? How are we in the storm? People are searching for Jesus. Will they find Him in me or you? "They came to Philip, who was from Bethsaida in Galilee, with a request. 'Sir,' they said, 'we would like to see Jesus.'" John 12:21.

Father God, forgive me when I give mixed signals. Strengthen me. May others see Your Son in me, and may it cause them to hunger and thirst after You.

November 20 – **The Divine Call**

Evangelist Billy Graham says he received his call to preach the Gospel while playing golf at the age of 19. Jeremiah is a youth when God commissions him to be a prophet. He argues with God that he is too young; God wins that argument (Jeremiah 1:7). God uses a blinding light to knock Saul to the ground and calls him to be the Apostle Paul and take the Good News to the

Gentiles (Acts 9:3). God uses different ways to call His servants into ministry. The important factor is that His spokespersons are divinely called and equipped for ministry. God puts His Word in their hearts.

"But if I say, 'I will not mention his word or speak anymore in his name,' his word is in my heart like a fire, a fire shut up in my bones. I am weary of holding it in; indeed, I cannot." Jeremiah 20:9. Jeremiah speaks out God's Word fearlessly and tirelessly in spite of the persecution.

"For when I preach the gospel, I cannot boast, since I am compelled to preach. Woe to me if I do not preach the gospel!" 1 Corinthians 9:16. The Apostle Paul obeys God's call on his life to the point of martyrdom and glad to do it.

Let us pray for those whom God has divinely called to preach and teach His Word in our churches and communities. May they be filled with His Word, anointed, and empowered by the Holy Spirit to preach the Word with boldness and clarity. May God divinely call others to follow Him into all the world, and may they obey His call.

November 21 – **Completeness Will Come**

We think we're so smart, but God's Word tells us we only know part of the story. "For we know in part and we prophesy in part," 1 Corinthians 13:9. However, there will come a day for the child of God when he or she will know the whole story and the whole truth. That day is the day of their death as we know it.

"but when completeness comes, what is in part disappears." (v. 10). That day came on the morning of November 17, 2012, for my daughter, Jamie. What is one of the saddest days of my life was by far the best day of her life. She experienced at that moment the perfection, the completeness of Jesus Christ, instantly released from months of excruciating physical and emotional pain, she found herself in the arms of her Savior – free, breathing pure life, rejoicing! At that moment, she understood; it all made perfect sense (Psalm 116:15). One day I will experience my own moment of completeness.

"For now we see only a reflection as in a mirror; then we shall see face to face. Now I know in part; then I shall know fully, even as I am fully known." (v. 12). We will see Jesus face to face; that one moment alone will make all the trials of this life fade into oblivion. We will know the answers to our questions, if it even matters then. Yes, we should keep learning and growing in Christ every day of this life, knowing all the while, our knowledge will only be in part until we meet Christ. "Let us acknowledge the Lord; let us press on to acknowledge him. As surely as the sun rises, he will appear; he will come to us like the winter rains, like the spring rains that water the earth." Hosea 6:3.

"A good name is better than fine perfume, and the day of death better than the day of birth." Ecclesiastes 7:1.

November 22 – **In Life and Death**

David knows there is more to this life than just this life. So much of God's Word applies to us in the life we live on earth today, and at the same time, to eternal life to come. Read these three verses and think of them in the context of today. "But I trust in you, Lord; I say, 'You are my God.' My times are in your hands; deliver me from the hands of my enemies, and from those who pursue me. Let your face shine on your servant; save me in your unfailing love." Psalm 31:14-16. As God's child, I trust Him for He is my God. Time and timing are in His hands. He delivers me today; He watches over me; He saves me by the power of His great love expressed through Jesus' death on the cross for my sins. Hallelujah!

Now, reread them from the standpoint of their ultimate fulfillment in heaven. When I step into heaven one day, I will be so thankful that I trusted Him on earth. I will bow before Him and say, "You are my God. You truly are all wise and knowing; you have delivered me from the enemy of my soul; I am safe. With my eyes, I see You in all of Your royal splendor and glory. Your wonderful love has saved me for all eternity, and I will forever praise You." Hallelujah!

Our God is the God of today and tomorrow. He rules over life, death, and the life to come. "If only for this life we have hope in Christ, we are of all people most to be pitied." 1 Corinthians 15:19. "Dear friends, now we are children of God, and what we will be has not yet been made known. But we know that when Christ appears, we shall be like him, for we shall see him as he is." 1 John 3:2.

November 23 – **Giving Them Over**

Paul makes no apologies for his strong teaching in Romans 1:18-32. He tells it like it is, because it is God's truth and we need to know it. This passage merits a slower reread and meditation. Paul knows we are prone to sin, thus his solid warning.

We do not have the license to pick and choose the parts of God's Word we will agree with, believe, and live by. Yet that is exactly what many of us do, professed Christians included. We buy into Satan's lies: This feels good, so I'm gonna do it! This doesn't hurt anyone, so it's okay. Society says this is acceptable, so I think I'll try it.

"Furthermore, just as they did not think it worthwhile to retain the knowledge of God, so God gave them over to a depraved mind, so that they do what ought not to be done." Romans 1:28. When it gets to this point, we don't even realize that what we're doing is contrary to God's holiness. At the first hint of conviction, we dismiss the thought. Basically, we don't care; we're trapped in a lie. "So I gave them over to their stubborn hearts to follow their own devices." Psalm 81:12. God has two purposes in "giving them over" to sin: to allow sin's consequences as part of His judgment on them (Romans 2:2), and to make them realize their need for salvation (Romans 2:4).

God doesn't offer us a smorgasbord of lifestyles from which to choose. He is God, and He has already made the rules for His creation; they are contained in the pages of the Holy Bible. "For whoever keeps the whole law and yet stumbles at just one point is guilty of breaking all of it. For he who said, 'You shall not commit adultery,' also said, 'You shall not murder.' If you do not commit adultery but do commit murder, you have become a lawbreaker." James 2:10, 11.

All is not hopeless for the one who wants to please God, for He has provided a way of escape. A person may repent of sin and turn in faith to Jesus Christ. "But God demonstrates his own love for us in this: While we were still sinners, Christ died for us." Romans 5:8.

November 24 – **I Am Blessed!**

I am so blessed, and let me tell you why! I was born into this world a sinner, but I have been born again in preparation for the next – all made possible by my Savior Jesus Christ, God's only Son. I could not save myself, but because I believe in Him and have faith in His Name, I will live forever with Him! How do I know this? Because His Holy Spirit lives in me! I have His joy, His peace, His strength, His love, His assurance! These come from Him, not me. God created each of us eternal beings; you and I will live forever – long past this life – somewhere. My destination is heaven. How about you?

"Blessed are those whose transgressions are forgiven, whose sins are covered. Blessed is the one whose sin the Lord will never count against them." Psalm 32:1, 2 and Romans 4:7, 8. These two verses describe me!

Let's "rightly divide the word of truth" (2 Timothy 2:15) and look at the three separate parts that make up these two verses. My transgressions are forgiven because one day… "Then Jesus said to her, 'Your sins are forgiven.'" Luke 7:48. Thank You, Jesus!

My sins are covered because… "You forgave the iniquity of your people and covered all their sins." Psalm 85:2. "and from Jesus Christ, who is the faithful witness, the firstborn from the dead, and the ruler of the kings of the earth. To him who loves us and has freed us from our sins by his blood," Revelation 1:5. His blood covers my sin!

The Lord will never count my sin against me because… "as far as the east is from the west, so far has he removed our transgressions from us." Psalm 103:12. My sin is gone! Praise His Holy Name forever!

What about you? Are you blessed?

November 25 – **To Whom Do You Belong?**

The practice of slavery was prevalent in ancient times. In Israel, slavery was a mild and merciful system compared to that of other nations. God put His guidelines in the Law of Moses on how slaves were to be treated, for all human life is important to God. Paul talks about slavery to the Romans, because it is something to which they can relate.

"When you were slaves to sin, you were free from the control of righteousness. What benefit did you reap at that time from the things you are now ashamed of? Those things result in death! But now that you have been set free from sin and have become slaves of God, the benefit you reap leads to holiness, and the result is eternal life." Romans 6:20-22.

We are all slaves to someone. To whom do you belong? There are really only two answers to that question: God or Satan. Satan wants us to believe that if we give our lives to God, we will lose our freedom and won't have any more fun. Nothing could be further from the truth! We find our freedom in Christ. Satan is the hard taskmaster. The end result of sin is eternal death, not just physical death; it's the eternal part about which we should be concerned. Physical death is over quickly; eternal death lasts – well, forever! Sin takes us down every time, but Jesus lifts us up. When we are born again, we realize how ugly our sin really was. Yes, I'm a slave to Jesus Christ; He is my Master, and I belong to Him.

"But all sinners will be destroyed; there will be no future for the wicked. The salvation of the righteous comes from the Lord; he is their stronghold in time of trouble." Psalm 37:38, 39.

November 26 – **When All Is Ready**

God is the Master Architect and Designer behind the construction of the temple and its furnishings. He gives Kings David and Solomon His plan, and they follow it. King Solomon completes the temple "in all its details according to its specifications" (1 Kings 6:38) and its furnishings "according to the specifications." It is God's house, and He knows exactly what He wants; Solomon obeys down to the last detail.

When all is ready according to God's stipulations, and the ark of the Lord's covenant is securely beneath the wings of the cherubim in the Most Holy Place, the priests and Levites begin the celebration. "The trumpeters and musicians joined in unison to give praise and thanks to the Lord. Accompanied by trumpets, cymbals and other instruments, the singers raised their voices in praise to the Lord and sang: 'He is good; his love endures forever.'

Then the temple of the Lord was filled with the cloud, and the priests could not perform their service because of the cloud, for the glory of the Lord filled the temple of God." 2 Chronicles 5:13, 14.

God has given us His plan of salvation. "If you declare with your mouth, 'Jesus is Lord,' and believe in your heart that God raised him from the dead, you will be saved." Romans 10:9. As we follow and obey God's plan for our lives, and praise and worship Him with exuberance, we will be filled with His Presence! "Give thanks to the Lord, for he is good; his love endures forever." Psalm 107:1.

November 27 – **From Meaningless to Meaningful**

No one is certain that Solomon wrote Ecclesiastes (translated teacher or preacher); but if he did, I wonder if it would read differently if he had remained humble and faithful to God throughout his life. "So I hated life, because the work that is done under the sun was grievous to me. All of it is meaningless, a chasing after the wind." Ecclesiastes 2:17. Perhaps the author's primary purpose is to warn others so they don't make the same mistakes he made. He makes it quite clear that earthly possessions and personal ambition do not bring contentment or add true meaning to life.

In fact, we learn from the complete story of the Bible that knowing Jesus Christ as Savior and Lord is the only way to have a meaningful life. And isn't that something we all want – a life that has meaning? We can find our purpose, the reason we're on this earth, only through a personal relationship with Jesus. Knowing Him makes life worth living; nothing else comes close. "For the kingdom of God is not a matter of eating and drinking, but of righteousness, peace and joy in the Holy Spirit." Romans 14:17.

Instead of amassing treasure here on earth, let's be more concerned about increasing our treasure in heaven. We're all just passing through this temporary life. For the child of God, the best is yet to come! I love these words from a poem by C. T. Studd: "Only one life, 'twill soon be past, Only what's done for Christ will last."

November 28 – **No Bible?**

I can't imagine walking through this life without God's Word. Where would we find direction, purpose, a reason to live, answers to our questions, wisdom, or a relationship with our Creator God? We would be lost, without a compass, stumbling in the dark, and would agree with the writer of Judges 17:6, "In those days Israel had no king; everyone did as they saw fit." I am so very thankful for the written Word of God.

God's Word is a bright and shining light in a dark sinful world. The Old Testament is extremely important to our spiritual life; it is the foundation for what we believe about God and His character. One purpose of God's Word is to authenticate the divinity of Jesus Christ, for we see Him in every book of the Bible. Reading, applying, and living God's Word adds eternal value to our lives.

"For everything that was written in the past was written to teach us, so that through the endurance taught in the Scriptures and the encouragement they provide we might have hope." Romans 15:4. The Bible teaches us about endurance. "Give thanks to the Lord, for he is good; his love endures forever." Psalm 118:1. "if we endure, we will also reign with him. If we disown him, he will also disown us;" 2 Timothy 2:12. When I need encouragement, the first place I go to is my Bible. "...But David found strength in the Lord his God." 1 Samuel 30:6. The KJV says this: "...but David encouraged himself in the Lord his

God." Learning endurance and finding encouragement from the Bible provide us with the hope we need to walk successfully through life and one day make an entrance into heaven. This world has no hope to give us. Jesus Christ is our Hope, and we find Him in God's Word.

Daily Bible reading is one of those good and healthy habits we must develop and practice. "All Scripture is God-breathed and is useful for teaching, rebuking, correcting and training in righteousness, so that the servant of God may be thoroughly equipped for every good work." 2 Timothy 3:16, 17.

November 29 – **Renewed!**

This body I'm living in is prone to aging. Tell me about it! Also wrinkles, gray hair, dry skin, aches and pains, fat, creaky joints, sickness and disease, and a general "slowing down." Need I say more? You get the idea. I can color, face lift, Botox, liposuction, eat more oatmeal, and dress like a 16 year old. Nothing really helps. I'm growing older! And I'm okay with that, because His Spirit within me is enabling my spirit to grow stronger every day! This body will return to dirt one day, and I'm okay with that too, because God will give me a new body that will never die!

Even though our outward is in decline, our spirit within should be on the incline. It's when both are headed neck and neck downward that we're in trouble. "and the dust returns to the ground it came from, and the spirit returns to God who gave it." Ecclesiastes 12:7. This body will decrease, but I want His Spirit increasing within me (John 3:30).

"Therefore we do not lose heart. Though outwardly we are wasting away, yet inwardly we are being renewed day by day." 2 Corinthians 4:16. My husband, Gene, and I observed God's finest work in death and life in our daughter, Jamie, during the last ten weeks of her life on earth. Her "tent" decayed at a rapid pace while the Spirit within her grew stronger and upward by leaps and bounds! During physically weak moments, her spirit would soar in praise, worship and song to her God. It was a precious and beautiful thing to witness. Could God have healed her at any moment? Absolutely! We prayed for that, but God had something far better for our Jamie.

Jamie is with the One she loved more than anything in the world. She lives on in our hearts, and the impact of her work and life continues on earth. Special Note: Mom, God's Got This! Is a biography of Jamie's young life well lived for Christ and is due to be published in 2015. "As for us, we cannot help speaking about what we have seen and heard." Acts 4:20.

How are you today? Are you being renewed day by day?

November 30 – **Giving**

If you've attended church for any period of time, you've probably heard a Scripture or two from 2 Corinthians 9: 6-11 just before the plate is passed/tithes and offerings received. Sowing and reaping is a physical law, spiritual law, and financial law. When you follow the Lord's instructions in giving financially, it's not necessary to pray for God's blessings, for He is faithful to His Word; He will bless you. It's similar to praying for God's justice, or asking for truth to be revealed in a situation, or asking Him to expose those things hidden in darkness; these things will be done; it is God's character; it's Who He is. At times we become impatient with God, because we generally don't enjoy waiting on anything. We give today; we expect to receive tomorrow – literally. We want God's justice today! We want the truth to be known by everyone today! We want those things hidden in darkness to come to light today! God's ways and timing don't usually resemble our own, so we must trust God. He is always faithful to His Word, and His timing will be perfect. Be patient.

"Remember this: Whoever sows sparingly will also reap sparingly, and whoever sows generously will also reap generously. And God is able to bless you abundantly, so that in all things at all times, having all that you need, you will abound in every good work. You will be enriched in every way so that you can be generous on every occasion, and through us your generosity will result in thanksgiving to God." 2 Corinthians 9:6, 8, 11. These verses are true as you sow financially and as you sow to the Spirit (Galatians 6:8).

Go to 1 Chronicles 29 and read how King David, the leaders of the people, and the people themselves give their gifts willingly and joyfully for the building of the temple. King David praises God. "The people rejoiced at the willing response of their leaders, for they had given freely and wholeheartedly to the Lord. David the king also rejoiced greatly. 'But who am I, and who are my people, that we should be able to give as generously as this? Everything comes from you, and we have given you only what comes from your hand.'" 1 Chronicles 29:9, 14.

DECEMBER

December 1 – **Boast in Your Weakness**

Watch out! When anyone draws attention to himself, putting self on a pedestal for all the world to see – like they say – something is "fishy." In other words, something stinks. Boasting in one's self and accomplishments, truth or not, is a sign of arrogance. People should not "toot" their own horn! If we're not careful, we will fall for their lie – or worse yet – be the guilty party. Remember Herod (Acts 12:23)!

The Apostle Paul finds himself in competition with false apostles in the Corinthian church. These "super-apostles" (2 Corinthians 11:5) pose as authorities and attempt to undermine Paul's character and his work among the people. They resort to boasting to make themselves look superior. Paul is so jealous over the Corinthians and so disturbed that they might be led astray, that he begins to list his credentials, which include imprisonment, floggings, and repeated exposure to death; he's been whipped, beaten with rods, pelted with stones, shipwrecked, and in constant danger. (You won't see those listed on many ministry related resumes today.)

"If I must boast, I will boast of the things that show my weakness." (2 Corinthians 11:30). "But he said to me, 'My grace is sufficient for you, for my power is made perfect in weakness.' Therefore I will boast all the more gladly about my weaknesses, so that Christ's power may rest on me. That is why, for Christ's sake, I delight in weaknesses, in insults, in hardships, in persecutions, in difficulties. For when I am weak, then I am strong." 2 Corinthians 12:9, 10. How many of us can say we delight in weaknesses, insults, hardships, persecutions, and difficulties? Rather, we pray for God to deliver us from such things!

"For it is not the one who commends himself who is approved, but the one whom the Lord commends." 2 Corinthians 10:18. When we commend ourselves, we may face God's disapproval. It is more important that we obtain God's commendation over man's. When we live holy and righteous lives before God, He is the One Who will commend and defend us; we don't have to worry about it. Let us focus on pointing people to Jesus. They need to see Jesus, not us.

"In God we make our boast all day long, and we will praise your name forever." Psalm 44:8. "Do not boast about tomorrow, for you do not know what a day may bring." Proverbs 27:1.

December 2 – **King of the Castle!**

My husband has been king of our castle for 42+ years, and I'm the queen! He's the head of our home, and I'm the neck; I turn the head! Our miniature kingdom is temporary, but we're both employed in an everlasting Kingdom.

Paul makes it clear he is not building his own kingdom. "However, I consider my life worth nothing to me; my only aim is to finish the race and complete the task the Lord Jesus has given me – the task of testifying to the good news of God's grace." Acts 20:24. He is not afraid to die and pass from the scene, because his life is not about him. His life's work is not about building "Paul's Kingdom," but all about advancing God's Kingdom on earth. He knows that when he "rests with his fathers," others will follow Him and also serve Christ and advance the Kingdom. He can't (and we can't) cling to anything in this life (what a relief!). We will wear ourselves out trying to do so! "What, after all, is Apollos? And what is Paul? Only servants, through whom you came to believe – as the Lord has assigned to each his task." 1 Corinthians 3:5.

King Saul, on the other hand, does everything he can to hold onto his personal kingdom; it just doesn't work and ends badly for the king and his son, Jonathan. "As long as the son of Jesse lives on this earth, neither you nor your kingdom will be established. Now send someone to bring him to me, for he must die!" 1 Samuel 20:31.

Ask yourself: Whose kingdom am I working so hard to build? Only God's Kingdom is eternal; everything else is inferior. The sooner we understand that truth, the more effective we will be. Let's do everything we can to further God's Kingdom on earth in the hearts and lives of men, women, and children, humbly serving God and others while we can (John 9:4).

December 3 – **What Are You Waiting For?**

Are you waiting for an airplane to amble across the sky trailing a banner that reads, "Today is your day!", or for all the pieces to come together in just the right way, or for the stars to be perfectly aligned? Can we wait too long or not long enough?

"And now what are you waiting for? Get up, be baptized and wash your sins away, calling on his name." Acts 22:16. Saul has just encountered the resurrected Jesus Christ, and the Lord has work for him to do. He mustn't waste any time. I know people who wait on "getting saved," going to church, or committing their lives to Christ, because they are busy right now. Maybe they want to experience certain "things/sins" or "have some fun" before they become a Christian. This is a perfect example of swallowing Satan's lie – hook, line, and sinker. The five foolish virgins in

Matthew 25:10 wait too long and miss their opportunity; the door is shut.

It is scriptural to wait on God. "Wait for the Lord; be strong and take heart and wait for the Lord." Psalm 27:14. However, Moses almost waits too long on God at the Red Sea. "Then the Lord said to Moses, 'Why are you crying out to me? Tell the Israelites to move on.'" Exodus 14:15. Joshua chides the Israelites in Joshua 18:3: "How long will you wait before you begin to take possession of the land that the Lord, the God of your ancestors, has given you?" King Saul also proves that sometimes we don't wait long enough (1 Samuel 10:8).

When it comes to salvation, what are you waiting for? God's Word tells us that today is the day of salvation (2 Corinthians 6:2). Regarding obedience to God, is it possible to get stuck in the waiting mode? Are we so concerned with our personal comfort that we avoid taking risks that could jeopardize that? We can rationalize God's will right out of our lives! When does taking that step of faith or living by faith come in to play? Only you can answer that question for yourself. "The following night the Lord stood near Paul and said, 'Take courage!'..." Acts 23:11.

December 4 – **A Full-Time Job!**

Let's talk about a full-time job. Personally, I think being a wife, mother, and homemaker is a full-time job. Throw in outside-of-the-home employment, and you have over-time in high gear! This full-time job is a major balancing act. I think of Nik Wallenda who successfully walked across Niagara Falls on a tightrope on June 15, 2012, the first person in the world to walk directly over the Falls, and he did it in 25 minutes! Talk about concentration, focus, resolve, and craziness wrapped up in one package!

"So I strive always to keep my conscience clear before God and man." Acts 24:16. In my opinion, Paul is describing a full-time job. He works hard to keep a clear conscience. "Always" is full-time! And not just before God, but before God and man! Yes, it takes work to pull that off! Paul must maintain an active and growing relationship with Jesus Christ and a strong knowledge of God's Word. A clear conscience before God and man will require the same from us. But what a blessing it is when our conscience doesn't condemn us! A crystal clear conscience is worth the investment! Keeping a clear conscience before God and man is much like walking a tightrope: One side is God, and one side is man. We must keep our eyes in front of us on the goal and never look down. We can't stop but must continue forward, putting one foot in front of the other. We can keep our balance; we can achieve our goal; we can make it to the other side – all with God's help!

Joseph's brothers carry a very heavy and guilty conscience for years. "They said to one another, 'Surely we are being punished because of our brother. We saw how distressed he was when he pleaded with us for his life, but we would not listen; that's why this distress has come on us.'" Genesis 42:21. This is a terrible burden that has weighed them down, affecting their lives for years, with no relief in sight. Only when they confront Joseph and receive forgiveness do they experience freedom from their guilt and shame.

It is work, but you can have a clear conscience; you can do the right thing. Stay balanced, move forward, and keep your eyes on Jesus. Whatever you do, don't give up and don't look down! You can't stop over Niagara Falls!

December 5 – **I Told You So!**

I must admit, I enjoy saying, "I told you so, but you wouldn't listen" to my husband when I'm right! Over the years, we've learned not to make it a big deal and laugh about it, but there is a teeny bit of satisfaction that goes along with the fact that I was right that time! I'm in good company, because the Apostle Paul and the Prophet Elisha say the same thing!

Paul tells the centurion on the ship that the "voyage is going to be disastrous," but he doesn't listen to Paul (Acts 27:10, 11). "When neither sun nor stars appeared for many days and the storm continued raging, we finally gave up all hope of being saved… 'Men, you should have taken my advice…'" Acts 27:20 21. Paul tells them, but they don't listen, and now here they are, in desperate trouble.

When God takes the Prophet Elijah to heaven in a whirlwind, the company of the prophets from Jericho want to go look for Elijah (2 Kings 2:15-18). "… 'No,' Elisha replied, 'do not send them.'" (v. 16). But they go anyway. The fifty men search for Elijah for three days and don't find him. "When they returned to Elisha, who was staying in Jericho, he said to them, 'Didn't I tell you not to go?'" (v. 18).

"Last night an angel of the God to whom I belong and whom I serve stood beside me and said, 'Do not be afraid, Paul. You must stand trial before Caesar; and God has graciously given you the lives of all who sail with you…Nevertheless, we must run aground on some island.'" Acts 27:23, 24, 26.

When you're in the middle of the hurricane, when hope is lost and strength is gone – nevertheless – God can save. He restores our hope and strength. It doesn't matter who of us is right or wrong. God is always right! Listen to God above all others. What does He say in His Word? "Be strong and take heart, all you who hope in the Lord." Psalm 31:24. I told you so!

December 6 – **A Tiny Blue Flower**

I remember hearing a story many years ago about a very old building of several hundred years torn down and its stones and foundation removed. The earth underneath the building, hidden from the elements for so long, is all that remains. A curious thing happens the following spring as rain showers and the warmth of the sun begin to soften and saturate the ground. A tiny blue flower blooms where once the old building stood, a flower thought to be extinct. Only God knew that tiny seed with life tucked inside was there, and with His light and living water, it emerges from its tomb, alive.

The Apostle Paul is definitely not a quitter. He takes advantage of every opportunity to share Jesus Christ with anyone and everyone. "Some were convinced by what he said, but others would not believe." Acts 28:24. That doesn't discourage him. He knows that everyone who hears his message will not believe; he cannot force anyone to believe the Good News of Jesus Christ. Everyone makes their own choice to believe or not.

God delivers the children of Israel out of Egyptian slavery. They see with their own eyes the amazing miracles that only the One True God can do. How can they not believe? "In spite of all this, they kept on sinning; in spite of his wonders, they did not believe." Psalm 78:32. Many people see and hear Jesus Himself when He walks the earth, and yet do not believe.

Child of God, do not be discouraged when people reject the Good News you share. Someone will believe, and it will be worth it all! Obey what God has called you to do. Share Christ at every opportunity. Remember that it is God Who gives the increase; He is in charge of the results. We plant and water and at times reap a harvest. God sees His seed tucked away in hearts. How do you know it will do no good to tell that person about the love of Jesus? Tell someone today what Jesus Christ means to you and what He has done in your life. "Who has believed our message and to whom has the arm of the Lord been revealed? Isaiah 53:1.

December 7 – **Please and Thank Him**

Paul's letter to the Ephesians is very blunt and honest. It hits everyone somewhere! I encourage you to read it prayerfully and humbly, and allow the Holy Spirit to do His work in your heart and life. "and find out what pleases the Lord." Ephesians 5:10.

As we grow in our walk with Christ and in the knowledge of His Word, we will learn what pleases Him. At the same time, we will discover what displeases Him as Paul so thoroughly brings to our attention, as well as the outcome (Ephesians 5:5). We need to know these things. Jesus Christ is not only our Savior, He is our Lord. It's crucial we understand how to live before Him. "...the prayer of the upright pleases him." Proverbs 15:8. "I will praise God's name in song and glorify him with thanksgiving. This will please the Lord..." Psalm 69:30, 31.

I will not only strive to please the Lord with my life, I will thank Him. "to him be glory in the church and in Christ Jesus throughout all generations, for ever and ever! Amen." Ephesians 3:21. "I will give thanks to you, Lord, with all my heart; I will tell of all your wonderful deeds." Psalm 9:1.

Lord, I want my life to please you. Help me to live my life in such a way as to bring You glory. Thank You.

December 8 – **Don't Quit!**

Do you remember Baruch, the Prophet Jeremiah's scribe (personal secretary)? Review Jeremiah 45:1-5. He is a faithful friend and servant to Jeremiah. He writes by hand on a scroll as Jeremiah dictates the Word from the Lord, but he becomes very discouraged in his work. It's difficult to write all those prophecies of doom and despair God decrees against his people. To top it all off, King Jehoiakim burns the first scroll, and Baruch must write everything down the second time at Jeremiah's dictation, plus many similar words are added. Even though Baruch is distraught about the apparent failure of Jeremiah's ministry and the events soon to take place, God's sorrow vastly exceeds that of Baruch. He is also worried about his own future. What will happen to him? God assures him he will be protected. "...but wherever you go I will let you escape with your life." Jeremiah 45:5.

You are important to God. He has given you something to do for Him and His Church. Every member of the body is essential to the overall function of the Church (1 Corinthians 12:12-31). You may feel unappreciated today; you may be discouraged and ready to quit. Don't quit! Your work is not in vain. "Whatever your hand finds to do, do it with all your might..." Ecclesiastes 9:10. Serve God by serving others and His Church, and God will bless you. "Serve wholeheartedly, as if you were serving the Lord, not people, because you know that the Lord will reward each one for whatever good they do, whether they are slave or free." Ephesians 6:7, 8.

December 9 – **What Are You Used to Using?**

"But David said to Saul, 'Your servant has been keeping his father's sheep. When a lion or a bear came and carried off a sheep from the flock, I went after it, struck it and rescued the sheep from its mouth. When it turned on me, I seized it by its hair, struck it and killed it.'" 1 Samuel 17:34, 35. Without knowing it, David has been preparing for this day all of his life. While in the field those many days and nights with the sheep, he has practiced knocking little rocks off of big rocks with his sling and a stone. He's chased, wounded, and killed predators. He has spent many hours worshiping God, meditating on His Word, and getting to know this God of Israel. He understands it is God's strength and not his own that gives the victory. He has learned and prepared well for the next thing on God's agenda – killing Goliath. Verse 35 can as easily be applied to Goliath.

"David fastened on his sword over the tunic and tried walking around, because he was not used to them. 'I cannot go in these,' he said to Saul, 'because I am not used to them.' So he took them off." (v. 39). He is used to his sling and a stone, because he has used them well in the past.

What are you used to? David isn't used to Saul's armor; it does him no good. God will use me in His Kingdom if I am a good steward of the gifts, talents, abilities, experience, wisdom, etc. that He has given me. "For you created my inmost being; you knit me together in my mother's womb." Psalm 139:13. Do I use what God has given me? Have I prepared well for the next thing on God's agenda for my life? I can only use what He gives me, not what He gives someone else. "Whatever you do, work at it with all your heart, as working for the Lord, not for human masters." Colossians 3:23.

December 10 – **Defend and Confirm**

"It is right for me to feel this way about all of you, since I have you in my heart and, whether I am in chains or defending and confirming the gospel, all of you share in God's grace with me." Philippians 1:7. Everywhere Paul goes, he defends and confirms the Gospel. As Christ-followers, we are called to do no less.

The Bible clearly teaches that God is our Defender, but when do we come to God's defense? A young David defends God's name when he stands against the giant Goliath who has challenged and defied the God of Israel. "David said to the Philistine, 'You come against me with sword and spear and javelin, but I come against you in the name of the Lord Almighty, the God of the armies of Israel, whom you have defied.'" 1 Samuel 17:45. God backs up the boldness and courage of this young man and causes the stone to hit its mark. Peter encourages us to always be ready to defend our faith in Christ and never shirk back. "But in your hearts revere Christ as Lord. Always be prepared to give an answer to everyone who asks you to give the reason for the hope that you have. But do this with gentleness and respect." 1 Peter 3:15. Never be ashamed of Jesus Christ (Mark 8:38).

In Elijah's contest with the prophets of Baal on Mount Carmel, God confirms the truth of Elijah's words and His own existence. "Then the fire of the Lord fell and burned up the sacrifice, the wood, the stones and the soil, and also licked up the water in the trench." 1 Kings 18:38. That was then; this is now: "So Paul and Barnabas spent considerable time there, speaking boldly for the Lord, who confirmed the message of his grace by enabling them to perform signs and wonders." Acts 14:3.

It's apparent to me that defending and confirming the Gospel go together! To defend is to speak in support of someone or something – to witness or testify, to preach or teach Jesus Christ. To confirm is to show that something is true. One should never be without the other. We are co-workers with Christ (1 Corinthians 3:9).

O Lord, help me to be bold and courageous in defense of the Gospel, for I am not ashamed of the Gospel, because it is the power of God that brings salvation to everyone who believes (Romans 1:16). And confirm Your Word with signs and wonders following (Mark 16:20). Amen.

December 11 – **God's Rightful Place**

"Nobody likes me, everybody hates me, I think I'll go eat worms! Big fat juicy ones, Eensie weensy squeensy ones, See how they wiggle and squirm!" I remember my children singing that when they were small and the disgust that registered on my face! If we are honest, we will admit that we have all felt that way at times; the whole world is against us! There are some things in life that only God can do for us. Everyone else is either clueless or completely incapable. The sooner we understand and accept that truth, the better off we'll be.

When our world is violently shaken by tragedy, heartbreak, disaster, illness, or the death of someone we love, where do we go? To the only One Who can help us. Family, friends, and our church can be a blessing when crisis rocks us to the core, but only Almighty God can give us peace. To expect more from people than they are able to give is unfair to them. Disappointment with others will add to our pain, and that's exactly what Satan wants to do – add sorrow upon sorrow (Philippians 2:27).

"Do not be anxious about anything, but in every situation, by prayer and petition, with thanksgiving, present your requests to God. And the peace of God, which transcends all understanding, will guard your hearts and your minds in Christ Jesus." Philippians 4:6, 7. "You will keep in perfect peace those whose minds are steadfast, because they trust in you." Isaiah 26:3.

"...continue to work out your salvation with fear and trembling, for it is God who works in you to will and to act in order to fulfill his good purpose." Philippians 2:12, 13. Just as salvation is not simply a one-time event, neither is growing in Christ. It's a process – a lifestyle. We live and learn each day as we walk with a loving Savior, One Who understands, loves us, forgives us, and stands by us. Take your eyes off of others and look into the face of Jesus. Trust Him. And no more worms!

December 12 – **Pollution**

Pollution is a serious problem in our world. Like all good mothers, I wanted to teach our young daughters to take care of their environment. Litter on the side of the road was a good place to start. One day as I was driving and they were in the back seat, I noticed a lot of newspaper pages scattered on the side of the road. We talked about litter and how horrible it was, so on the way back home, I pulled over on the side of the road and we started picking up all the trash. They were less than excited, but I was trying to teach them a valuable lesson. We did our good deed for the day. Several days later, we were in the car again and were following a pick-up truck with open boxes in the back and Styrofoam peanuts started flying everywhere! They looked at each other in the back seat and in unison began wailing, "Nooooooo! Momma, Nooooooo! Don't stop!" I smiled and kept driving.

"Religion that God our Father accepts as pure and faultless is this: to look after orphans and widows in their distress and to keep oneself from being polluted by the world." James 1:27. Sin contaminates our lives. When we come to Jesus Christ and receive Him as our Savior, He purifies us from sin. It is impossible to clean ourselves; we bring all the filth and trash in our lives to Him, and He removes it. It is then our responsibility "to keep oneself from being polluted by the world" again. A daily intake of God's Word teaches and helps us guard our lives from the world's pollutants (sin).

Have you ever thought about environmental pollution in Bible days? Elisha's first miracle is the healing of polluted water and is recorded in 2 Kings 2:19-22. "Then he went out to the spring and threw the salt into it, saying, 'This is what the Lord says: "I have healed this water. Never again will it cause death or make the land unproductive."'" (v. 21). Jesus freely gives us living water (John 7:38).

God is concerned that we be good stewards of the earth He has given us, but even more important to Him is that our hearts and lives remain pure before Him. One thing we know for sure is that heaven has no pollution of any kind! Everything is pure and clean and fresh and new forever! "Nothing impure will ever enter it..." Revelation 21:27.

December 13 – **Shoulder to Shoulder**

I think we give the devil way too much credit. Have you ever heard someone say, "The devil made me do it"? We blame him for a lot of things. Yes, he is a liar and a deceiver; and if we listen to him long enough, we may follow him. We all make decisions – some right and some wrong. I'm reminded of the cartoon where a little angel is sitting on one shoulder saying, "Do this." On the other shoulder is a little devil saying, "No, do this." We go back and forth. What do we do? We've all been there. We decide who we listen to and obey. If we do what Satan tells us to do long enough, he will bind us with his chains and take away our freedom. "Submit yourselves, then, to God. Resist the devil, and he will flee from you." James 4:7. This is a powerful truth in God's Word which we should obey every day.

In Ezekiel chapter seven, God says to the children of Israel that He will judge, repay, or deal with them according to their conduct, and He says it five times (vs. 3, 4, 8, 9, 27). He is making a strong point here that we are responsible for our conduct. "...I will deal with them according to their conduct, and by their own standards I will judge them. Then they will know that I am the Lord." Ezekiel 7:27.

"For we must all appear before the judgment seat of Christ, so that each of us may receive what is due us for the things done while in the body, whether good or bad." 2 Corinthians 5:10.

You must submit your life to God first. Then, you can tell that devil on your shoulder to take a hike. Resist him in the Name of Jesus, and put your hand in the hand of the Savior and follow Him.

December 14 – **A Consuming Fire**

Nadab and Abihu are PKs, the older sons of Priest Aaron, following closely in their father's footsteps. A quick look back at Exodus 24:9, 10 shows them in the literal presence and glory of God. In Leviticus 8:24, we see them consecrated (set apart) and anointed for the priesthood. Things are going great for them, but then what happens? "Aaron's sons Nadab and Abihu took their censers, put fire in them and added incense; and they offered unauthorized fire before the Lord, contrary to his command. So fire came out from the presence of the Lord and consumed them, and they died before the Lord." Leviticus 10:1, 2. "For the Lord your God is a consuming fire, a jealous God." Deuteronomy 4:24.

Do Nadab and Abihu defiantly rebel against God and His law? Where is the fear of God in their lives? Are they serving their own desires? Are they intoxicated? They are clearly disobedient, and God does not tolerate it. We do know a few things to be true. 1) God is holy. 2) He says what He means, and means what He says. 3) We don't know better than God, so we must obey Him fully and walk closely to Him. 4) The incident is a solemn warning against every sin of presumption. 5) No man is indispensable to God. 6) Those who are called to teach God's laws must take His commandments seriously.

It is a grave responsibility, privilege, and high honor to teach and preach God's Word. Read 1 Timothy 3 for the qualifications God gives us for overseers in His church. "He must not be a recent convert, or he may become conceited and fall under the same judgment as the devil." 1 Timothy 3:6.

December 15 – **Burn Brightly for Jesus!**

God commands Moses to keep the lamps burning in the tabernacle always. "The Lord said to Moses, 'Command the

Israelites to bring you clear oil of pressed olives for the light so that the lamps may be kept burning continually.'" Leviticus 2:1, 2. It is the same for Solomon's temple (2 Chronicles 4:20). The light represents the presence of God and should always burn brightly. You and I are God's temple today. Is His light burning brightly within us?

"For this reason I remind you to fan into flame the gift of God, which is in you through the laying on of my hands. For the Spirit God gave us does not make us timid, but gives us power, love and self-discipline." 2 Timothy 1:6, 7. We must be reminded to fan into flame the gift of God. What is the gift of God – the Holy Spirit. Living a Spirit-filled life is more than a one-time experience of being baptized in the Holy Spirit with the evidence of speaking in tongues. This should be an on-going experience in our lives. If it is not, there exists the danger of growing cold and dim, and what good is that to God? Spend time in the presence of God and allow Him to breathe on you and increase the fire of the Holy Spirit within you. With the baptism of the Holy Spirit, we receive power to be His witnesses and boldness to live this life to its fullest. Fan into flame His fire within you! We not only need more boldness and power, but more love and self-discipline as well; and it all comes about as we fan into flame the gift of God within us.

"But you, dear friends, by building yourselves up in your most holy faith and praying in the Holy Spirit, keep yourselves in God's love as you wait for the mercy of our Lord Jesus Christ to bring you to eternal life." Jude 1:20, 21. Praying in the Holy Spirit is praying in tongues (1 Corinthians 14:15). Keep on being filled. "Be dressed ready for service and keep your lamps burning." Luke 12:35.

December 16 – **But I Like Chocolate!**

If I look hard enough, I will always find someone to agree with me. I don't want to change what I'm doing (It's too much work!), so I'll find a way to justify my lack of self-control, my beliefs, my sin. I happen to enjoy chocolate, so now I'm proclaiming its health benefits! The same goes for coffee. Some news sources would have us believe that marijuana is good for us. Really? We've all heard how too much salt in our diet is unhealthy, but now it's reported that salt reduces stress. What about my aversion to exercise? Have you read 1 Timothy 4:8 in the KJV recently?

"For the time will come when people will not put up with sound doctrine. Instead, to suit their own desires, they will gather around them a great number of teachers to say what their itching ears want to hear." 2 Timothy 4:3. The time has come. Anyone can prove a point by pulling a Scripture out of context and make it say just about anything they want. It's called scratching an itch.

Change and growth require something from us, and most of us are just too lazy. To know the truth, we must approach God's Word empty with no preconceived ideas, and just let God's Word say what it says. Read it cover to cover. Afterwards, repentance and prayer for divine strength are usually in order. It does take our time and energy to grow in Christ, but it's so worth it. Jesus wants this for us more than we do, and He will team up with us, so that we can become more like Him.

I want and need to know the truth, the whole counsel of God, not just rearranged bits and pieces. God knows what He is talking about; my knowledge is questionable. Jeremiah 5:30-31 gives us this warning: "A horrible and shocking thing has happened in the land: The prophets prophesy lies, the priests rule by their own authority, and my people love it this way. But what will you do in the end?"

December 17 – **Spiritually Healthy**

Watching a movie one time is enough for me. I don't enjoy reading a book more than once either – every book, that is, except the Bible. What's the difference? God's Word is the only book that is alive. It feeds my spirit. I'm hungry for it. I can't tell you what I ate for dinner thirty days ago. I do know that my body assimilated the food I ate, sending nourishment to blood, bones, tissue, organs, and muscle. The human body is an amazing organism. I am also a spiritual being, and a steady diet of God's Word feeds and strengthens my spirit man. I may not understand perfectly everything I read; nevertheless, it is powerful in its working in me. We tend to over-feed our physical body and starve our spiritual man. That's not healthy! Are you a spiritual skeleton? And we wonder why we feel so spiritually weak.

The Bible not only feeds my spirit, but it is also a skilled surgeon. "For the word of God is alive and active. Sharper than any double-edged sword, it penetrates even to dividing soul and spirit, joints and marrow; it judges the thoughts and attitudes of the heart." Hebrews 4:12. As I dig deep into God's Word, God's Word goes deep within me. More than a pin-prick, it is a double-edged sword dividing, exploring, exposing, excising ungodliness; it is spiritual surgery that only God's Living and Written Word can do. Surgery can be painful but at times necessary to save a life. God's Word is a skilled surgeon accomplishing what it must do in order to bring abundant life to the spirit man.

"As the rain and snow come down from heaven, and do not return to it without watering the earth and making it bud and flourish, so that it yields seed for the sower and bread for the eater, so is my word that goes out from my mouth: It will not return to me empty, but will accomplish what I desire and achieve the purpose for which I sent it." Isaiah 55:10, 11. A generous diet of God's Word will keep me spiritually healthy.

December 18 – **Our High Priest**

Parents sacrifice for their children. Pastors sacrifice for their congregations. Soldiers sacrifice for their country. You will gladly sacrifice something you want to help someone you love or a cause you care deeply about. A fulfilling and satisfying life will include personal sacrifice. But any and all sacrifices I make in my lifetime will never compare to Christ's sacrifice for me on the cross.

In the Old Testament, the High Priest was required to make a sacrifice for his own sins before he could sacrifice for the sins of the people. And this had to be done on a regular basis, because the blood of animals was insufficient to make atonement for the sins of man. "He said to Aaron, 'Take a bull calf for your sin offering and a ram for your burnt offering, both without defect, and present them before the Lord.'" Leviticus 9:2. "Without defect" points to Jesus Christ Who was without sin.

"Unlike the other high priests, he does not need to offer sacrifices day after day, first for his own sins, and then for the sins of the people. He sacrificed for their sins once for all when he offered himself." Hebrews 7:27. Jesus Christ knew no sin; He was and is the perfect Lamb Who willingly gave Himself on the altar of the cross for our sins, once for all time. He did for me what I could not do for myself. Praise His Holy Name!

"Son though he was, he learned obedience from what he suffered and, once made perfect, he became the source of eternal salvation for all who obey him." Hebrews 5:8, 9. Jesus Christ is the only source of eternal salvation; there is no other (John 14:6). Notice what this Scripture says: for all who obey Him. Our obedience is extremely important to God. "If you are willing and obedient, you will eat the good things of the land;" Isaiah 1:19.

December 19 – **Commended Faith**

"Let us hold unswervingly to the hope we profess, for he who promised is faithful." Hebrews 10:23. "Not one of all the Lord's good promises to Israel failed; every one was fulfilled." Joshua 21:45. We love these verses of God's faithfulness and fulfilled promises. Then we read this in Hebrews 11:39, 40 concerning Old Testament saints: "These were all commended for their faith, yet none of them received what had been promised, since God had planned something better for us so that only together with us would they be made perfect." I see no contradiction here.

Yes, God's promises were fulfilled to the nation of Israel in the days of Joshua. And, yes, God is faithful to fulfill His Word today. But just because the Old Testament heroes did not see with their eyes the fulfillment of God's promises for which they believed, does not mean they will never be fulfilled. God's Word was, is, and always will be true. He decides the best timing; we continue to believe and allow nothing to shake our faith. Some of God's promises are fulfilled in eternity. God, in His providence, has reserved the consummation of His crowning blessing for all His sons and daughters to share together. "Then the angel said to me, 'Write this: Blessed are those who are invited to the wedding supper of the Lamb!' And he added, 'These are the true words of God.'" Revelation 19:9. Praise His Holy Name!

December 20 – **Who Through Faith**

I have an older brother with whom I have never had a conversation; we never played games together as children; he never married and had a family of his own. He is a toddler in what is now a senior citizen's body. Billy is mentally retarded, and he's always been a small child. I look forward to going to heaven one day. I want to see Jesus and my daughter and many loved ones. But one of the things I am really looking forward to is talking to my brother for hours and hours. I believe I will hear him say, "Remember the time when….I wanted to say this to you, but I couldn't." This is just one more reason that heaven will last forever – to make up for lost time!

When King David's infant son dies, he says, "I will go to him, but he will not return to me." (2 Samuel 12:23). When a child dies, he goes to heaven, because he has no sin to separate him from God (Isaiah 59:2). Jesus tells us that His Kingdom belongs to little children (Luke 18:16), and we must become as a little child in order to enter the Kingdom of Heaven (Matthew 18:3).

For the rest of us (adults) we need faith in God to enter heaven. Hebrews 11:6 tells us we will never please God without faith, and He will allow only those who please Him to enter His domain. "who through faith conquered kingdoms, administered justice, and gained what was promised; who shut the mouths of lions," Hebrews 11:33. David says this: "The Lord who rescued me from the paw of the lion and the paw of the bear will rescue me from the hand of this Philistine." 1 Samuel 32:37.

Complete and everlasting freedom will come when we enter heaven. Billy will be set free at last from that which has confined him all his life. He will be free to worship and praise His God forever and always! "He upholds the cause of the oppressed and gives food to the hungry. The Lord sets prisoners free," Psalm 146:7. (See also Isaiah 61:1 and Luke 4:18.) Keep the faith!

December 21 – **Good and Unchanging**

Babies can be very expressive. Have you ever fed a baby sitting in a high chair squash or peas for the first time? I don't know about yours, but my babies made the funniest faces whenever they tasted something different! There was never any doubt when they liked something and when they didn't!

"Taste and see that the Lord is good; blessed is the one who takes refuge in him." Psalm 34:8. "now that you have tasted that the Lord is good." 1 Peter 2:3. God is good, and He invites us to taste and see for ourselves that He is good. There is no one good but Him (Mark 10:18). There is nothing good in me except Him. "I say to the Lord, 'You are my Lord; apart from you I have no good thing.'" Psalm 16:2.

One of the good things about God is that He never changes. We change every day. We change clothes, hairstyles, diets, deodorants, jobs, plans, schedules, our tone of voice, friends, churches, the way we set the table, and our minds. Some of these things need to change on a regular basis! Life is full of change. However, one thing is absolute: God never changes. "He who is the Glory of Israel does not lie or change his mind; for he is not a human being, that he should change his mind." 1 Samuel 15:29. "Jesus Christ is the same yesterday and today and forever." Hebrews 13:8.

It doesn't matter who you think you are, God will not change Who He is or His Holy Word to suit you. He is already perfect. You must change for Him. If you are looking for better results, you are the one who must change. Don't expect another person to change. The only one you have any control over is you. He will help you when you ask and trust Him. Remember: God is good; He is unchanging; and He loves you.

December 22 – **Details**

"The Lord said to Moses, 'Tell the Israelites to bring me an offering...'" Exodus 25:1. "Make the tabernacle..." Exodus 26:1. "Build an altar..." Exodus 27:1. God not only tells His people what to do but how to do it. He gives precise details, explicit instructions, because He is a God of details. Just look at His creation. From microscopic to massive, God is interested in details.

He leaves nothing to chance. He gives us His owner's manual, the Holy Bible, so we are without excuse; He tells us exactly what He expects of us. It is our responsibility to read God's Word and apply it to our lives. "Jesus replied: 'Love the Lord your God with all your heart and with all your soul and with all your mind. This is the first and greatest commandment. And the second is like it: Love your neighbor as yourself.'" Matthew 22:37-39.

Since God is involved in every facet of life, He is interested in whatever concerns me or you, no matter how great or small. If it's important to me, it's important to God. I am so thankful for His love and care. "Cast your cares on the Lord and he will sustain you; he will never let the righteous be shaken." Psalm 55:22. "Cast all your anxiety on him because he cares for you." 1 Peter 5:7.

December 23 – **Keep Going Forward**

The people who live in Jerusalem in the day of the Prophet Jeremiah (597 BC) refuse to believe his prophecies that God is about to destroy their beloved city. How could God destroy His city and His temple where He put His Name? After all, they are Israelites, God's chosen people. "Will you steal and murder, commit adultery and perjury, burn incense to Baal and follow other gods you have not known, and then come and stand before me in this house, which bears my Name, and say, 'We are safe' – safe to do all these detestable things? Has this house, which bears my Name, become a den of robbers to you? But I have been watching! declares the Lord." Jeremiah 7:9-11. Jeremiah says the people went backward and not forward (v. 24).

This same mindset is common today. Some people think they are safe to do whatever they want to do and live however they want to live – all because they said a prayer of commitment to Jesus Christ one day. We can't keep sinning and God not care;

He does care. When we are truly born again, we become part of God's family; we're born into it. The way we live our lives must change, because we now belong to Him. We must move forward with Christ and never go backward, and the way to keep going forward is to continue growing in grace and knowledge of our Lord and Savior. Peter says that if we become entangled in the world again and are overcome, we are worse off than we were before (2 Peter 2:20). "Therefore, dear friends, since you have been forewarned, be on your guard so that you may not be carried away by the error of the lawless and fall from your secure position. But grow in the grace and knowledge of our Lord and Savior Jesus Christ. To him be glory both now and forever! Amen." 2 Peter 3:17, 18.

December 24 – **Lip Service**

I have been known to cry at a sad movie. My husband gently puts his arm around me and says, "Honey, it's okay. It's not real. It's just a show. They all get up and go have dinner and go home after a long day's work." It helps – a little.

The Book of First John contains some strong words for us today. Why? Maybe it's because we're almost at the end of God's Book, or maybe it's because we are living in the last hour (1 John 2:18). Regardless, it's obvious that God does not appreciate lip service without a life to back it up. To Him, it's all for show, and He knows the truth about us. "Dear children, let us not love with words or speech but with actions and in truth." 1 John 3:18. "Like a coating of silver dross on earthenware are fervent lips with an evil heart." Proverbs 26:23. His warnings to us include:

- "Whoever says, 'I know him,' but does not do what he commands is a liar, and the truth is not in that person." 1 John 2:4.

- "But anyone who hates a brother or sister is in the darkness and walks around in the darkness. They do not know where they are going, because the darkness has blinded them." 1 John 2:11.
- "No one who lives in him keeps on sinning. No one who continues to sin has either seen him or known him." 1 John 3:6.
- "This is how we know who the children of God are and who the children of the devil are: Anyone who does not do what is right is not God's child, nor is anyone who does not love their brother and sister." 1 John 3:10.
- "Anyone who hates a brother or sister is a murderer, and you know that no murderer has eternal life residing in him." 1 John 3:15.

These are serious words! We must remain in Him (1 John 2:27). Back up what you say with a heart and life of service. "And now, dear children, continue in him, so that when he appears we may be confident and unashamed before him at his coming." 1 John 2:28.

Heavenly Father, forgive me for any show of lip service only. You know the truth about me; I can't hide anything from You. Forgive me for lies and hatred. Cleanse me. I want my life to accurately reflect truth and love as You are truth and love. In the Name of Jesus I pray. Amen.

December 25 – **The Son of God Has Come!**

There is no doubt that we live in turbulent times. But how exciting is that! No, I'm not crazy. I'm just glad that I'm alive today – today – lodged in time between Jesus Christ's first coming to earth 2,000 years ago and His soon return to earth! You and I are so blessed! We are living in "Bible days." Don't be nervous. Don't be anxious. Be glad! Rejoice! For we are closer to seeing

Jesus today than we were yesterday! "And do this, understanding the present time: The hour has already come for you to wake up from your slumber, because our salvation is nearer now than when we first believed." Romans 13:11.

"And we have seen and testify that the Father has sent his Son to be the Savior of the world." 1 John 4:14. "For to us a child is born, to us a son is given, and the government will be on his shoulders. And he will be called Wonderful Counselor, Mighty God, Everlasting Father, Prince of Peace." Isaiah 9:6. "But the angel said to them, 'Do not be afraid. I bring you good news that will cause great joy for all the people. Today in the town of David a Savior has been born to you; he is the Messiah, the Lord.'" Luke 2:10, 11. So do not be afraid. God the Father will soon send His Son back to earth to take His children home! Our eyes won't see the baby Jesus or the young man Jesus. Your eyes and my eyes will see the glorified Jesus! Each day that passes draws us closer to that reality. Whether in death or life, we will see Jesus!

"We know also that the Son of God has come..." 1 John 5:20. And we know that He is coming again soon. "The armies of heaven were following him, riding on white horses and dressed in fine linen, white and clean." Revelation 19:14.

December 26 – **Your Church**

A church consists of people. People have personalities; therefore, churches have personalities and distinctive characteristics that reflect those of the pastor, leadership, and congregation. What does God know about your church? John's vision of Christ and His message to the churches carry implications for our churches today. The seven lampstands are identified as the seven churches (Revelation 1:20), and He walks among the seven golden lampstands (2:1). Does Jesus Christ walk in your church? Could the seven stars, identified as angels or messengers, be the pastors of these churches? Is His Word, that sharp double-edged sword, going forth in your church (1:16), or does the preaching and teaching more resemble a flimsy plastic toy sword that couldn't cut paper if it tried.

God knows the good and the bad about us and our churches. In His letters to these first four churches, He affirms the good first, points out the bad, and then gives the solution and the consequences. Are we listening?

- The Church in Ephesus is known for its good deeds, hard work, and perseverance, yet it has forsaken its first love. "Consider how far you have fallen! Repent and do the things you did at first. If you do not repent, I will come to you and remove your lampstand from its place." (2:5).
- The Church in Smyrna lacks worldly wealth but is rich in God. God warns them of coming persecution. "…Be faithful, even to the point of death, and I will give you life as your victor's crown." (2:10).
- The Church in Pergamum has remained true to the name of God in its city, yet it is tolerating blatant sin and sexual immorality in the church. "Repent therefore! Otherwise, I will soon come to you and will fight against them with the sword of my mouth." (2:16).
- The Church in Thyatira possesses love, faith, perseverance, and works hard for God. God commends them, but are they allowing people to teach and hold positions within the church for which they are not qualified, thus doing more harm than good? "…I am he who searches hearts and minds, and I will repay each of you according to your deeds." (2:23).

If Jesus sent a letter to your church today, what would it say? "You gave your good Spirit to instruct them…" Nehemiah 9:20.

"Whoever has ears, let them hear what the Spirit says to the churches." (2:29).

December 27 – **A Blot in God's Book**

"The Lord replied to Moses, 'Whoever has sinned against me I will blot out of my book.'" Exodus 32:33. It's the exodus, and God already has a book with names in it! Apparently just because God writes our names in His book of life is no guarantee that He won't ever remove our names from that same book. He has the power to write them in, and He has the authority to blot them out. Man's sinful nature has not changed over the centuries. The children of Israel are literally following the Presence of God; they see His miracles every day; yet they quickly turn their back on God, disobey Him, and do evil.

"May they be blotted out of the book of life and not be listed with the righteous." Psalm 69:28. May we walk humbly and closely to the Savior every day, obey His Word, serve Him, and point others to Him. May we never let our guard down and allow ourselves to be deceived by Satan and swallow his lies. God never takes away our capacity to choose; we choose to make Him Lord of our lives every day. I want my name to remain sharp and clear and never be reduced to a smeared blot in God's book. "The one who is victorious will, like them, be dressed in white. I will never blot out the name of that person from the book of life, but will acknowledge that name before my Father and his angels. Whoever has ears, let them hear what the Spirit says to the churches." Revelation 3:5, 6.

December 28 – **Take and Eat**

Have you ever eaten something that tasted delicious, but then later did a number on your stomach and up it came! It tasted, looked, smelled, and sounded quite differently going down than it did coming up. Okay, maybe this is not the best illustration for today's reading, but it's all I've got!

God commissions His prophets in different ways. A seraphim touches Isaiah's lips with a burning coal from the altar (Isaiah 6:6-7). The Lord reaches out His hand and touches Jeremiah's mouth (Jeremiah 1:9). Ezekiel and John's experiences are very similar. Compare their accounts in Ezekiel 2:9-3:4 and Revelation 10:8-11. Both are commissioned as prophets and have to literally eat God's Words and then go speak them. "Then he said to me, 'Son of man, eat this scroll I am giving you and fill your stomach with it.' So I ate it, and it tasted as sweet as honey in my mouth." Ezekiel 3:3. "…He said to me, 'Take it and eat it. It will turn your stomach sour, but in your mouth it will be as sweet as honey.'" Revelation 10:9.

Eating the scroll in both cases causes sweetness and bitterness due to the mixture of blessings and curses to be announced. Ezekiel and John are required to receive God's message and make it their own before proclaiming it. Men and women who declare God's Word today must do the same. We eat God's Word; it is sweet to the taste. We chew it and digest it; it goes deep within us and becomes a part of who we are. When we speak it forth, it comes from the very depths of our being. We've experienced it; God has made it real to us first. But this isn't regurgitated mush; it is life and strength and health. It's the powerful Word of God that drives out demons and ushers in new life.

"While they were eating, Jesus took bread, and when he had given thanks, he broke it and gave it to his disciples, saying, 'Take and eat; this is my body.'" Matthew 26:26.

December 29 – **Evil's Pay Day**

Crime doesn't pay. We've all heard that expression before. Oh, but crime does pay; just not in good ways. When it seems evil has won, God makes it clear that evil never succeeds for long. Israel is ensnared in the throes of ungodliness once again. Even the one committing evil believes everything is just fine; his sin will never be exposed; and God has looked the other way. Deception can be so subtle. "After Abimelek had governed Israel three years, God stirred up animosity between Abimelek and the citizens of Shechem so that they acted treacherously against Abimelek." Judges 9:22, 23. "Thus God repaid the wickedness that Abimelek had done to his father by murdering his seventy brothers. God also made the people of Shechem pay for all their wickedness..." (9:56, 57).

"The wicked plot against the righteous and gnash their teeth at them; but the Lord laughs at the wicked, for he knows their day is coming." Psalm 37:12, 13. "Do not take revenge, my dear friends, but leave room for God's wrath, for it is written: 'It is mine to avenge; I will repay,' says the Lord." Romans 12:19. In this fallen world, it is comforting to know that God's Word is unchanging and Satan's days are numbered. "Therefore rejoice, you heavens and you who dwell in them! But woe to the earth and the sea, because the devil has gone down to you! He is filled with fury, because he knows that his time is short." Revelation 12:12.

December 30 – **Stay Awake!**

God always knows exactly what He is doing – today and tomorrow. I don't always know, but I trust Him completely. He is true and just in all His judgments (Revelation 16:5, 7). Justice doesn't always come as quickly as I think it should, but it always comes. I praise Him for His supreme justice in every situation.

He will ultimately judge every sin that hasn't been covered by the blood of Jesus. Jesus will soon come back to earth like a thief in the night, when we least expect Him. "Look, I come like a thief! Blessed is the one who stays awake and remains clothed, so as not to go naked and be shamefully exposed." Revelation 16:15.

I must stay awake. This is no time to get lazy in my spiritual life. I must remain ready to meet Him in the clouds at any moment. As a mother gently rocks her baby to sleep, I can be lulled to sleep if I'm not aware of the enemy's devices. "So then, let us not be like others, who are asleep, but let us be awake and sober." 1 Thessalonians 5:6.

We are intentional about schedules for this and routines for that. It's time to be intentional with spiritual fitness. Design a plan to get spiritually fit (let's not call it a New Year's resolution!). Work out your routine, establish good spiritual habits (like reading through your Bible in a year!), and watch yourself get into shape spiritually. However, like anything else, you must stick to the plan; make it a lifestyle. This is not a two-week crash diet to lose ten pounds, then fall away and be worse off than when you started. Make small gradual changes; increase your intake of the Word and your time in prayer; be faithful to church; find a place to serve others, obey the Lord in tithes and offerings. Simply stated: Just grow in your relationship with Jesus Christ. When you come near to God, He will come near to you (James 4:8). When you take one step toward Him, He takes two steps toward you – but you first.

"The great day of the Lord is near – near and coming quickly…" Zephaniah 1:14.

December 31 – **The Holy City**

I have read the last chapter of God's Book, and He wins; therefore, I win, because I am His child! "I saw the Holy City, the new Jerusalem, coming down out of heaven from God, prepared as a bride beautifully dressed for her husband." Revelation 21:2. I will see that city; better yet, I will live as a citizen in that resplendent Holy City forever! The things God has prepared for His children cannot be described by any earthly tongue. It's a grand feeling to know I am on the winning team! Jesus Christ, by His death on the cross, has made eternal life with God in heaven possible for you and me. Praise His Holy Name!

References to heaven are throughout the Bible. Nehemiah proclaims in 9:6, "…and the multitudes of heaven worship you." "After this I heard what sounded like the roar of a great multitude in heaven shouting: 'Hallelujah! Salvation and glory and power belong to our God,'" Revelation 19:1. The Psalmist in 47:8 announces, "God reigns over the nations; God is seated on his holy throne." "No longer will there be any curse. The throne of God and of the Lamb will be in the city, and his servants will serve him." Revelation 22:3.

"There is a river whose streams make glad the city of God, the holy place where the Most High dwells." Psalm 46:4. "Then the angel showed me the river of the water of life, as clear as crystal, flowing from the throne of God and of the Lamb" Revelation 22:1.

"Look, I am coming soon! My reward is with me, and I will give to each person according to what they have done. The grace of the Lord Jesus be with God's people. Amen." Revelation 22:12, 21.

CONNECTIONS TOPICAL INDEX

BIBLIOGRAPHY

Donald C. Stamps, Gen. Ed., The Full Life Study Bible NIV, Life Publishers International (Grand Rapids, Michigan: Zondervan Publishing House, 1992).

NIV Archaeological Study Bible (Grand Rapids, Michigan: Zondervan, 2005).

Merrill F. Unger, Unger's Bible Dictionary (Chicago, Illinois: Moody Press, Eleventh Printing, 1964).

Professor F. Davidson, Ed., The New Bible Commentary (Grand Rapids, Michigan: Wm. B. Eerdmans Publishing Company, 1960).

CPSIA information can be obtained
at www.ICGtesting.com
Printed in the USA
LVOW11s1321040117
519714LV00002B/85/P